Praise for Low

'This is a remarkable book. Very few we ~~~~ ~hors
have embraced, and as a result very fe ~~~~ the
choices we must make as a society. I hop ~~~~ ply,
about
Bill McKibben, ~~~~

'If we are to deal with the crisis of climate change as seriously as it demands, all of us need to overcome our addiction to our unsustainable carbon-based lifestyles. The Delaneys, a family who have lived a low-carbon life in the slums of India and the suburbs of Australia, show us how we can do it in style.'

Dave Andrews, author of *Building A Better World*

'This book is a rare gem. It comes out of hard-earned experience, genuine concern, and heartfelt passion for a rapid and robust response to climate change. Perspectives are underpinned by a simple, holistic and rare combination of Knowing, Doing, and Being. By advancing knowledge (covering the basic climate science), promoting practice (suggesting practical implementation steps), and advocating a more wholesome way of life (inspiring self-awareness, authenticity and restraint), this book makes a timely and critical contribution to a decarbonised and habitable future.'

Dr Johannes Luetz
*(Senior Lecturer; Ph.D. Environmental Policy and Management;
Thesis on Climate Migration @ UNSW Sydney)*

'In a fast-changing world, many are confused by science, baffled by statistics, and overwhelmed by the enormity of the challenges we face. What we need is stories - human experiences that resonate and engage, and in which we can imagine ourselves. Mark and Tom Delaney have given us a story that is both remarkable - because not many educated westerners have lived for years (and in Tom's case grown up) in an Indian slum - but also inspiring and challenging. Their story is accessible, honest, moving, informative, funny and also very uncomfortable for those of us who try to square affluent high-consumption lifestyles with knowing the facts on climate change and global poverty. I dare you to read this book and not be changed. And like Mark, Tom and their family, you may discover that giving something up enables you to receive so much more.'

Dave Bookless, *A Rocha International*

'This book by Mark Delaney and his son Tom, who live in India and can speak from the heart about what sustainable living really means, provides fantastic insight into how we can all think about and change how we impact the planet every day. Thoughtful, creative and sensible, their book covers the breadth of how we can all take action to protect our climate, including "small picture solutions" that are particularly inspiring. From the Aussie suburbs to the streets of India, Mark and his family's story calls into question what we really need to live and be happy and challenges all of us to do more to protect the planet we depend on.'

Blair Palese, CEO, *350.org Australia*

Low-Carbon and Loving It

Mark & Tom Delaney

First published in 2018

by Mark Delaney and Thomas Delaney

E-mail: low.carbon.and.loving.it@gmail.com

Blog: www.lowcarbonandlovingit.wordpress.com

ISBN 13: 978-0-6482477-0-8

NON-FICTION

Cover design and layout by Alistair Craig
seriousmedicine.co.nz

This work is licensed under the Creative Commons Attribution-NonCommercial-ShareAlike 4.0 International License.
To view a copy of this license, visit http://creativecommons.org/licenses/by-nc-sa/4.0/.

Printed and bound by **InHouse Print & Publishing**

In memory of
Anthony

Contents

A Father, a Son, and the Climate   i

CLIMATE PROBLEMS

Part A.   The Birthday Chicken – why care anyway?

1.	Career Path from Hell – lawyer to slum dweller	2
2.	Home Sweet Home – an Indian slum	7
3.	Return to the West – reverse culture shock	14

Part B.   Climate Science Demystified – what's happening to our planet?

4.	Fossil Fuels – ancient energy to power modern lives	17
5.	A Blanket for the Earth – the greenhouse effect	22
6.	Can We Believe This? – climate change myths	27

Part C.   Clear and Present Danger – what happens if we do nothing?

7.	Storm Ahead – extreme weather events	32
8.	Goodbye Reef – a coral calamity	37
9.	Take Me Higher – sea level rise	41
10.	Snow Leopards and Koalas – extinction	50
11.	Is There Enough? – food insecurity	55
12.	Arms or Alms? – geopolitical tensions	59
13.	Margaret Thatcher's Warning – three options for the earth	63

Part D.   Ruksana versus Bruce – who is responsible?

14.	Our Carbon Budget – the ultimate overspend	66
15.	Bruce – high-carbon culprit	72
16.	Ruksana – low-carbon champion	78

Part E. Head in the Sand – why have we done so little?

17.	Desire. Consume. Repeat. – corporate and media manipulation	84
18.	Someone Else Will Fix It – over-confidence in science and politics	90
19.	It's Their Fault – blaming others	97
20.	What Can I Do? – psychological excuses for inaction	102

Contents - continued

CLIMATE SOLUTIONS

Part F. Big Picture Solutions – how can science and politics help?

21.	Cars, Planes and Trains – alternative fuel solutions	107
22.	Nature's Power – renewable energy solutions	113
23.	Farts, Forestry and Fugitives – agricultural and industrial solutions	118
24.	Winning and Losing in Paris – international political solutions	122
25.	Incentives for Good – national political solutions	127
26.	Why Didn't You Do Something? – protest solutions	132

Part G. Small Picture Solutions – what can you and I do?

27.	The 5 R's – low-carbon 'stuff'	138
28.	Waists and Wastes – low-carbon diets	144
29.	Cycle to Freedom – low-carbon local travel	149
30.	Rail and Sail – low-carbon long-distance travel	153
31.	Produce on Your Roof – low-carbon electricity	158
32.	A Castle or a Home? – low-carbon housing	162
33.	Mel and Joe – low-carbon living	166

Part H. Building a Movement for Change – where to begin?

34.	The Middle Path – between fatalism and fantasy	169
35.	The Rubber Hitting the Road – 8 steps to a low-carbon life	172
36.	Spreading the Word – talking with others about climate change	175
37.	Kallu and a Kid – ordinary people making an extraordinary difference	178

Appendices 184
1. Australians who live on slumdog millionaire's row – and love it 184
2. Abbreviations 186
3. Index of Illustrations, Science Geeks, Myth-busting and Tables 187
4. Test Your Understanding (including answers) 189
5. Vital Statistics in *Low-Carbon and Loving It* 191

Acknowledgements 195
Copyright Notices 196
Endnotes and References 199

A Father, a Son, and the Climate

Our world is in trouble. If our atmosphere warms more than 2°C above pre-industrial levels, we will face more frequent natural disasters, the extinction of thousands of species, sea level rise measured in metres, food shortages and possible climate-related wars. These changes will happen within this century unless we, as a global community, limit our carbon dioxide emissions to around 800 gigatonnes for the remainder of the century. That might sound like a lot, but it averages about two tonnes per head per year for everyone on the planet. At the moment, Australians emit 23 tonnes per year*. As a global community, we'll blow our budget by 2040 if we continue at the current rate. The awful consequences of climate change will increase in intensity within our own, and even more so, within our children's lifetimes.

This book is for those of us who are sick of passively watching this crisis unfold and are ready to do something about it. Tom and I believe that it is ordinary people like you and me who must take the initiative in the fight against climate change by leading low-carbon lives. Only then will politicians and business leaders follow by creating the solar farms, high-speed rail networks and international agreements necessary to usher in a sustainable world.

The good news is that leading a low-carbon life is not only doable, but can be a fulfilling and fun way to live. We should know. We've done it, not only in middle class Australia, but also in the slums of India. In fact, our love for the natural world has, somewhat ironically, grown out of living in places with very little natural beauty – poor urban neighbourhoods in north India, places that many would call slums.

Slumdogs

My wife Cathy and I, along with our sons, Tom and Oscar have lived in slums for over 13 years. Why would anyone in their right mind choose to do that? The answer is simple. We believe life isn't just about earning money and getting comfortable, but rather about attempting to make the world a better place.

We came to India to help the poor. But first, it was important to get to know

---

* North Americans emit 20 tonnes, New Zealanders 17 tonnes, and Britons 8 tonnes per year.

Our neighbourhood (2007)

what life was like for the people we wanted to help. So we moved in with them. Over the years, we've attempted to help our friends and neighbours in slums find employment, access health care, and get better educated. Sometimes we've succeeded and sometimes we've failed. We've also tried to just be good friends with our neighbours. You can read more about our work in Chapter 2.

Initially, we knew that living in a slum was highly unusual, but as with anything strange one does in life – growing cacti or riding a unicycle – over time, it became normal for us. So we were somewhat surprised when Matt Wade, the South Asia correspondent for a major Australian newspaper, *The Sydney Morning Herald*, asked to do a story about our experiences. That article, entitled 'Australians who live on slumdog millionaire's row – and love it',* generated significant media interest, both in India and Australia. For several weeks, weary Indian journalists, tired from finding their way through slum alleys, wandered up to our room asking: *'Are you the Delaneys – the ones in the newspaper?'* Various TV shows too, including *Australian Story*, showed interest in getting a TV crew into our slum for a documentary about us. After considering our options for

---

* The article is reproduced in Appendix 1. The title refers to the Oscar-winning film in 2008 'Slumdog Millionaire'.

a while, we declined all offers. As nice as it would have been for our egos, we decided that such attention wouldn't be terribly useful to our neighbours. It would also have treated us as heroes, which, compared to our friends – Ruksana, Kaneez and Kallu – who you'll meet in this book, we certainly were not.

However, the prospect of a book had more appeal. Since Matt's article in 2009, we had become passionate about climate change, so when our good friend, Dave Andrews, suggested weaving our Indian story into a book on low-carbon lifestyle, the idea felt right.

Father and son

Part way through an initial draft, I began to wonder whether the message might be better coming from both father (me) and son (Tom). Tom was born in India in 1996, a year after Cathy and I arrived. Tom and our younger son, Oscar, have spent most of their lives in north Indian slums – not the usual childhood for western* kids. It has given them a unique perspective on life. One consequence of Tom's experience is his passion for the environment. That passion initially grew out of a love for animals and nature, but when coupled with his love for science and keen interest in international politics, Tom came to understand climate change very well. He also felt the gravity of the problem, not just for our neighbours in India, but for our friends and family in Australia too – indeed for all of humanity.

Tom is young – 21 at time of writing. To avert a climate crisis, it will be young people like him who will most likely usher in the necessary changes, since they have the most to lose. For these reasons, I asked Tom to co-author the book with me – to allow him to express his views in his own way and hopefully inspire young people to become as low-carbon as he is. We've indicated the sections Tom has written (most of Parts B, D, F & H) in another font, as you'll see below. I hope you'll enjoy our different voices and styles, noting in Tom's sections that he's a warm, generous, mature young man with barely a whisker, while I'm a less optimistic, grey-bearded 50-year-old.

---

* We use the term 'West' to refer to richer industrialised countries, compared to poorer 'developing' nations.

Why us?

In 2016, when Dad first asked me to co-author a book on climate change, I was a bit sceptical. Having spent much of my life in India, at that time I was living in Australia, working as a disability support person, studying at university, and enjoying sport and friends. I wasn't keen on what would surely be a tricky project. I was also concerned that this would be 'just another book on climate change'. Dad and I aren't at the cutting edge of climate science, or working for a renewable energy company. We aren't government consultants, or professional writers. What new information or insight could we possibly add to the voices of many experts?

I was gradually persuaded to join Dad in writing, as I realised we could make an important contribution after all. Our role is not to create new information, but to re-arrange the existing information, making it more accessible. Our book straddles the divides between complex science and simple writing, between personal anecdotes and global analysis. Our aim is to give you a broad but thorough understanding of the problem of climate change and to show that solutions are possible, interesting, and even fun.

Another reason Dad and I are well placed to contribute something fresh to the discussion on climate change is that we have lived several years in both high-carbon and low-carbon contexts. Perhaps more importantly, as a family, we do have a very low carbon footprint compared to most Australians (and North Americans, Europeans, Britons, and New Zealanders). We've been able to do that without much difficulty, even having plenty of fun along the way. In writing about our journey as a low-carbon family, we hope to offer a way forward for everyday people who want to personally do something about the worsening climate crisis. You might not want to adopt all our methods for lowering your carbon footprint, but we're confident that you'll find some of our suggestions doable, interesting and worthwhile.

The evolution of this book

After living in India for 19 years from 1995 to 2014, we returned to Australia for three years. During our time in Australia, we became more acutely aware of the gravity of climate change and the alarming lack of interest in the issue shown by many westerners. We began this book in Australia, partly to address this indifference. Along the way we visited politicians to talk about their response to climate change, only to be infuriated by their unwillingness to look past the next election. Sometimes we spoke out against mining companies wanting to dig up even more coal. Once we took a longer break from writing to visit the

Great Barrier Reef, which is threatened by ocean-warming and acidification. Australia, therefore, was a very relevant place to write about climate change.

In early 2017, Cathy, Tom, Oscar and I returned to India. Now we're back in a poor neighbourhood in a big north Indian city of concrete and brick. Temperatures regularly hit 45°C. We and our neighbours bear the brunt of these temperatures without air-conditioning. India is also a country where Australian coal is burned – releasing vast amounts of carbon emissions. In fact, India reigning in its emissions is now key to the global community limiting temperature rise to 2°C.[1] So India is also a very relevant place to write about climate change. We finished our book in India. That's got a nice symmetry to it — coming back to the place where we started our environmental journey.

In writing this book, we have attempted to be honest about our own efforts, our mistakes, and the ways in which we've *not* done well on our journey towards a low-carbon life. We are ordinary people, trying to follow our consciences and responding to the changing world around us. We've been lucky to stand outside western culture for long enough to see that many of our high-carbon ways aren't actually necessary and that lower-carbon alternatives may be better for us.

We offer many examples of our and our friends' low-carbon choices in Part G (Small Picture Solutions). I'll just give one story here. I recently turned 50 and was looking for a new leisure activity to help me not feel so old. I had plenty of high-carbon options before me: jet-skiing, 4-wheel driving, or skydiving. Instead, I'm learning to surf. I love sitting out there behind the break, feeling the breeze, marvelling at the power of the ocean. And I love the thrill of catching a wave. Give me a low-carbon surfboard over a high-carbon jet-ski any day.

Framework and features of the book

Our book is divided into two halves. In Parts A-E we lay out the problem of climate change. Part A tells the story of how our time in India helped birth a passion for the natural world, the climate and the people affected by it. Through our lives with the poor in India, coming back to Australia, and then returning to India, we realised the magnitude of the climate crisis. Part B explains the science of climate change: how we humans have upset the carbon cycle and exacerbated the greenhouse effect. Part C then describes what the world will look like by the end of this century if we don't act in the coming decades to 'de-carbonise' our society. The picture of extreme weather events, rising sea levels, species extinction and decreased food production is not pretty. Part D examines who is responsible for this mess. We'll see that, without trying, or even knowing it, most of us in the West have adopted very high-carbon lifestyles. This becomes especially clear when we compare our carbon footprints to those of poorer people – some of whom happen to be our friends – in countries like India. Finally, in our description of the problem of climate change, Part E looks at why we've done so little to address it. We'll see that powerful corporations have a vested interest in the continuation of our high-carbon lives. Additionally, we pin false hopes on scientists and politicians – wanting them to fix the problem without us needing to do anything. Ultimately, we must face the fact that many of us in the West just don't want to change our high-carbon lifestyles.

In the second half of the book (Parts F-H), we discuss solutions to climate change. In Part F we consider 'big picture' solutions – the ways scientists, governments and corporations can help address the problem. While these are the fixes most talked about in the media and around dining tables, we'll see that they are unlikely to happen quickly enough to save us from catastrophic climate change, unless everyday people like you and me first change our own behaviour. Therefore, in Part G, we look at 'small picture' solutions: changing our diets, travel patterns, and leisure activities. We'll see that only when we adopt these small picture solutions, will we force the hand of politicians and corporations to implement the big picture solutions. Finally, Part H offers practical suggestions on how to actually make these changes in our lives. At the end of the day, unless we substantially alter our lifestyles, this book will have been entertaining, but useless. However, we dare to believe that we *can* live differently. Together with thousands of others making similar changes, we can bring about a sustainable world.

To aid your enjoyment of the book, we've included a number of different features, so you can choose the ways in which you'd like to engage:

- **Reflection Questions** at the end of most chapters will help you think about your own life – on where you are now and how you might live differently, especially with respect to your environmental footprint. These will be particularly useful if you read the book as a small group and together discuss the questions after reading each chapter.

- For those who enjoy a little more detail on the science, we've included **Science Geek boxes**. We think the facts are pretty interesting, but feel free to skip over those boxes if you're not into science.

- For those who are confused by misinformation about climate change in the media and on the web, we've included **Myth-busting boxes** at various points, to debunk false or misleading information that you might have come across.

- For those wanting to extend their understanding on a topic of interest, we've included **Want to Learn More?** sections at the end of many chapters. There are also several hundred references at the end of the book, detailing the various sources of our information. Small numbers like this[1] point you to those references.

- Finally, if you like quizzes, you could try the **Test Your Understanding** questions in Appendix 4 (followed by the answers).

The low-carbon path, with courage and joy

I remember as a kid hearing the story of 'The Emperor's New Clothes'. You'll recall how the cunning tailor pretended to make new clothes for the emperor. The clothes didn't actually exist, but the tailor and other 'yes men' around the emperor acted as though they did. The emperor proceeded to walk around naked, much to everyone's mirth. But since people didn't want to offend the emperor, nobody said anything. That is, until a brave little kid simply said, *'He's naked.'* That act of speaking the truth changed everything.

In a way, climate scientists are like that little kid. Deep down, most of us know the truth: our lifestyles are unsustainable. However, very few people have been willing to speak this truth plainly and clearly. Many climate scientists have, in fact, been criticised for emphasising the enormous seriousness of climate change. In some small way, it feels like Tom and I are also trying to speak the truth in a context of denial. Being away from the West and its carbon-intensive ways for many years, the truth seemed all the more clear when we returned. Climate change is happening, it is human-caused and it is a catastrophe affecting our homes, our biodiversity, our food supply, and even the very habitability of our planet.

Climate change is a matter of life and death, so demands passion. On the other hand, facts and figures should be discussed calmly and objectively. This tension made it difficult to know what tone to use in the book. Given that people in the West emit far more greenhouse gases than our friends in Indian slums, and that many westerners seem apathetic about climate change, it would have been easy to be harsh. However, we've tried to avoid writing judgmentally. Why? Because we assume that if you've picked up this book, you're a well-intentioned, caring person who recognises that climate change is a very serious issue and who wants to play a part in addressing it.

Tom and I are Australians. We know the Australian context better than that of the US, Canada, UK or New Zealand, so many of our stories are from Australia. Even so, we hope that readers in other English-speaking countries (including India) will be able to relate to the message in these pages. Climate change is truly a global problem: it requires people from every country to join together to solve it.

It's our sincere hope that you join us in embarking on a low-carbon journey. Not only because it's the surest way to safeguard a sustainable future for us and our children, but also because it's a great way to live.

Mark and Tom
December 2017
India

Low-carbon and loving it (2016)

CLIMATE PROBLEMS

 The Birthday Chicken
— why care anyway?

1. Career Path from Hell
— lawyer to slum dweller

We've lived in slums for a long time. After years in these exotic, vibrant and terrible places, I still find myself surprised as to how I got here. Certainly, there was little in my childhood to suggest such a bizarre 'career path'. In fact, my childhood was quite normal.

I grew up in a middle class family on the east coast of Australia. Dad was a builder. Mum mostly stayed at home to look after my siblings and me. Having grown up in farming families, Mum and Dad had learnt to live simply. Their experience translated into simple lifestyle choices once we five children (of whom I'm the youngest) came along. Growing up, I remember camping at the beach instead of staying in hotels, because it was the simple, low-cost way to holiday. There were few sweets or fizzy drinks in the house. I recall Mum even hand-making some of our school clothes to save money. Readers who grew up in the 70s may relate to that type of frugal lifestyle. Learning to make our own things (clothes, food, fun) and to repair broken things, rather than buy new ones, was largely an enjoyable challenge.

After completing high school, I studied Law and Commerce at the University of Queensland in Brisbane. In my second year of university I started to take my faith more seriously. At its core, that faith challenged me to move from a purely self-centred life towards being mindful of others around me, especially those at the bottom of society. Intriguingly, my new-found faith also suggested that to the extent to which I shifted my orientation from myself to others, life would actually become more meaningful and fulfilling. As a result, I began to question the normal 'life map' laid out by society for middle class young people like me: completing a university education, getting progressively higher-paying jobs, buying a house and retiring early to a life of leisure.

1. Career Path from Hell - lawyer to slum dweller

The Life Map

Credit: David Nagai

Disturbingly, it seemed my role models did not advocate such a life map at all. People like Gandhi, Martin Luther King, Mother Teresa and Jesus directed most of their energy toward caring for the outcasts of society – the homeless, the lonely, the sick, the marginalised and the misfits. Even worse, they confronted

Part A: The Birthday Chicken - why care anyway?

those in power – the politicians, religious leaders and wealthy rulers – who were largely responsible for pushing people to the margins. If I were to model my life on these heroes, it seemed to require using whatever skills and resources I was privileged enough to possess to care for *others*, rather than 'feathering my own nest' as the life map told me to do.

So while finishing my law studies and working for a few years, I started to look at the bigger picture of the world and consider careers through which I might somehow make a difference. Practising law may have led to a career within the UN or politics through which I may have eventually been able to bring about some positive change for the poor, but that was going to be a long road. I wanted a more direct path to responding to the broken world around me.

The nature of the 'brokenness' of the world has changed over the years. In recent decades, it has taken on a new dimension – climate change. But back then, the brokenness that struck me was the huge gulf between the rich and the poor. From a couple of months in India during my university holidays, I knew that the needs in the developing world were enormous.[*] I witnessed people struggling to feed their families with less than a dollar a day. I saw woefully

Friends in India outside their house (1995)

[*] The term 'developing' is contentious, as it implies that the western model of economic development is one that all countries should follow. In this book we use the term simply to mean relatively poor countries in Asia, Latin America and Africa.

inadequate healthcare systems, where patients would wait for hours, often to only get two minutes with a doctor. I learned that the government school system was terribly under-resourced, often with 50 or more children in a class.

During that first trip to India, one incident in particular had a profound impact on me. I met a man outside his house (a plastic shack). With my limited Hindi, I learned that his wife had just given birth to their child, right there in their hut, without any medical help. As I said goodbye, I shook his hand. It felt like ice. It was the middle of winter and he was clearly struggling to stay warm. It was a very simple interaction, but one that changed my life. I was deeply affected by the realisation that I was leading a privileged life, with world-class education and healthcare, purely by virtue of being born in the West. Meanwhile, this man's life was incredibly difficult, simply because he was born into a poor family in India. That difference seemed terribly unjust to me, so I decided to attempt to redress it.

For Indian readers who may take offence at this bleak assessment of their country, I hasten to add that India also has some world-class health and education centres (not to mention cricket teams). However on my first short trip, I'd intentionally sought out everyday Indians and found that for all those other than the top 20%[2], who make up the professional middle class, life was very difficult. I knew this poverty was of an order of magnitude worse than that in the West.*

Cathy had been on a very similar life journey. She studied Maths and Computer Science at university. Largely because of her faith, Cathy's perspective on life had also been reoriented from, '*life is all about me*', to focusing on those at the bottom of society. Instead of pursuing academia or professional life, she decided to work with homeless kids in a poor part of Brisbane. So when I met Cathy, we already had plenty in common. It helped that she was a spunky, fun and adventurous woman. After a year or so of getting to know (and love) each other, we married. When we did so, in 1993, we hoped and planned to spend a significant part of our lives overseas, living and working with the poor.

We knew, however, that India had suffered enormously under British colonial rule. Given that, we wondered whether Indians today would tell westerners like us to stay at home and mind our own business. If that happened, we could

---

* Except in some indigenous communities where, damningly, the poverty is on a par with that in the developing world.

hardly blame them! We were also aware, from our brief experiences in India and our involvement in international development agencies like TEAR Australia, that there were many highly capable Indians doing an excellent job at bringing about positive change. Cathy and I didn't want to presume that we, as relatively inexperienced outsiders, could add anything to the fight against poverty in India. One of the things that convinced us to at least explore the option was talking to our friend, Dave Andrews. Dave and his wife Ange had worked in South Asia for many years. Dave thought that our deep questions regarding our usefulness in the developing world were appropriate, but suggested that they weren't questions that could or should be answered in the West. He suggested that we go to India for a couple of years and attempt to answer those questions there, rather than from the comfort of the West. That sounded good to us, so in 1995, with me 28 years old and Cathy 30, we packed our bags and set off for Delhi.

Reflection Questions

- Mark's family, as with many families in the 1970s, led a relatively frugal lifestyle. What lifestyle did you experience in your childhood? How has that affected you as an adult?
- Mark's short experience in India during his university days was confronting. Have you ever spent time in a poorer country? If so, did it change the way you live in the West?
- To what extent do you think the 'life map' Mark describes is a reasonable summary of aspirations in life for many people in the West?
- What factors helped Mark and Cathy follow a very different life path? Are any of those factors present in your own life?

2. Home Sweet Home
— an Indian slum

When Cathy and I first moved to India, neither of us expected to be here for so long. We went initially to see if there was any role that we, as middle class westerners, could play in helping to alleviate the dehumanising conditions in which so many lived. We weren't at all sure there was. In the face of overwhelming poverty, it was difficult to know how to respond.

We first needed to understand the situation before attempting to help. So we moved into a poor neighbourhood, hoping to learn a little about the life of the poor. We initially needed to learn how to 'do life'. First, there were the simple things, like how to use a squat toilet with no toilet paper. We soon found that water cleans a lot better than paper! Then there was learning to cook on a little kerosene stove on the ground. Getting used to sleeping in temperatures regularly over 40°C was another challenge. Trying to live as much like our neighbours as possible, we didn't use air-conditioning, so instead used a local method to sleep in the heat. We would lie on the floor directly under the ceiling fan, then wet a sheet, lay it on top of us, and try to get to sleep before the sheet dried!

While these challenges were quite fun, the toughest part was the language. The first year or so was very difficult. We had little Hindi, and in our poor neighbourhood there wasn't a lot of English spoken. So we would learn a couple of Hindi phrases each day (*'How are you?' 'What are you doing?'*) and go around the neighbourhood using the same phrases with several people, until we perfected them. Our neighbours were good-hearted and often laughed with us about our stumbling efforts.

During that first year, we also made a concerted effort to ask various Indian development workers and social activists whether they felt there was a role that we, as foreigners, could play. In summary, they said we were welcome to stay, if we could satisfy three conditions:

- Stay for the long-term, rather than just a few months, as long-term change takes many years;
- Learn good Hindi, so we could converse with everyday Indians, not just the middle class; and

- *Not* set up our own development projects, nor try to be 'the boss' as many foreigners do, but rather, work with Indian co-workers under their direction.

These conditions seemed entirely reasonable to us, so we planned to stay for several years, proceeded to learn Hindi, and found an Indian social welfare organisation, Emmanuel Hospital Association*, in which I could work and be accountable.

Barapula

Barapula (2002)

The neighbourhood Cathy and I lived in for our first few years was poor, but not *very* poor. Perhaps 30% of Delhi's population lived in even poorer neighbourhoods. One such place, Barapula, was nearby, so we considered moving in. Being by nature more fearful than Cathy, I was reticent, imagining that we might get sick, or even worse, that Tom, our 18-month-old baby, might become ill. I also feared that we would attract too much attention from the police, standing out as the only foreigners in the neighbourhood. But Cathy

* For more information on Emmanuel Hospital Association go to www.eha-health.org

spurred me on, saying that we still had to learn about life for the *very* poor. So in May 1999, we moved in.

Barapula was a mainly Muslim neighbourhood of about 900 families – 6,000 people in all. It was built on a 30-metre-wide strip of land running about a kilometre along the bank of a drainage canal. Slums are often built in such places – on land that is otherwise useless. In terms of natural beauty, you couldn't say Barapula had much going for it. There was one decent tree and several pigs rooting around in the mud, but that was about it.

Cathy and I and baby Tom lived in a single room. It had brick walls and a wood and plastic roof. Our water supply was from a hand pump shared with our landlord's family. The lack of a toilet meant we needed to go to the community toilet 500 metres away. That was OK under normal circumstances, but when we got the 'runs' it was a long run! So we built our own little toilet on the bank of the canal. That 'fix it yourself' mentality from our childhoods was serving us well.

As is often the case, my fears were unfounded, and while living in Barapula we generally had very good health. Eventually Barapula was demolished by the Delhi Government and its residents 'relocated' to a desolate patch of land 27 kilometres away. You can read more about that eviction in Chapter 37 (Kallu and a Kid). But, looking back, those 18 months in simple conditions in the Barapula slum were very formative and enriching. We forged genuine friendships with our poor neighbours, some of whom, like Kallu, are still good friends to this day. We also learned to be less fearful of slums. While our middle class friends and the police warned us that slums were full of thieves and thugs, we learned that most residents were just everyday people trying to get by. In fact, they are some of the most generous and hospitable people we've met. The poor know how to identify someone who is really struggling, having 'been there' themselves. They often sacrificially give their limited resources to help others who are worse off.

A persistent widow

After Barapula, we moved to another poor neighbourhood, Janta Colony, in Delhi's east, where we lived for about 10 years. While it was difficult at times, it was a hugely rewarding experience. It was inspiring to see our poor friends'

Part A: The Birthday Chicken - why care anyway?

resilience and courage in dealing with incredible vulnerability and adversity. For example, our friend Ruksana (who you'll meet again in Chapter 16) was amazing. She was married by her parents when she was 14 years old and became a mother by 16. She had no formal schooling, yet worked hard to have her own three children educated. She eventually passed grade 12 herself, by correspondence schooling, before going on to help many mums have safe pregnancies, and to help enrol their older children in school.

My main role in India for many years was helping poor people to become informed about government services available to them, and then assisting them to access those services. That wasn't easy, as there were many barriers to accessing even basic services like a widow's pension. Often people don't have the necessary identity documents to apply for a particular service, or if they do, a corrupt official may demand a bribe before accepting the application.

Our friend Kaneez, her husband and four children lived in a makeshift hut across the alley from us in Janta Colony. In 2008, Kaneez's 11-month-old baby girl died – probably of diarrhoea – one of those thousands of preventable deaths that happen every day in the developing world. Except this time, for us, it wasn't a statistic, but a neighbour. A few months later, Kaneez's husband died. This time it was probably tuberculosis, another huge killer. Kaneez was left with her three surviving children, no income, and living in a tiny hut. She was very vulnerable.

The Delhi government provides a widow's pension of Rs1,000 (US$15) a month. However, the government officials said that Kaneez was not eligible because she didn't have a bank account. Kaneez had never had a bank account, so we went to the local bank to get one. *'No,'* the manager informed us, *'we need some identity documentation to open an account.'* Kaneez had no such documentation, so the next stop was the Electoral Commission to ask for a Voter ID Card. After several days, the officials visited her at her hut. They shook their heads and said: *'No, sorry, because she lives in a slum hut, we won't give her a Voter ID Card.'* I protested that all adult Indian citizens are eligible for a Voter ID Card, whether they live in a palace or a slum hut. After a little more hand wringing, they finally agreed.

Armed with the ID Card, we went back to the bank, which thankfully opened Kaneez's account. Triumphant, we went back to the pension official, confident we'd now succeed. *'No,'* came the answer, *'even with the bank account, she still needs some official document proving she's been resident in that hut for five years!'* Exasperated, we wrote a letter of appeal to the head of the Social Welfare Department, who finally agreed to our request. After 12 months of battling with the bureaucracy, Kaneez finally got her pension. It wasn't much, but the regular amount has helped her survive.

During our time in Janta Colony we helped many people like Kaneez access government services.[*] Ruksana also joined in that work and became an expert at helping children who weren't getting any education to enrol in government schools.

Kaneez and children outside her house (2007)

Children and chickens

I can say with some conviction that raising Tom and Oscar in slums in north India has been a wonderful parenting experience. The boys have had a chance to see both sides of the huge economic divide in our world, from the middle class in Australia (and India), to poor friends and neighbours like Kallu, Kaneez and Ruksana.

[*] For more about Mark's work in India, see the document at: www.eha-health.org and click on Downloads, then Advocacy Manuals.

Part A: The Birthday Chicken - why care anyway?

Little did we know that as the years unfolded, it would primarily be Tom who would drive our environmental awareness. When he was three, Cathy cooked a special chicken dish for his birthday. When Tom saw the food, he asked, quite innocently, as children are so good at doing: *'Was this chicken alive an hour ago?'* That question might sound strange to the western reader, but it made perfect sense in India, where chicken is bought, not frozen from the supermarket, but from the 'chicken man'. He has a cage of live chickens. He pulls one out, kills it and skins it right there in front of you. Minutes later, you carry the chicken meat home, ready to cook. On learning the chicken had indeed been alive only an hour ago, Tom refused to eat it, reasoning, in a lovely three-year-old way, that he didn't want to have another living thing killed for his enjoyment. I think that moment was the birth of genuine environmental awareness for me. I'd already had a love for the wilderness and the beach, but I'd never really changed my lifestyle to care for that natural world. But now, my willingness to change had begun, thanks to my three-year-old son.

Over the years, our environmental awareness has grown considerably and become more focused on climate change. When Matt Wade wrote the story about us for *The Sydney Morning Herald* in 2009, he closed the piece saying: *'A striking feature of the Delaneys' lifestyle is their small environmental footprint. They use very little electricity, create only a small amount of waste and rely exclusively on public transport.'*

That began us thinking a little more about carbon footprints and their effect on the world. Around the same time, friends started sending us copies of *The Guardian Weekly*, a newspaper that had excellent coverage of international news and often ran articles about the growing climate crisis. All of this led to many family discussions over dinner. We also started asking our friends in India about their experiences of the climate. One friend, Kamran, told us that the climate is very different now from when he was a child. He reported that it now rains less in monsoon, the rivers are drying up, winters are not as cold and summers are hotter. We also heard stories of how farmers used to know which week of the year they could plant, and then harvest their rice or wheat, as the climate used to be more predictable. Now it is not so. Sometimes the monsoon starts early, sometimes late, and occasionally not at all. Even though these residents and farmers may have never heard of 'climate change', they know from experience that the climate is changing.

Our growing concern about climate became even sharper when we returned to Australia in 2014 and found that most Aussies were not taking the issue as seriously as it deserved.

Reflection Questions

- Mark and Cathy spent their first year in India learning, rather than helping. What do you think of this approach? Why do many people feel the need to help immediately when visiting a poor country?

- Mark and Cathy 'dived in the deep end' of Indian culture with squat toilets, a kerosene stove and 40°C temperatures. Have you ever 'dived in' to a culture like that? If so, how was it? If not, does it sound exciting or scary?

- Mark claims that an Indian slum was a very good place to raise their children. Why was it so good? Could any of those positives be replicated in the West?

- Mark reports his environmental awareness beginning with Tom's realisation that the chicken died for his birthday lunch. Has a child's innocence ever changed the way you see the world?

- Have you experienced the climate where you live changing in any way?

- What factors have influenced your growing awareness of climate change?

3. Return to the West
— reverse culture shock

In 2014, after 19 years in India,* we returned to Australia for a break and to reconnect with friends and family. However, with a change of Indian government in 2014, visas for development workers like us became harder to obtain and our visa application to return to India in 2015 was not approved. We needed to come to terms with being in Australia longer-term.

Our friends in India view Australia as heaven-on-earth. In a way they are right. Compared to India, life is efficient. Traffic flows fairly well, the Internet is fast and government helplines tend to work (eventually). Health and education systems are efficient and of a high quality. People are generally friendly and helpful.

Australia's natural beauty is also striking. It's not just the postcard beauty of the oceans or deserts – even the simple greenery in suburban parks and gardens gives me joy. My delight in Australian nature is all the greater because of the stark contrast with the urban slum environment in north India, where there is barely a blade of grass. I still marvel at the blue skies of Australia, even more so as I imagine our friends living under the 'pollution grey' skies of Delhi – now one of the most polluted cities in the world.[3] We are sometimes even corrected by Indian children for colouring the sky blue in drawings, being told: *'The sky's not blue, it's grey!'*

But our re-entry to Australian society wasn't all easy. Returning to our home culture after a significant period overseas gave us new eyes to see our own society. For some aspects of Australian culture, we gained a new appreciation, but other parts we found unpleasant and annoying. Sociologists call this 'reverse culture shock'. Perhaps the strongest part of this shock for us was what seemed to be a disturbing lack of concern about climate change.

When we left Australia initially in 1995, climate change was barely on the radar. While we were in India, however, the climate did become a serious issue in the West, perhaps the highest point of concern being in the mid-2000s, thanks to Al Gore's famous documentary, *An Inconvenient Truth*.

---

* Our 19 years were in periods of 2-3 years at a time, interspersed by breaks of several months in Australia. Of the 19 years, 12 were spent living in slums.

3. Return to the West - reverse culture shock

Australia's natural beauty (2016)

During our time in India, we've seen evidence and heard stories of climate change actually happening. We have also done enough reading to be convinced that climate change is real, human-caused and hugely problematic. There is now clear evidence that unless we significantly change how we live in the coming decades, we will be facing 3-5°C temperature increase, massive sea level rise, severe weather events, drastic biodiversity loss and food shortages

When Matt's article in 2009 praised our small carbon footprint, it suggested to us that everyday Australians were now also thinking more about environmental issues. So when we returned to Australia in 2014, we were expecting to find Australians working hard to reduce their carbon emissions. How wrong we were!

Australians have one of the highest average carbon footprints in the world. Despite this, we were aghast to find that climate change was rarely being discussed.[4] Most people, it seemed, were more concerned about the latest iPhone and how their favourite sports team was faring, than about the future of life on earth. Climate change was old news and as a nation we were happily carrying on carbon-intensive lives as if it didn't matter. How did that happen?

Part A: The Birthday Chicken - why care anyway?

After a couple of years reflecting on Australians' inaction on the climate, we now understand it a little better. We'll look more closely at the reasons for that lack of action in Part E (Head in the Sand).

First though, we need to get a clear understanding of just what climate change is. In the next Part, Tom explains the science simply and clearly. If you feel like you know that science well enough already, try the 'Test Your Understanding' questions in Appendix 4 and then feel free to skip straight to Part C (Clear and Present Danger).

Reflection Questions

- Have you ever lived in another culture for a significant period? If so, did it give you any new insights into the aspects of your own society for which you are grateful, and into those aspects which you don't like?

- Why do you think climate change dropped off the agenda in the West until more recently?

Want To Learn More?

→ Film: *An Inconvenient Truth.* 2006. Al Gore's famous documentary.

Climate Science Demystified
– what's happening to our planet?

4. Fossil Fuels
— ancient energy to power modern lives

The first time I saw a petrified tree stump – at the botanic gardens in Brisbane – it was with awe that I stroked its rings, each of which represented a year's growth some 200 million years ago. What a rare privilege to get a glimpse of this ancient past, seemingly so far removed from our day-to-day lives. In reality though, it is plant growth hundreds of millions of years ago that has created the cornerstone of our modern lives: fossil fuels.

For many years I've enjoyed learning climate science. From Dad's beach-ball and tennis-ball model of the solar system, to browsing the university library for books on the climate, I have thirsted to understand our natural world. Over the years, though, this sense of excitement at new understandings has grown sombre, as I've realised the profound changes we're inflicting on our planet.

In this Part, we'll look at the science of climate change. We will briefly explain the carbon cycle, and how people have put it out of balance, primarily through our burning of fossil fuels. We'll then see in the next chapter that this excess carbon in the atmosphere is exacerbating the greenhouse effect, leading to rising temperatures. Along with building your understanding of the science, in Chapter 6 (Can We Believe This?) we'll also develop your ability to explain it to others by helping you rebut the many myths circulating about climate change.

Carbon is the building block of all life. Plants use energy from the sun, water from the ground and carbon dioxide (CO_2) from the atmosphere to create carbohydrates, which they need to live and grow. This process – photosynthesis – is also vital for all animals (including humans) as it produces both our food and, as a by-product, the oxygen we need to breathe. We use the carbon

Part B: Climate Science Demystified - what's happening to our planet?

from our food and the oxygen from our breathing to produce energy which drives our movement and growth. This reaction – respiration – is the reverse of photosynthesis. While plants use CO_2 and energy to make complex carbon molecules, animals and humans break down these complex carbon molecules to release energy and CO_2.* To a person like me who loves patterns, this symmetry is beautiful.

We humans have always relied primarily on plant matter both for our food, and the means to cook it. One of our earliest innovations – controlling fire – was essentially a way to get energy (heat) out of the carbon in plant matter that couldn't be eaten (wood). In fact, some of our friends in India still use wood and dung to cook by. It is the method that their ancestors have used for millennia and is, especially for rural people, the simplest: just go to the forest and gather firewood or dry the buffalo dung produced in great quantities every day. However in the world's cities, where a billion people live in slums, cooking with wood and dung is expensive and very bad for people's health.

All living things are made primarily from carbon. When those living things die in the presence of oxygen, they decompose and the carbon escapes into the atmosphere. When people burn wood or dung, the carbon is also released into the atmosphere. However, when living things die in the *absence* of oxygen (imagine a tree falling into a river or lake), the carbon may *not* escape into the atmosphere. Over millions of years, under pressure from the water, silt and rock above it, that organic material can undergo a chemical transformation into what we call fossil fuels: coal, oil and gas. Which of those fossil fuels is produced depends on the original vegetation, the length of time, the amount of pressure and heat, and the type of the rock in which it is embedded.[5]

Eventually, we humans figured out that we could dig up coal to burn on a large scale, releasing tremendous amounts of energy. Fossil fuels enabled the widespread use of the steam engine, the spinning jenny and railways: in short, the industrial revolution. Over the next 200 years, we continued to learn better ways to release the energy of coal (then oil, and later gas) to generate electricity and power cars and aeroplanes. In addition, scientists learned how to convert oil into all sorts of plastics and other products, which we use in a huge variety of ways. Thus, modern life is, to a large extent, enabled by fossil fuels.

The great advantage of fossil fuels is their easy availability. Massive deposits of coal, oil and gas embody huge amounts of energy that have been stored up for millions of years. It's the equivalent of discovering that you had inherited millions of dollars. Unfortunately, we have since been splurging this inheritance at an ever-increasing rate. *Illustration 1* shows the total energy consumption in the world since 1800. You'll see that there has been a massive increase in the use

---

* Plants respire too, to generate energy for themselves. This is why Illustration 2 shows vegetation and land (and animals) releasing 440 Gt of carbon into the atmosphere.

4. Fossil Fuels - ancient energy to power modern lives

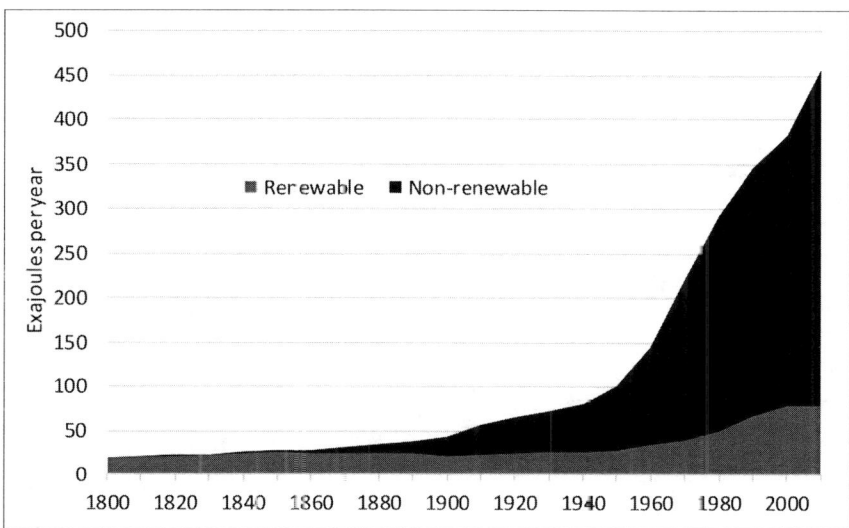

Illustration 1: Global energy use over time Credit: Oscar Delaney. Data: Vaclav Smith

of non-renewables (fossil fuels), especially in the latter half of the 20th century.

What happens to the carbon when we burn fossil fuels? Some of it is absorbed by forests and oceans. Huge amounts of carbon are exchanged between oceans, land and atmosphere naturally, and this carbon cycle has the capacity to absorb some of the excess we are pumping into the atmosphere *(Illustration 2)*. Sadly, we have cut down 20 million square kilometres of the earth's original 60 million square kilometres of forests.[6] However, you'll see that forests and land still absorb a net 11 gigatonnes (Gt)[*] (451-440) of CO_2 a year. Oceans absorb a net 7 Gt (337-330) of CO_2 a year. However, that extra 18 Gt (11+7) isn't enough to cope with the 36 Gt of CO_2 people are putting into the atmosphere every year by burning fossil fuels. Thus, about half of our emissions remain in the atmosphere.[7] We have upset the balance of the carbon cycle.

We've released lots of CO_2 into the atmosphere, and the concentration of CO_2 has greatly increased. It seems obvious that this is no coincidence. However, some people still suggest that the higher concentration of CO_2 in the atmosphere we've seen in the last several hundred years is natural. Science Geek (1) examines evidence that it is we humans who are causing the rise in CO_2 concentration in the atmosphere by burning fossil fuels.

---

[*] A gigatonne (Gt) is a billion tonnes, that is, a thousand million tonnes.

Part B: Climate Science Demystified - what's happening to our planet?

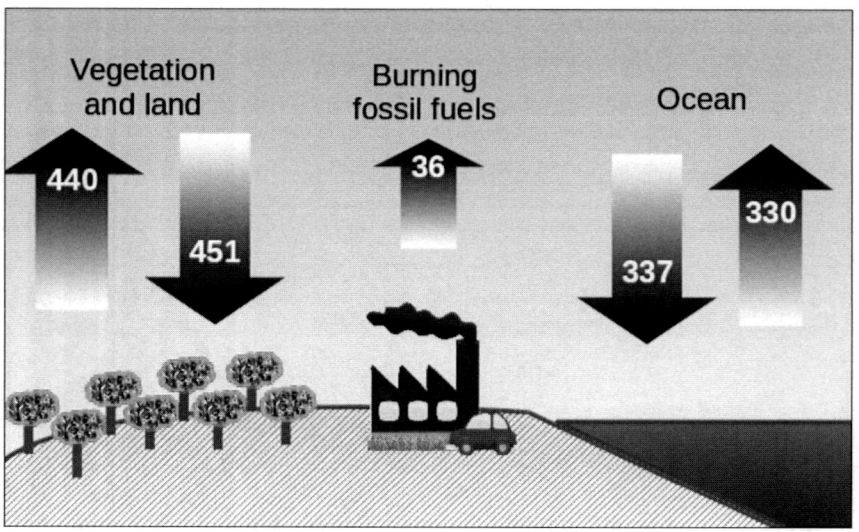

Illustration 2: CO_2 cycling between air, land and water (in gigatonnes per year)

Credit: Cathy Delaney. Data: Skeptical Science

SCIENCE GEEK 1

Are humans really causing an increase in CO_2 concentration?

There are different types of carbon in the air, known as carbon isotopes. The most common type is Carbon-12, while Carbon-13 is a rarer isotope. In photosynthesis, plants prefer Carbon-12. Fossil fuels, like coal or oil, come from ancient plants. So when we burn fossil fuels, we're sending more Carbon-12 into the air. Thus, we expect to see the ratio of Carbon-13 to Carbon-12 fall. This is exactly what has happened. If the extra carbon in the atmosphere were from another source, this ratio would be unaffected.[8]

In the next chapter we'll see how this extra carbon in the atmosphere is causing temperatures to rise, due to the greenhouse effect.

Reflection Questions

- Have you ever thought about how our modern lives are reliant on fossil fuels?
- How do you feel about the fact that we humans have significantly altered the carbon cycle, to such a degree that the world's oceans and forests can't absorb the excess carbon?

Want To Learn More?

→ Website: *Khan Academy*. A high school educational resource dealing with the carbon cycle. *https://www.khanacademy.org/science/biology/ecology/biogeochemical-cycles/a/the-carbon-cycle*

Part B: Climate Science Demystified - what's happening to our planet?

5. A Blanket for the Earth
— the greenhouse effect

On the same trip to the botanic gardens (where I saw the petrified tree), my brother Oscar and I entered its greenhouse. Initially, we enjoyed the exquisite tropical plants, but within minutes, the temperature and humidity, so conducive to these plants' growth, had become unbearable. We had experienced the 'greenhouse effect'.*

As we saw in the last chapter, our rate of burning fossils fuels has increased dramatically, so much so that our oceans and forests can't absorb carbon dioxide at the rate we're pumping it out. Consequently, the amount of carbon in the atmosphere has increased alarmingly. Over hundreds of thousands of years, the level of CO_2 in the atmosphere had cycled between about 180 and 300 parts per million (ppm). About 12,000 years ago, the level of CO_2 gradually increased from 180 ppm to 280 ppm. This caused temperatures to rise, ending the last ice age. That spelt trouble for woolly mammoths, but it provided a climate conducive to human progress, and agriculture was soon developed. For the last 10,000 years, the climate has been quite stable, allowing humans to develop elaborate civilisations. *Illustration 3* shows the clear correlation between CO_2 levels and temperatures.

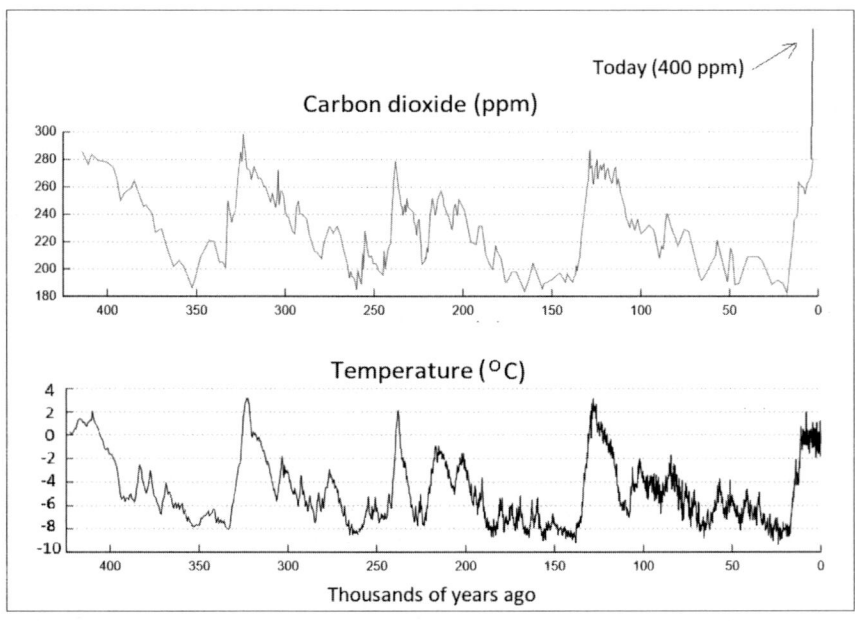

Illustration 3: Correlation of CO_2 and temperature   Credit: Wikimedia Commons

* The greenhouse effect in relation to climate change does work somewhat differently from a glass greenhouse.

5. A Blanket for the Earth - the greenhouse effect

Unfortunately, the climate is no longer stable. Over the past several hundred years, we've shot CO_2 concentrations over 400 ppm – far greater than at any stage over at least 400,000 years. This is a bigger shift than that which pulled us out of an ice age. The concentration is still going up, at about 2.5 ppm per year.[9]

SCIENCE GEEK 2

How do scientists know about the history of the earth's climate?

Scientists learn about temperature and CO_2 levels hundreds of thousands of years ago primarily by taking ice samples from Greenland and Antarctica, where some ice-sheets have remained frozen for that long. When water freezes, there are tiny pockets of gas trapped in the ice. These can be analysed to estimate the concentration of gases in the atmosphere when the ice froze. A similar, but more complex method is used to estimate the atmospheric temperature when the ice froze.[10]

How do increased CO_2 levels lead to increased temperatures? The answer is known as the 'greenhouse effect'. The sun emits a lot of high frequency radiation, while the earth, being at a lower temperature, emits lower frequency, infra-red radiation. The greenhouse effect involves a 'blanket' of CO_2 and other greenhouse gases (GHGs) in the atmosphere. Much like a blanket traps our body warmth on a cold night, these GHGs trap infra-red radiation, reducing how much energy is lost to space *(see Illustration 4)*. With climate change, the difficulty is that we're pumping *too much* carbon into the atmosphere. Put most simply, it is as if the 'blanket' of atmosphere around the earth is becoming too heavy.

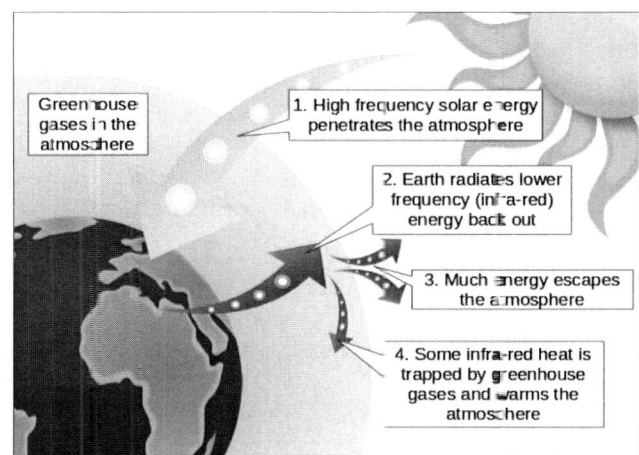

Illustration 4:
The greenhouse effect
Credit: Cathy Delaney

Part B: Climate Science Demystified - what's happening to our planet?

Illustration 5 shows the effect this increased carbon dioxide concentration has had on temperature over the last 130 years.

You can see that since 1880, the concentration of CO_2 has risen from about 290 ppm to 400 ppm. Over the same period the average global temperature has risen from 57°F to 58.5°F (a rise of about 1°C). In fact, 15 of the 16 hottest years

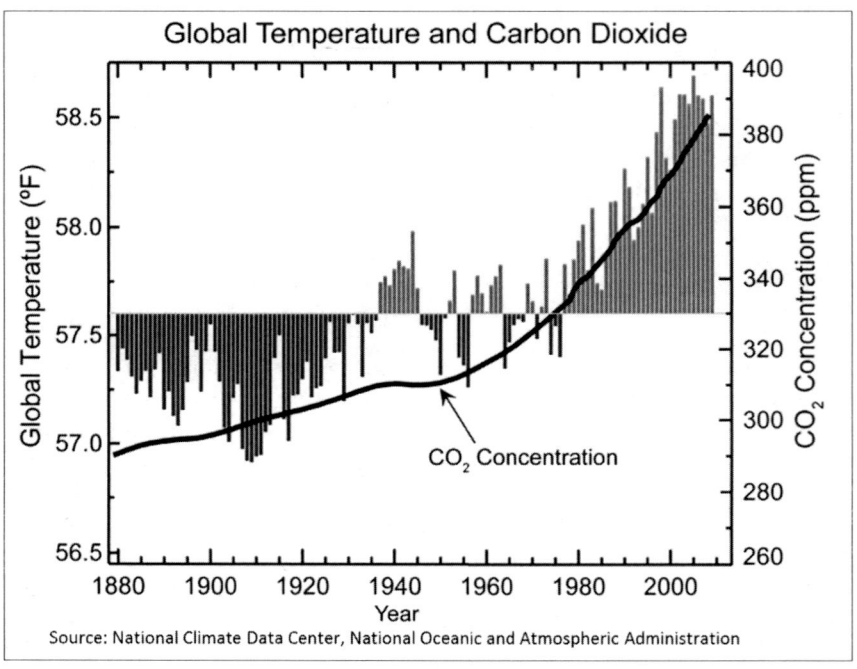

Illustration 5: Global temperature and CO_2 concentration 1880 - 2014   Credit: EPA

since temperature records began in the 1800s have occurred since 2000.[11] An unfortunate aspect of these temperature records is that they correspond almost exactly with our years in north India. Mum and Dad report summers being incredibly hot (40-45°C) in 1996 when I was born, but now it's even hotter. And with few of our friends being able to afford air-conditioning, any extra heat makes more misery for our neighbours (and us).

This all seems like strong evidence that increased carbon levels have caused increased temperatures – but it is circumstantial. Any scientist should be thinking: *'Just because CO_2 concentrations and temperatures are correlated, doesn't necessarily mean that increased CO_2 concentration causes the rise in temperature. It could be the other way around, that increased temperature causes the rise in CO_2 levels.'* Thus, some climate sceptics suggest that increased temperatures may be happening, but due to other *natural* causes.[12]

Science Geek (3) rebuts this by showing several pieces of evidence that point to increased CO_2 concentrations causing the rise in temperatures, not vice-versa.

SCIENCE GEEK 3

Is temperature rise really caused by the greenhouse effect?

1) **Cooling upper atmosphere.** Detailed measurements from thousands of weather stations around the world show a steady average surface temperature increase. Interestingly, satellites have recorded progressively lower temperatures in the upper atmosphere. This indicates that the increased concentration of GHGs doesn't allow as much heat to escape the lower atmosphere to heat the upper atmosphere. If temperature rises on earth were caused by the sun heating up, the upper atmosphere would be warmer too.[13]

2) **Nights and winters warming faster than days and summers.** We only receive radiation from the sun during the day, heating the ground, while at night we cool off as the earth radiates heat into space. The greenhouse effect reduces the amount of this radiation getting back to space, making nights warmer. Consequently, measurements showing that nights are warming faster than days, and winters faster than summers (for a similar reason), indicate the warming we are experiencing is greenhouse-induced.[14]

3) **More infra-red radiation hitting earth.** Scientists have been measuring the amount and type of radiation hitting the earth for decades, and know that infra-red radiation has been increasing. The best explanation for this is the greenhouse effect: infra-red radiation from earth back towards space being trapped by the extra GHGs in the atmosphere and radiated back down.[15]

In the next chapter we'll address several other popular climate change myths.

Part B: Climate Science Demystified - what's happening to our planet?

Reflection Questions

🔎 The atmospheric CO_2 concentration is now more than it has been for at least 400,000 years. Why do you think this has not been more widely discussed?

🔎 After reading this chapter, how would you explain climate change to a 10-year-old?

Want To Learn More?

→ Video series: *Global Weirding.* Climate scientist Katharine Hayhoe explains a range of climate science issues. *https://www.youtube.com/channel/UCi6Rk-daEqgRVKi3AzidF4ow*

6. Can We Believe This?
– climate change myths

I place high value on enquiry, scepticism and doubt. From the age of two, I've loved to ask '*why?*', a tendency my parents were gracious enough to humour by patiently answering my hundreds of questions. With a nickname of 'doubting Thomas', I understand the importance of being sceptical. However, on the issue of climate change, I find myself perplexed by the doubters. Their so called 'doubt' is usually not genuine enquiry, but rather an unwillingness to accept very uncomfortable facts.

Despite the very strong scientific consensus that climate change is real and human-caused, many people in the West still don't accept it. This is a major problem in the US, where about half the population believes that climate change is either not happening or is caused naturally.[16] Australia is little better, with an estimated 35–55% of people doubting the science.[17] This chapter is devoted to debunking some myths popularised by climate sceptics, as well as taking a big-picture look at what can be a ferocious debate.

First, let's examine the depth and breadth of scientific consensus on the basic material outlined in the previous two chapters. The pre-eminent global scientific body for climate change is the UN's Intergovernmental Panel on Climate Change (IPCC). It is made up of top climate scientists from all over the world. The IPCC has, over the last 20 years, become progressively more certain that climate change *is* human-caused. Two decades ago, in its 1995 report, the IPCC said: '*The balance of evidence suggests a discernible human influence on global climate.*'[18] By contrast, 18 years later, the IPCC wrote: '*It is extremely likely (more than 95%) that human influence has been the dominant cause of the observed warming since the mid-20th century.*'[19]

97% of climate scientists have concluded that human-caused climate change *is* happening. This figure is not plucked from thin air. A number of independent studies have quantified the scientific consensus on climate change, finding that 90 to 100% of climate scientists agree that humans are causing global warming, with a number of studies converging on 97% agreement.[20] In any field of science 97% is very robust consensus. Academies of Science in 80 countries have also endorsed the consensus. No national Academy of Science has rejected it.[21] As historian of science Naomi Oreskes says: '*the basic reality of anthropogenic (human-caused) global climate change is no longer a subject of scientific debate.*'[22]

Of course, there are still uncertainties in the field of climate science: exactly how

27

Part B: Climate Science Demystified - what's happening to our planet?

much warming a particular level of CO_2 will cause, and how severe the effects of warming will be in different locations over different time-scales. Climate sceptics latch on to any semblance of debate about climate change to cast doubt on the basic science discussed in the previous two chapters – issues which are no longer questioned by climate scientists. A primary way sceptics cause this doubt is by creating climate myths: ideas which sound plausible but are simply wrong. There are several common techniques used to create myths. We explore six of these techniques in the 'Myth-busting' boxes below.*

> ⚡ **Myth-busting 1: Cherry-picking**
>
> Evidence from thousands of weather stations shows a steady, long-term rise in global average surface temperatures. However some climate sceptics 'cherry-pick' data to suggest warming is not happening. Cherry-picking involves taking only certain pieces of data to 'prove' one's point, while ignoring other data which do not support the desired conclusion. In a bizarre scene in 2015, US congressman Jim Inhofe threw a snowball in Congress to 'prove' that climate change is not happening.[23] In reality though, climate change is about a long-term rise in global temperatures: it cannot be 'disproven' by the occasional cold day or cold year in a particular part of the world.[24] *Illustration 6* shows how cherry-picking is used by some people to claim temperatures are not changing. So whenever we hear anyone pointing to one instance to 'prove' something, we need to ask ourselves: *'What does the whole picture say?'*

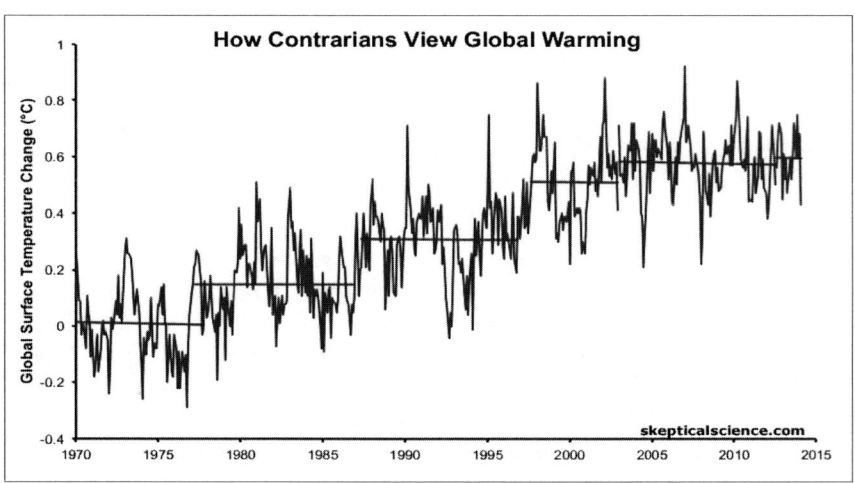

Illustration 6: The sceptic's 'escalator'. By cherrypicking the temperature records for only 10 years at a time, the natural variability of climate allows sceptics to claim warming has stopped (the horizontal lines). When the whole record is seen, the warming trend is clear.
Credit: Skeptical Science

* We owe this framework to John Cook, Research Assistant Professor at the Centre for Climate Change Communication at George Mason University and founder of the Skeptical Science website (see 'Want to Learn More?' for details). Throughout the book, we explore various other myths that use these six techniques.

⚡ Myth-busting 2: False experts

There is very strong scientific consensus for human-caused climate change. Despite this, in the US, a group called the 'Global Warming Petition Project' convinced 31,000 scientists to sign a petition claiming climate change was not happening. The only criterion for signing was a science degree of any sort. 99.9% of signatories were *not* climate scientists, so were 'false experts'*. Just because someone is a scientist, doesn't mean they'll have anything sensible to say on the topic. It's like having a geologist commenting on the value of a vaccine. So when we hear a so-called 'expert', we need to ask: *'What are his/her qualifications?'* and *'How respected is she/he in this field?'* While Mark and I are not experts on climate change ourselves, this book draws from and refers to expert sources such as the IPCC, NASA, the World Health Organisation, the Australian Institute of Marine Science and numerous climate scientists.

⚡ Myth-busting 3: Logical fallacies

There is clear logic behind the science of climate change. However some myths cast doubt on the science using logical fallacies, such as: *'Carbon dioxide levels have increased naturally in the past, so their current increase must be natural too.'* That is an illogical argument – it is like saying that because some fires start naturally, *all* fires must have started naturally. When we hear such arguments, we should ask: *'Does this really follow logically?'*

Credit: Chris Madden. Used with permission

⚡ Myth-busting 4: Oversimplification

This technique takes a surface look at the facts to draw a false conclusion. A deeper look will reveal the true story. Some sceptics say, for example, that human-caused CO_2 emissions are small compared to those happening naturally, and are therefore not significant. This oversimplifies the situation and ignores delicate balance of the carbon cycle, which human-caused emissions has severely disrupted *(see Illustration 2)*.

---

* Many of these scientists are no doubt experts in some field of science, but not climate science.

Part B: Climate Science Demystified - what's happening to our planet?

⚡ Myth-busting 5: Red herrings (irrelevant facts)

This technique uses facts that appear relevant but, on further inspection, are not. Some sceptics, for example, claim that CO_2 can't be a problem because it is a colourless, odourless gas, or because it is in such small concentrations (400 ppm is 0.04%). This is irrelevant information: nobody would accept nuclear waste being dumped in their backyard just because its radiation is invisible. Similarly, some climate sceptics believe that climate change is 'just a couple degrees – big deal.' But the size of a number is irrelevant. What matters is its effect. Nobody would argue that a fever of 40°C is 'just a couple degrees' over the normal body temperature of 37°C. When we hear facts bandied around, we need to ask: 'Is this really relevant?'

⚡ Myth-busting 6: Conspiracy theories

Donald Trump tweeted in 2012: *'The concept of global warming was created by and for the Chinese in order to make US manufacturing non-competitive.'*[25] Faced with the facts of climate change and hoping to shift the focus onto an enemy group, some sceptics resort to conspiracy theories. However even a little thought reveals how implausible many of these theories are. In this case, Mr Trump would have us believe that all climate scientists have been paid or threatened by the Chinese government to produce false scientific papers showing climate change is real. Seldom do these conspiracy theories explain how difficult it would be for all climate scientists to coordinate their actions and to keep their real motives quiet. So when we hear a conspiracy theory, we need to ask ourselves: *'How plausible is this theory?'* and then, *'What is the promoter of this theory trying to deflect my attention from?'*

It's now time to take a step back from analysing these myth-creation tactics to consider which group – the climate scientists or the sceptics – deserves our trust. Lonnie Thompson, an expert on glacial melt says:

> *Climatologists, like other scientists, tend to be a stolid group. We are not given to theatrical rantings about falling skies. Most of us are far more comfortable in our laboratories or gathering data in the field than we are giving interviews to journalists or speaking before Congressional committees. Why then are climatologists speaking out about the dangers of global warming? The answer is that virtually all of us are now convinced that global warming poses a clear and present danger to civilization.*[26]

6. Can We Believe This? - climate change myths

This statement encapsulates the main reason Mark and I accept the strong scientific consensus on climate change. Climate sceptic organisations, many of which are backed by the fossil fuel industry,[27] have every motivation to disregard the evidence for climate change (we'll explore this further in Chapter 17). By contrast, climate scientists have no ulterior motive to lie about the seriousness of climate change. In fact, speaking the truth about it often makes them unpopular and opens them to attack.[28] Given this, who would you rather believe – the climate sceptics or the climate scientists?

In the next Part, we look at what will happen to our world over the remainder of this century if we don't act quickly enough to reduce our carbon emissions, but go on with 'business as usual'.

Reflection Questions

- After reading this much of the book, what, if any, doubts remain that climate change is happening and is human-caused?

- Look at a denialist website like *www.globalclimatescam*. Try to find examples of the myth creation techniques discussed in this chapter.

Want To Learn More?

→ **Website:** New York Times; *17 Frequently Asked Questions with straight forward answers.* *https://www.nytimes.com/interactive/2017/climate/what-is-climate-change.html?smid=pl-share*

→ **Website:** *Skeptical science.* Presents clear climate science and rebuts climate sceptics' claims. *https://skepticalscience.com/*

→ **Short course:** *Making Sense of Climate Science Denial.* Seven-week free on-line course through the University of Queensland. *http://sks.to/denial101x*

Part C: Clear and Present Danger
– what happens if we do nothing?

7. Storm Ahead
– extreme weather events

We have friends in the Philippines who, like us, attempt to live simply with the poor. Shortly after Typhoon Haiyan struck in 2013, our friend Dave visited the devastated area and described the apocalyptic scenes – buildings destroyed, entire villages wiped out, and people desperately searching for family members not seen since the massive storm. It was the poor, especially those without solid housing, who were worst hit, their homes completely levelled. We'll see in Chapter 16 (Ruksana) that the poor are least responsible for causing climate change. It is a great injustice that those who have contributed least to the problem are suffering most, not only from extreme weather events, but also from the other problems discussed in this Part.

We've just seen how human-caused emissions have led to an increased concentration of CO_2 in the atmosphere and how that causes increased temperatures. Next, we need to take a cold, hard look at what the world will be like by the end of the century if we continue emitting CO_2 and other greenhouse gases at our current levels. In this Part, we will see that climate change will bring a number of devastating problems: extreme weather events will increase in frequency and severity; coral reefs will be severely damaged, affecting much marine life; sea levels will rise by metres, displacing hundreds of millions of people; there will be catastrophic loss of biodiversity; and global food production will be under significant stress. While all this might sound dramatic, these are not wild predictions, but rather, scientific projections based on many pieces of evidence. While less certain, we'll also consider the geopolitical strife, or even wars, that may ensue as the world struggles to cope with the effects of climate change. But first, let's look at extreme weather events.

7. Storm Aheac - extreme weather events

Aftermath of Typhoon Haiyan Credit: Wikimedia Commons

Extreme weather events – storms, floods, droughts, heatwaves and wildfires have always occurred, but with climate change they are increasing in frequency and severity.[29] Extreme weather events are the effect of climate change most visible to people in the West. They are also the most dramatic, so make the news frequently. Some extreme weather events you might remember from the news in recent years include the following:

- 2003: In Europe, a heatwave led to 70,000 deaths.[30]

- 2009: In Australia, record heatwaves and bushfires caused more than 170 fatalities.[31]

- 2010: In Russia, extreme heatwaves, drought, and bushfires led to 50,000 deaths.[32]

- 2010: In Pakistan, the worst floods in its history saw more than 1,700 deaths and 20 million people affected.[33]

- 2012: In the Caribbean and the US, Super-storm Sandy hit Haiti and Cuba before reaching the United States, killing almost 200 people.[34]
- 2013: In the Philippines, Typhoon Haiyan, one of the most intense tropical cyclones on record, with winds of up to 315 km/h, devastated many areas, killing over 6,000.[35]
- 2016: In Canada, huge fires burned across 220,000 km² and required Fort McMurray, a city of 80,000, to be evacuated.
- 2017: In the horn of Africa, famine (contributed to by drought) threatened 20 million people with starvation.[36]
- 2017: In the Caribbean, Hurricane Irma, with sustained wind speeds of 295 km/h for 33 hours, was the longest storm of such intensity since satellite monitoring began.[37]

It's impossible to say definitively whether a particular extreme weather event was caused by climate change. However, there is strong correlation between the number of extreme weather events striking in the last two decades and the increasing temperatures that are occurring due to climate change. While correlation doesn't necessarily show causation, scientists conclude that climate change is 'loading the dice' towards a greater frequency of such events.[38] Here are some statistics from which we may draw inferences:

- Of the ten deadliest heatwaves in recorded history, six have occurred since 2003.[39]
- Between 1980 and 2017, 218 different extreme weather events, each causing over US$1 billion damage, occurred in the US. That's an average of 5.9 per year. The number of such events in each of the last seven years from 2011 to 2017 was considerably higher than average (16, 11, 9, 8, 10, 12, 15).[40]

The Intergovernmental Panel on Climate Change (IPCC) stated in its 2014 report that climate change is likely to have contributed to the observed changes in heatwaves and flooding. It also noted that storm surges have become more destructive due to higher sea levels.[41]

It's easy to understand how a warming planet will cause more extreme temperatures and heatwaves.[42] Some of the hottest places on earth are already becoming almost unliveable. In the Iraqi capital Baghdad, for example, temperatures regularly reached 48°C in the summer of 2017.[43] If you've ever lived in places with those temperatures, you'll know that life is very difficult, especially if you don't have air-conditioning, as most of the poor do not. Where we live, in north India, summer days often hit 45°C. We can attest to it being miserable, especially during the regular power outages when the fan stops!

The science as to how a warming atmosphere causes more frequent storms, floods and droughts is still evolving. We do know that the extra heat alters ocean and atmospheric currents. It also causes higher humidity levels, since warmer air can hold more moisture. Together these changes cause greater rainfall in some areas and less in others.

In climate change terminology, 'mitigation' means reducing greenhouse gas emissions to lessen the extent of climate change, while 'adaptation' means better coping with the effects of climate change.[44] Both mitigation and adaptation are crucial. Regarding extreme weather events, we need to rapidly reduce our emissions to curb the frequency and intensity of such future events (mitigation). But we also need to deal with and prepare for the disasters that are happening now and will continue to happen, given how much we've warmed the earth already (adaptation). What does adaptation to extreme weather events look like? Depending on the context, it may involve early warning systems, stronger buildings, sea walls or drought-resistant crops.

Extreme weather events are estimated by the World Health Organisation to kill 60,000 people each year.[45] Rich countries can lessen the human costs through adaptation measures. However, developing world countries, like the Philippines, suffer much more, as they lack the economic resources for such adaptation. The great majority of deaths from extreme weather events occur in poorer countries.[46] This is not at all surprising to me, in that we've met many people in India who still live in houses made of mud, wood and plastic. These huts are cheap to construct and stay cooler than concrete and brick during summer, but they don't stand up well to severe wind, rain and flooding. Our good friend Kallu (who you'll meet again in Chapter 37) told me that he, his wife and children even had to relocate to a large unused concrete pipe for several days during one flood, because of the vulnerability of their housing.

The prospect of massive human and economic damage from climate change led the Paris climate agreement in 2015 (discussed in Chapter 24) to include provision of a US$100 billion per year fund to '*support low-carbon growth and climate resilience in developing countries.*'[47] Unfortunately, we are far from raising that amount of money. The Australian government, for example, has only pledged 0.05% of this total (despite having 1.7% of the world's GDP)[48] – and that too, from its existing aid budget.[49]

Aid to help developing countries adapt to climate change is not a handout. Given that it's our (wealthy countries') emissions which contribute most to these disasters, it is a matter of justice.[*] Our responsibility for extreme weather events linked to climate change should also spur us on to mitigation measures to reduce our own emissions. The IPCC warns that it will be much cheaper to mitigate climate change now (by working to keep temperature rise to under 2°C), than to pay for the increased damage bill should we delay acting and so see temperature rise exceed 2°C.[50]

In the next chapter, we'll examine the devastating effects of climate change on our coral reefs.

Reflection Questions

🔍 Have you, or anyone you know, ever suffered injury or property damage from an extreme weather event? How did you or they cope with that?

🔍 How confident are you that your government can protect you from the worst impacts of extreme weather events?

Want To Learn More?

→ Report: *IPCC. Climate Change 2014, Synthesis Report, Summary for Policy-makers.* The latest report from the world's leading body on climate change. Pages 7-8 discuss extreme weather events. *https://ipcc.ch/pdf/assessment-report/ar5/syr/AR5_SYR_FINAL_SPM.pdf*

---

* See *Illustration 10* in Chapter 11.

8. Goodbye Reef
– a coral calamity

Charlie Veron, the Chief Scientist at the Australian Institute of Marine Science, has travelled all over the world studying coral. He says of his role: '*When I first worked on the Great Barrier Reef, inshore fringing reefs were very interesting. In fact I described a lot of the new species from that work. And now most of them are all gone.*'[51]

The Great Barrier Reef is an Australian icon. As Australians, we are immensely proud that one of the natural wonders of the world is in our country. I was lucky enough to visit the Great Barrier Reef on a holiday with Cathy, Tom and Oscar in 2016. It was stunning and I'll forever have fond memories of snorkelling with vibrantly-coloured and magically-shaped fish. Yet even while we were snorkelling at the southern end of the reef, we were reading reports about vast swathes of reef further north being bleached.

Climate change is bringing about two major changes in the world's oceans: temperature rise and acidification. Together, these changes are leading to the degradation of the world's corals and therefore its marine ecosystems. We'll consider each of these changes in turn.

The temperature of the oceans is increasing as the greenhouse effect escalates and more energy is trapped in the earth's climate system, much of it in the oceans. Over the last 200 years the world's oceans have increased in temperature by an average of 0.5°C, more in the polar regions and less in the tropics.[52] This is less than the rise in air temperature, which is now almost 1°C hotter than in pre-industrial times.

SCIENCE GEEK 4

Rising ocean temperatures

The oceans have stored over 90% of the heat accumulated on the earth due to the greenhouse effect. That is because the oceans have a far greater mass than the atmosphere, and thus contain a vastly greater quantity of heat. We might think of this like a large, outdoor swimming pool. The temperature of the water changes more slowly than the air

Part C: Clear and Present Danger - what happens if we do nothing?

temperature, so at the start of summer the air temperature increases more quickly than the water, making the water relatively brisk for the first few swims of the season. By the end of summer, however, the water has accumulated a lot of heat. The pool retains that heat well after air temperatures drop in winter. In the same way, it takes a lot of the sun's energy to make a small change in ocean temperature, but that change in temperature stays for much longer.

The rising ocean temperature leads to a 'bleaching' phenomenon in our coral reefs. Corals get their vibrant colours from algae living within them. When oceans warm, even a little, the coral becomes stressed and expels the algae, thus losing its colour. While the loss of the algae and the colour doesn't necessarily lead to the death of the coral, it does make it more likely.[53]

Bleached coral   Credit: Wikipedia

Large swathes of the Great Barrier Reef are already bleached. The Australian Institute of Marine Science found that: *'The impact from this bleaching event, the most widespread and severe ever recorded on the Great Barrier Reef, is still* unfolding. Based on in-water monitoring surveys, overall coral mortality is (as of June 2016) at 22% for the entire Great Barrier Reef.'[54]

The second major effect of climate change on oceans is acidification. This occurs as oceans absorb more carbon from the atmosphere.[*] Over the last 200 years the world's oceans have increased in acidity[†] by 26%.[55] This has very adverse effects on coral reefs. The increased acidity of the water lowers the concentration of calcium carbonate, which is the main 'building block' for coral. This weakens the coral, making it less resistant to storms which, as we saw earlier, will become more severe and frequent with climate change.

Sadly, these two major changes – increasing ocean temperature and greater acidity – mean that the outlook for the Great Barrier Reef and other coral reefs around the world is grim. With a quarter of all marine species globally having part of their life cycle in coral reefs, this has massive implications.[56] We'll consider this further in Chapter 10 (Snow Leopards and Koalas).

> ⚡ **Myth-busting 7: The reef is fine, isn't it?**
>
> In November 2016, Pauline Hanson, an Australian senator, conducted a media event snorkelling at the Great Barrier Reef to show Australians that the reef was 'fine'.[57] Ms Hanson, who is not a scientist, let alone a climate scientist, is a good example of a false expert. Who would you rather trust, Ms Hanson or Charlie Veron, the Chief Scientist at the Australian Institute of Marine Science?

The Great Barrier Reef is a natural wonder that we all have the right to enjoy, but also the responsibility to protect for future generations. David Attenborough, in a recent documentary on the Great Barrier Reef, closes the series by saying: '*Do we really care so little about the earth on which we live that we don't wish to protect one of its greatest wonders from the consequences of our behaviour?*'[58]

Next, we'll consider another change to the ocean that is already having a major effect, not only on marine species, but on humans – sea level rise.

---

[*] For the chemists among you, the chemical process is: $H_2O + CO_2 \rightarrow CO_3 + 2H \rightarrow H_2CO_3$ (carbonic acid).
[†] The pH level (scale from 1 to 14, with 1 most acidic and 14 most basic) of the oceans has reduced from 8.2 to 8.1.

Part C: Clear and Present Danger - what happens if we do nothing?

Reflection Questions

🔍 Have you ever visited the Great Barrier Reef? If so, how was that experience for you?

🔍 If you are not Australian, are there coral reefs off your country's coast? If so, do you know how they are faring with climate change?

Want To Learn More?

→ Podcast: ABC Radio. *The evolution of the Great Barrier Reef's first scientist, Charlie Veron.* *http://www.abc.net.au/radio/programs/conversations/conversations-charlie-veron/7924128*

→ Documentary: ABC TV. *The Great Barrier Reef: David Attenborough.* *http://www.abc.net.au/tv/programs/david-attenboroughs-great-barrier-reef/*

→ Report: *IPCC. Climate Change 2014, Synthesis Report, Summary for Policymakers.* The latest report from the world's leading body on climate change. Pages 13-14 discuss coral reefs. *https://ipcc.ch/pdf/assessment-report/ar5/syr/AR5_SYR_FINAL_SPM.pdf*

9. Take Me Higher
– sea level rise

As a boy, I remember seeing the sand dunes on Australia's east coast being decimated by cyclones. It was sobering to witness the power of the sea. In more recent years, houses near my home town of Brisbane have become unliveable as their foundations are weakened by rising sea levels and storms.

Sea levels have risen about 20 cm since 1870, and are currently rising at about 3 mm/year.[59] While that doesn't sound like much, it has been enough to cause difficulties in many places. In this chapter, we'll see that these problems will become much greater over the remainder of this century, as the rate of sea level rise increases. We'll examine the main causes of sea level rise, the rate and scale of the rise, and finally consider which countries will be most affected.

Causes of sea level rise

Sea level rise is caused by two factors: thermal expansion and ice-melt. Thermal expansion is the technical term for the fact that as water heats, it expands. An easy way to understand this is the old (non-digital) type of thermometers. They contain mercury, which is highly responsive to temperature change. As temperature increases, the mercury expands and moves up the thermometer. Water, while not nearly as responsive to temperature change as mercury, still does expand when heated. Therefore, as water temperature rises, it increases the volume of the ocean, causing sea levels to go up. It's not known exactly what proportion of sea level rise is caused by thermal expansion, but it's probably around half.[60]

When massive sheets of ice on land melt, the water runs off into the ocean. Every year, about 565 Gt of land-ice melts – amounting to 75 tonnes per person on earth!* The four major bodies of land-based ice of concern to us are: glaciers, Greenland, the West Antarctic ice-sheet, and the East Antarctic ice-sheet. Some people might wonder, given the enormity of the oceans, how melting ice-sheets could significantly affect sea levels. However, rising sea levels become easier to imagine when we consider that these ice-sheets cover millions of square kilometres and are, in places, over two kilometres thick.[61] These ice-sheets and their implications for sea level rise are summarised in Table (1) and detailed thereafter.

* From Table 1, 565 Gt of ice melts each year, divided by 7.4 billion people on earth = 75 tonnes per person.

41

Part C: Clear and Present Danger - what happens if we do nothing?

Table 1: Ice-sheets and associated sea level rise[62]

Location	Area (mill km²)	Equivalent area	Sea level rise if melts (metres)	Stability
Glaciers	-		0.41	90% unstable and melting. Losing 150 Gt ice per year
Greenland	1.7	3 times the size of Texas	7.3	Unstable. Losing 281 Gt ice per year
West Antarctic	2	The size of Mexico	3.2	Unstable. Losing 134 Gt ice per year
Entire Antarctic (including West and East Antarctic)	14	80% of the size of Russia	58.3	Relatively stable (except for West Antarctic)

⚡ Myth-busting 8: Glaciers growing?

There are 170,000 glaciers in the world, not counting those in Greenland and the Antarctic.[63] Until the late 1800s most glaciers were increasing in size, but since then, 90% of them have been melting.[64] One climate myth uses the fact that some glaciers are increasing in size as 'evidence' that climate change is not happening. This myth cherry-picks data by ignoring the 90% of glaciers which have been shrinking.

Comparison of McCarty Glacier (Alaska) in 1909 and 2004   Credit: Wikimedia Commons

9. Take Me Higher - sea level rise

Greenland is a massive ice-covered island north of Europe and Canada. With the ice-sheet on Greenland already beginning to melt, mining companies are eyeing the rich mineral and oil deposits under the ice.[65]

The West Antarctic ice-sheet is separated from the East Antarctic by the Transantarctic Mountains. While the West Antarctic isn't currently losing ice as quickly as Greenland, the signs are troubling. Eric Ringot, lead author of a study by NASA and the University of California, says that the melting of the West Antarctic ice-sheet '*appears unstoppable*' and '*comes with a sea-level rise of between three and five meters. Such an event will displace millions of people worldwide.*'[66] By contrast, the East Antarctic ice sheet is still relatively stable.

How much and how quickly will the sea rise?

Global temperatures have already risen by about 1°C, but sea levels have only risen by about 20 cm since 1870.[67] At first glance, this is cause for some comfort. Maybe that means that if temperatures rise by another degree, it will translate to only another 20 cm of sea level rise over the next hundred years, which seems manageable. Unfortunately, that's not the case, because of the interrelated phenomena of positive feedback loops, tipping points and time lag.

Positive feedback loops: Thus far, we have been discussing ice on land. Melting of sea-ice, like the Arctic ice cap, doesn't affect sea levels directly because the ice floats, with 90% of its volume below the surface of the ocean* (remember the icebergs in *Titanic*). Arctic ice-melt does, however, contribute to sea level rise indirectly, by a 'positive feedback loop'. Parents and child-carers will know intuitively about positive feedback loops. When we praise a child for a particular behaviour, such as being helpful around the house, the praise tends to produce more of that good behaviour. This prompts even more praise, which produces more of the behaviour and so on – a positive feedback loop.

Ice-melt generates a positive feedback loop of a different sort. Much of the sun's radiation is reflected from the earth's surface back into space. That reflection happens very efficiently from white ice. Oceans, on the other hand, are relatively dark and absorb much more radiation. As temperatures rise and the white Arctic ice melts, less radiation is reflected and more is absorbed by the dark Arctic Ocean. Thus the oceans heat even more, more ice melts and the

---

* Ice is also 10% less dense than water, so sea-ice melting has no effect on sea levels.

whole cycle is exacerbated. This feedback loop is not positive in the sense of being good, but only in the sense of building on itself. Increasing temperatures have already led to significantly less ice in the Arctic ice cap over the last 30 years *(see Illustration 7)*, thus reducing the reflectivity of earth and contributing to increased temperatures. In recent decades, the September (summer) average

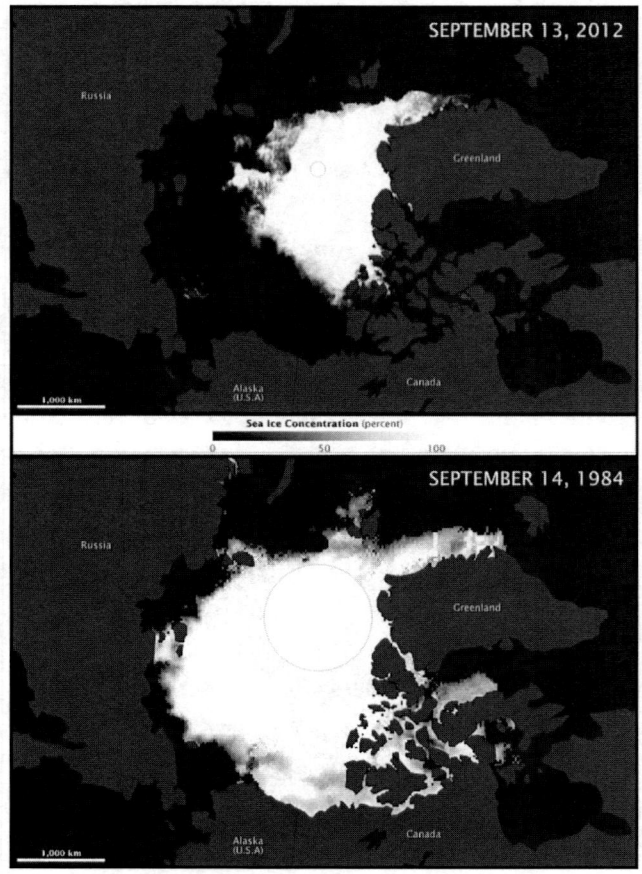

Illustration 7: Reduction in Arctic sea-ice   Credit: Wikimedia Commons

sea-ice in the Arctic has halved from 6.8 million square kilometres in 1984 to 3.4 million square kilometres in 2012.[68] The melting is so significant that shipping companies are now planning routes through the Arctic regions in summer, rather than taking the much longer routes through the Suez or Panama canals.[69]

A second positive feedback cycle of great concern in climate change is related to permafrost. This frozen soil, in places like Siberia and Canada, is beginning to thaw. As it does, it releases methane that had been trapped in the ground for thousands of years. Methane, a greenhouse gas, exacerbates warming, so thawing more permafrost, releasing even more methane and so on.[70]

Tipping points: This term refers to a phenomenon whereby if you change one factor, you may see very little change in a second factor; but at some point, a similar small change in the first factor will cause a huge change in the second. It's where we get the saying, 'the straw that broke the camel's back' – the owner puts on many straws with no change in the camel's ability to bear the load, but that last tiny change (the last straw) breaks the camel's back – a huge change. Another way to understand tipping points more literally is by placing a pencil flat on a table, perpendicular to the edge. Pushing the pencil a little towards the edge makes no change – it's still on the table. Push it a little more – still no change. But eventually you push it that little bit more and it literally tips off the table – a big change.

So how do tipping points work with ice-melt? Imagine a block of ice in the freezer. Warm the freezer from -4°C to -2°C and there will be no change to the block of ice. Warm it to -1°C and still no change, but warm it to +1°C and the ice will start to melt – a very big change.*

So what is the tipping point for these huge ice-sheets? There is not an exact figure, but scientists think that 2°C will be close to it for the West Antarctic ice-sheet. The World Bank says: *'As global warming approaches and exceeds 2°C, there is a risk of triggering non linear tipping elements. Examples include the disintegration of the West Antarctic ice-sheet leading to more rapid sea-level rise...'*[71]

A tipping point does not mean that massive melting will happen suddenly and dramatically. Just as a block of ice at 1°C doesn't melt immediately, so too the huge ice-sheets won't melt instantly. It will take several decades or even a century to melt enough to have catastrophic sea level rise. However, these tipping points do mean that once reached, there is no going back.

If we don't act to reduce emissions quickly, we will reach these tipping points and massive sea level rise will be unavoidable. Unfortunately, the fact that these changes are gradual and long-term mean they're less dramatic and 'newsworthy'. We may well pass these tipping points without even noticing at the time. Like the proverbial frog in water that is gradually brought to boiling

---

* In reality ice melting is more complex than just moving above 0°C, but it does illustrate the idea of tipping points.

Part C: Clear and Present Danger - what happens if we do nothing?

point, change that is initially gradual can ultimately be lethal. If we don't act on greenhouse emissions quickly enough, these changes will gather pace as the century progresses. Scientists are now predicting 0.5-1.3 metres sea level rise by the end of this century and six metres by 2200.[72]

Time lag: CO_2 remains in the atmosphere for decades after we emit it.* This fact, together with positive feedback loops and tipping points, creates a time lag between stopping the cause of the heating (carbon emissions) and the heating itself. It's a little like turning the gas off on the stove, but the pot continuing to heat the contents. This means that for decades after emissions have started to decline, ice will continue to melt and water continue to expand, leading to sea level rise. Rises of 4-6 metres may already be 'locked in', given the carbon already in the atmosphere.[73]

Credit: www.CartoonStock.com

⚡ Myth-busting 9: Sea levels falling?

One climate myth says that a small drop in sea levels in 2010 'proved' that sea levels aren't rising. This myth is another example of cherry-picking, using the data from 2010, but ignoring other years. There is a rational explanation for the anomaly. In 2010 there were huge floods in Australia. All of that water, which had evaporated from the sea and then dropped as rain far inland, took several months to eventually find its way back to the oceans. During that period, the sea level dropped minimally. Once the huge volume of water found its way back to the ocean, however, sea levels were back up and continued to rise.[74]

---

* For more detail on CO_2 remaining in the atmosphere, see Chapter 14 (Our Carbon Budget).

9. Take Me Higher - sea level rise

Who will be impacted?

Naturally enough, it will be lowest-lying areas that are worst hit by sea level rise. Some Pacific islands are already becoming unliveable. Sirilo Sutaroti, 94, a resident of the Solomon Islands, describes having to relocate because of sea level rise: *'The sea has started to come inland, it forced us to move up to the hilltop and rebuild our village there away from the sea.'*[75] This extreme vulnerability of the Pacific islands led participants at the Paris climate summit in 2015 to aim to restrict warming to 1.5°C. The Pacific Islanders' catch-cry was *'1.5 to stay alive.'*

Even places in the West will be significantly affected. Cities like Amsterdam, New York and Miami are already planning sea walls and other measures to protect themselves. *Illustration 3* shows The Netherlands. The dark areas show the parts of the country which will be underwater with just two metres of sea level rise.

However, much more significant damage will be done in low-lying developing world cities like Mumbai, Dhaka and Jakarta, which don't have as much capacity to protect themselves against sea level rises.

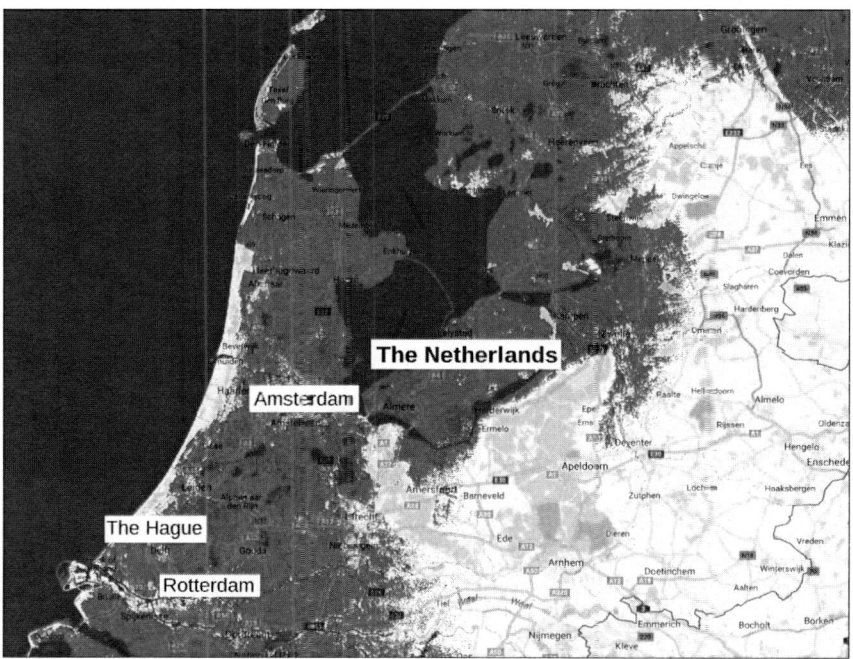

Illustration 8: The Netherlands with 2-metres sea level rise

Credit: Alex Tingle and http://geology.com/sealevelrise/

47

Part C: Clear and Present Danger - what happens if we do nothing?

Bangladesh, a country of 160 million residents, will also have large swathes of its land become unliveable, displacing tens of millions of people. Our journalist friend Matt Wade told us that these effects are already taking place. In one of his visits to Bangladesh he found coastal communities that had been displaced by unprecedented tidal surges. Residents reported how fearful they were of sea level rise.

During a war or famine, refugees flee across borders to safer places. Kolkata, across the border in India, is the obvious choice for Bangladeshis fleeing rising waters. But Kolkata will also be significantly waterlogged with two metres of sea level rise. In fact, our friend Asad, who runs a social welfare organisation in India, already responds to flooding emergencies near Kolkata every couple of years. With more sea level rise, that part of India will become less habitable. So where will those tens of millions of Bangladeshis and Indians go?

Such sea level rise will cause human migration on a scale never before known. Some predictions are that 500 million people will be displaced.[76] The world is currently (2017) struggling to deal with millions of refugees fleeing Syria and North Africa. How will we deal with *hundreds* of millions fleeing rising waters?

Sea level rise will have a profound effect on humanity. In the next chapter, we'll see that climate change will also have devastating effects on thousands of other species.

9. Take Me Higher - sea level rise

Reflection Questions

- Go to *http://geology.com/sea-level-rise/*
  Put in 2 metres sea level rise and then zoom in to where you live. Do you know anyone whose home will go underwater with 2 metres sea level rise? Reflect on that eventuality a little.

- Even if we limit warming to 2°C, scientists suggest this may result in 6 metres sea level rise by the end of 2200.[77] Enter 6 metres rise on the website. Zoom to where you live. How is it faring?

Want To Learn More?

→ Podcast: *Radio National; 2016. Rising Seas to Push out 500 million.* http://www.abc.net.au/radionational/programs/scienceshow/rising-seas-to-push-out-500-million/4831836.

→ Website: *National Snow and Ice Data Centre.* Authoritative information on ice-melt and sea level rise. *https://nsidc.org/cryosphere/quickfacts/icesheets.html*

→ Website: *Antarctic Glaciers.* Interesting diagrams, illustrations and graphs on Antarctic glaciology. *http://www.antarcticglaciers.org/antarctica/west-antarctic-ice-sheet/*

Part C: Clear and Present Danger – what happens if we do nothing?

10. Snow Leopards and Koalas
– extinction

Our friend Jeph, who lives in the mountains in India, tells us that the snow leopard, a rare Himalaya-dwelling cat, is facing extinction. Many more species are endangered, such that we face the real prospect of never being able to show our children iconic animals like tigers, gorillas, chimpanzees and polar bears. However, the problem of species extinction from climate change goes well beyond these 'poster animals'. Climate change will cause thousands of species to become extinct.

Just because most species are not as visible as large vertebrates does not mean they are unimportant. Think, for example, of krill, a tiny marine species, but the primary food of blue whales.[78] If the tiny krill become extinct, so too will the mighty blue whale. Vital too are our coral reefs – created by tiny marine organisms. As we saw in Chapter 8 (Goodbye Reef), one quarter of all marine species have some part of their life cycle in coral reefs. If we lose our reefs due to climate change, it will have a massive effect on many marine species.

> **SCIENCE GEEK 5**
>
> **Species on earth**
>
> There are approximately 1.7 million known species of multicellular life on earth. That will surprise many, as we tend to think only about the species of big animals. However, the vast majority of species are barely noticed. Approximately 1 million are insects. Then there are 0.3 million species of plants. Only 66,000 species are vertebrates (mammals, birds, fish, reptiles and amphibians). Of the vertebrates, there are 5,513 species of mammals, of which we humans are only one.

The World Wildlife Fund has surveyed sample populations from 3,700 animal species for almost half a century. It found that animal numbers plummeted (on average) 58% between 1970 and 2012.[79] Three main factors are responsible: loss of habitat, over-hunting/fishing and climate change. It's easy enough to understand how habitat loss and over-hunting leads to animal populations decreasing, and sometimes to extinction, but just how does climate change contribute to extinction? There are several factors:

- Some species just can't keep up with the increase in temperature. Corals become stressed with slight increases in ocean temperatures, expel their colour-giving algae and may eventually die. Bats become stressed when temperatures exceed 42°C.[80] Koalas struggle above 38°C.[81]

- Some species lose their access to food. This is clearest for polar bears, which need sea-ice to hunt seals. As Arctic ice melts, the bears' hunting range becomes compromised and they lose their access to food (see Myth-busting (10)).

- Other species need to move their habitat to cope with the temperature changes. Some animals (such as various species of moth)[82] live at a particular altitude where the temperature is just right. As temperatures increase, however, they need to move up the mountain to find cooler temperatures. Sometimes the mountains they live in just aren't high enough. Other species, like the caribou and Arctic fox, are migrating north to stay cool, but are simply running out of room to move north.[83]

- As some animals move their habitat, this may bring them into more contact with humans, creating conflict. And guess who usually wins? In Australia, for example, koala populations tend to move east, away from the heat, but toward human population centres, with the associated roads and dogs, neither of which are good news for koalas.

- As some species of animals move, the plants on which they feed aren't as prolific. Plants can grow in new areas, but generally don't move as quickly as the animals feeding on them.[84] Plants often require decades or centuries to propagate in new areas.[85]

- Some plant species pollinate according to temperature changes. With increasing temperatures, some species are pollinating earlier. However their *pollinators* (birds and insects) have not changed the time of the year in which they are active, thus creating a mismatch between the pollinators and plants that need pollinating.

Part C: Clear and Present Danger - what happens if we do nothing?

⚡ Myth-busting 10: Polar bears thriving?

Polar bears live in the Arctic regions. They need sea-ice to hunt for seals, their primary food source. In the last 35 years, 40-50% of Arctic sea-ice has disappeared,[86] so polar bears are struggling to maintain their hunting range.

One climate myth says that polar bears are thriving, noting that there are more polar bears now than in the mid-20th century. While this is true, it is an oversimplification which obscures the real situation.

In the mid-20th century polar bears were hunted at a rate of 1,000 a year, so their numbers were declining rapidly. Since then, governments have banned most hunting, so numbers have recovered to a degree. However after the numbers recovered from hunting-times, populations have started to struggle again. So while the raw numbers of polar bears may be better than during hunting times, they do appear to be in decline again, this time because of climate change rather than hunting.[87]

Polar bear (compulsory in all literature on climate change)
Credit: Christopher Michel. www.flickr.com

Over the history of the earth, many species have become extinct. The evolution of new species and extinction of others is normal over the course of geological history. Biologists estimate that, over millions of years, we lose on average 1-5 species a year.[88] Extinctions themselves are not so much the problem as the *rate* of extinction.

There have already been five 'mass extinctions' in the earth's history – periods when there has been a relatively rapid loss of species. These extinctions wiped out 75-90% of the species on earth during those periods. The last of those 'mass extinctions' was in the late Cretaceous period, about 65 million years ago, during which the dinosaurs perished.

Over the last several hundred years, the rate of extinction has increased dramatically from five per year to more like 1,000 per year. That is a rate not dissimilar to – indeed, probably higher than – the rates in those five mass extinctions. Many biologists now see this as the beginning of the sixth great extinction.[89]

There are two important distinctions, however, between this sixth great extinction and the previous five. Firstly, this one is happening over a much shorter time frame. While the previous extinctions have taken tens of thousands of years to play out, the current one is happening in only a couple of hundred. Secondly, while all six extinctions have involved the greenhouse effect, the *cause* of that effect is different. In previous extinctions the greenhouse effect increased because of exceptional volcanic activity, while in the current one, *human*-caused emissions are responsible. In recognition of the profound effects that humans are having on the planet, some scientists suggest that we have now entered a new geological epoch, the Anthropocene (*anthro* meaning human).[90]

Species extinction is much more serious than not being able to show our children a polar bear or a koala. The interconnectedness of life means the extinction of other species threatens our own existence. A species of bee becoming extinct, for example, may make it difficult for a particular species of plant to be pollinated. That plant may in turn be the main source of food for a herbivore (plant-eater), which may be important to a species of carnivore (meat-eater) and so on, all the way up the food chain to humans.

Renowned biologist, professor Jeremy Kerr of the University of Ottawa says:

> *When you're a global change biologist a lot of the time it feels like what you're studying is like global catastrophe that's unfolding in slow motion... It's really important that globally the oceans are acidifying or that we are losing species at the rate at which we lost them at the end of the age of the dinosaurs. I mean, this is disaster movies, it's just unfolding at a hundred-year time scale. We have to tell people that that's what's happening. Failing to do this, adding unnecessary layers of caution that is inaccurately conveying that these processes may or may not be happening is doing the public a disservice.* [91]

This is the tragic irony of climate change: extinctions are happening hundreds of times faster than the natural rate, yet, for many of us humans, it's still too slow to take notice. One factor humans will take notice of, though, is a lack of food. It is to that we turn next.

Part C: Clear and Present Danger - what happens if we do nothing?

Reflection Questions

- Have you noticed any change in the wildlife where you live over your lifetime? What do you think are the reasons for that change?

- What do you think about the notion of the interconnectedness of different species? What implications does that have for us as humans?

- Is it reasonable to name this epoch 'Anthropocene' in recognition of the human impact on the earth?

Want To Learn More?

→ Podcast: Columbia University, *Climate Change Poses Challenges to Plants and Animals.* *http://blogs.ei.columbia.edu/2015/02/03/climate-change-poses-challenges-to-plants-and-animals/*

11. Is There Enough?
– food insecurity

We have met mums in India who simply don't have enough food to feed their children. They are real people and their physical and emotional pain is enormous. If you're reading this, it is highly unlikely that you will have ever experienced food insecurity, chronic hunger or malnourishment. We sometimes see images of malnourished children, but we have little idea how awful it is to not have enough to eat or, even worse, to watch your children waste away from lack of nutrition. An incredible 45% of Indian children are stunted due to malnutrition.[92] Not only in India, but across the developing world, millions of people are food insecure – not knowing where their next meal will come from. The awful reality of climate change is that food insecurity will worsen.

The map in *Illustration 9* shows projected food production changes between 2003 and the 2080s due to climate change.

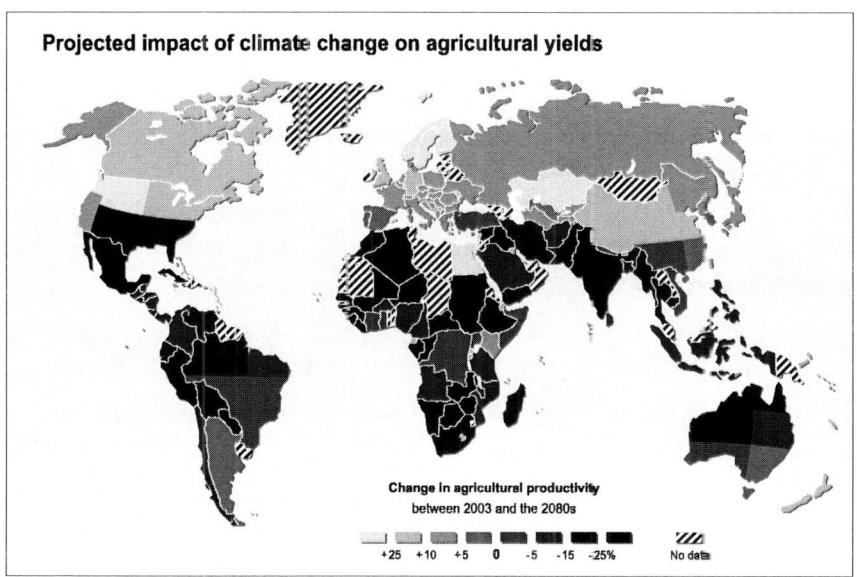

Illustration 9: Projected change in food production   Credit: Wikimedia Commons

Note that some northern areas like Europe, Russia, and significant parts of North America and China are lighter in shade, meaning they are likely to become more abundant food producers.[93] That is because as they warm, areas which were previously too cold for much agriculture will become better able to produce crops. More significantly though, most of Africa, Latin America, Australia and South Asia, which are currently abundant food producers, are darker in colour, meaning their food production will *decrease*.

> ⚡ **Myth-busting 11: Increased food production?**
>
> Plants use carbon dioxide in photosynthesis. One climate myth says that the increased carbon levels in the atmosphere will help plants grow and therefore increase food production. However, this is an oversimplification. Plants require not only CO_2, but also a reliable water source and stable temperatures – which climate change threatens. Extreme weather events like storms, heatwaves and droughts further impinge on agriculture. These effects outweigh the benefit from increased CO_2 concentrations. The IPCC now predicts that food yields will decrease by 2109.[94]

Some of the world's most productive agriculture occurs in low-lying river deltas, which tend to have fertile soils and abundant water availability. Sea level rise threatens the viability of agriculture in many of these deltas. Sea level rise also poses a major threat to coastal agriculture in general, through groundwater becoming contaminated with salty seawater.[95]

Another way climate change impacts global food production arises from the vulnerability of the world's coral reefs. Fish provide 17% of humanity's total animal protein consumption.[96] But with one quarter of all marine species having some part of their life cycle in coral reefs, fishing is likely to become less productive due to climate change.[97]

Given expected population increase, the world may not be able to feed itself by the end of the century. Disturbingly, in 2017, for the first time this century, the UN reported that the number of hungry people in the world increased. One of the factors it cited was climate change.

Another sobering point emerges when we compare changes in food yields to the map in *Illustration 10*, showing which countries have been most responsible for carbon emissions from 1850 to 2007. Countries which appear bloated have emitted most carbon to date, whereas countries which appear withered have emitted least. Clearly 'fat' USA, UK, Japan and Europe are most responsible for emissions to date. Meanwhile, barely recognisable Africa and Latin America

11. Is There Enough? – food insecurity

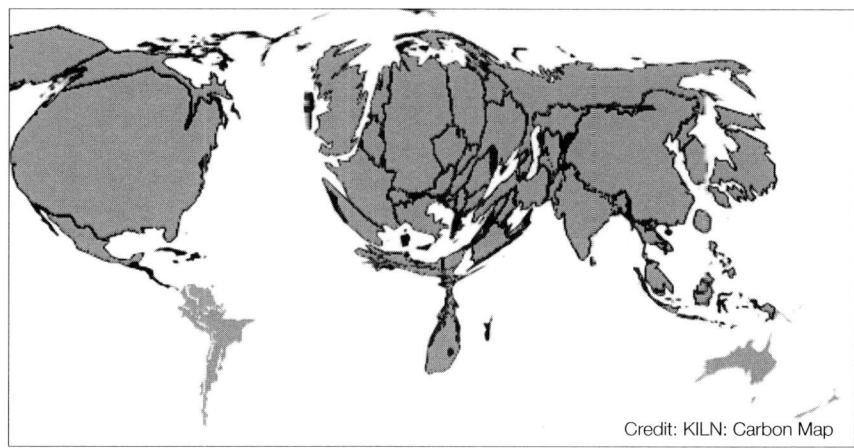

Illustration 10: Countries most responsible for historic carbon emissions

have been responsible for very few emissions.*

When we compare *Illustration 9* and *10*, we see that the countries which have been responsible for most emissions to date may actually benefit in terms of food production, while the regions least responsible for emissions may have significantly impaired food production. This is terribly unjust and creates one of the great difficulties for global action on climate change – those nations most responsible for the problem have less incentive to address it, at least in terms of food production.

Amidst questions of whether there will be enough food in the future, we must emphasise that there *is* enough now. Without food wastage and huge amounts of grain fed to animals, there would be more than enough food for everyone in the world. We will revisit these issues in Chapter 28 (Waists and Wastes).

While wealthy countries and people may be able to produce adequate food as climate change unfolds, they may not escape the global political fallout. We will examine that next.

---

* Australia and Canada appear withered, despite their large per capita footprint, because they have such low population densities.

Part C: Clear and Present Danger - what happens if we do nothing?

Reflection Questions

- How many generations ago were your forefathers farmers? Have you heard stories from relatives or friends about how difficult it is to grow food when rainfall and weather is unpredictable?

- For readers in Australia, Africa, Latin America and Asia, where might your country import food from, should agricultural production decline as the century unfolds?

Want To Learn More?

→ Report: IPCC. *Climate Change 2014, Synthesis Report, Summary for Policymakers.* The latest report from the world's leading body on climate change. Pages 14-16 discuss food production. *https://ipcc.ch/pdf/assessment-report/ar5/syr/AR5_SYR_FINAL_SPM.pdf*

12. Arms or Alms?
– geopolitical tensions

I (Tom) remember studying geography in primary school, learning about the difference between 'natural' and 'man-made' disasters. It all seemed so clear-cut back then: some disasters, like droughts, floods and storms, are caused by nature, while other calamities, such as war, are wrought by humankind. Climate change blurs this distinction between natural and human disasters, as each is linked to the other. As we've seen, human emissions are changing the climate system, increasing the frequency and severity of some 'natural' disasters. Just as profound as the impacts of human actions on natural systems, though, are the impacts of natural systems on human actions.

There are significant reasons to suggest that climate change will exacerbate conflict.[98] Of course, human behaviour can be harder to predict than even the most complex natural systems. This means that the speculations in this chapter have a lower degree of certainty than the projections in preceding ones. Nevertheless, it is worth considering how our societies might react to climate change. There are several ways new conflicts might be triggered and existing ones exacerbated.

Water: Water is essential to life. Seldom do we realise, though, just how much water our modern lifestyles consume. For instance, producing a kilogram of beef requires about 15,000 litres of water.[99]

Climate change is already affecting rainfall patterns, impacting how rivers flow. Many rivers are also fed by seasonal glacial melt in summer months – 40% of the world's population relies on this glacial melt for their drinking water.[100] As we saw in Chapter 9, 90% of these glaciers are shrinking. Once glaciers have permanently melted, some of these crucial rivers, like the Ganges system in India, will be severely depleted. People relying on these rivers to irrigate farmland – and to drink – will be desperate for more water. When whole countries face acute water shortages, they will be tempted to dam the river, reducing the water access of countries downstream. This 'water stress' may become so severe in some parts of the world that it leads to war. Conflicts may erupt between, for example, Ethiopia and Egypt over use of the water from the Nile or between India and Pakistan over the Indus.

Indo-Pakistani relations have been strained ever since these countries were established in 1947. They have already fought four wars.[101] Mum and Dad tell me that there were such high tensions in 2001 that people feared a nuclear war. A number of foreigners left Delhi, but Mum and Dad stayed and thankfully the tension subsided. On that occasion, the hostilities weren't over water. However, tension over the Indus water supply is already increasing the strain between these two nuclear powers. The Indus Water Treaty (1960) has survived the test of time so far, but was not written with climate-change-caused water scarcity in mind. The Indian government recently hinted that it may revoke the treaty, and Pakistan has responded that this would be viewed as an act of war.[102]

Food: Some analysts argue that the Arab Spring became such a powerful movement because of popular discontent fuelled by the high price of bread in those Middle Eastern countries.[103] We saw in Chapter 11 that climate change will likely cause a net decline in global agricultural production. Some current food exporters, such as Australia, may no longer be able to produce food at the same scale. Others which are self-sufficient now (like India) will become desperate for imports. This will likely lead to food prices rising. Rather than a steady, gradual rise in global food prices, we may see sudden spikes caused by disasters wiping out crops, or even by governments banning food exports. These price spikes may lead to many dying from hunger. Our neighbours know too well how price volatility affects their lives. Every year, the price of fresh vegetables spikes around monsoon, leaving many with no option but to curb the variety of their already meagre diet. Understandably, starving countries and people will stop at nothing to acquire food, potentially leading to war with countries which do have food.

The Arctic: The Arctic Ocean, like other oceans, is international territory: it doesn't belong to any one country. In the past, few people cared too much about the Arctic, as its thick ice-sheets prevented it being of significant economic value. As the planet warms – especially at the poles – this is all changing. The Arctic is likely to become a major shipping route, saving travel time from East Asia to Europe. While the Antarctic, in the south, is subject to an international treaty banning mineral exploration and fishing, the Arctic, in the north, is not. Large reserves of oil and gas under the Arctic are already being explored by fossil fuel corporations. It may also become a significant fishing area. It is possible that conflict will break out as different countries vie for control over this increasingly valuable area.[104]

Unilateral geoengineering: The costs of climate change will be unevenly distributed. Some countries, like Russia and Canada, may experience a net benefit; while others, including many Pacific islands, will literally be wiped off the map. As we'll see in Chapter 18 (Someone Else Will Fix It), there are a range of controversial geoengineering techno-fixes which might allow us to reduce the temperature of the earth, such as shooting sulphur particles high into the atmosphere, where they'll block sunlight. We definitely do not endorse these highly risky 'solutions', and it would be extremely difficult for the international community to agree on any such measures. However, a country like Bangladesh,

12. Arms or Alms? - geopolitical tensions

understandably desperate to gain respite from sea level rise and cyclones, could potentially implement such a 'solution' itself. As disastrous as geoengineering might be in itself, the conflicts it triggers could be even more devastating. For instance, countries suffering unintended side effects of geoengineering (such as sudden rainfall changes) might retaliate against the state that took those measures.[105]

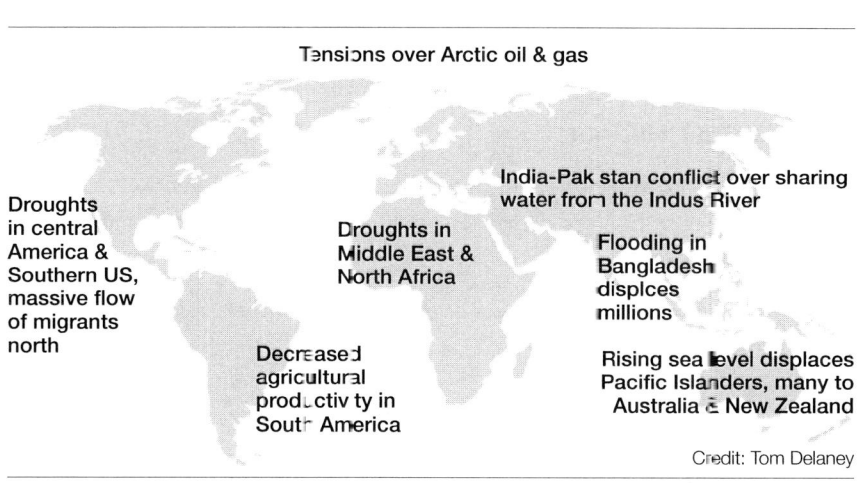

Illustration 11: Possible mass displacements and conflicts due to climate change

In summary, climate change is likely to exacerbate conflicts, as people and countries struggle over access to resources. With conflicts come refugees. Add these to the numbers of people displaced by natural disasters and sea level rise, and it is likely that climate change will be responsible for hundreds of millions of people being forced to migrate. Indeed, this is only natural: like all animals, when humans find that food and water are no longer available where we're living, we migrate. As we've seen in recent years with the refugee crisis in the Mediterranean, if there is food, water and security on the other side of a border, people will do whatever it takes to cross that border.

It is my sincere hope that the world will be generous in its response to the victims of disasters – 'natural' and 'man-made' – caused by climate change. Perhaps we'll welcome refugees, apologetic for the calamities wrought upon them by our emissions. Maybe we will be more generous in our foreign aid, helping people adapt to climate change. Hopefully, climate change will result in more alms-giving, rather than accumulating arms.

However, given the West's current stinginess regarding aid and refugees,* I find it hard to imagine we'll become more generous as we face climate stresses

---

* Apart from some European countries like Germany, which have very generous refugee policies.

within our own nations. Scariest of all is a possible positive feedback cycle: the more conflict globally, the harder it will be to maintain global cooperation in tackling emissions. This could lead to runaway climate change in a dog-eat-dog world – an awful possibility.

Reflection Questions

- Which of the four sources of possible geopolitical conflict have already begun to some degree? In which parts of the world is that happening?

- Which of the potential sources of geopolitical conflict are most likely to affect your country?

Want To Learn More?

→ Report: CNA Corporation; 2007. *National Security and the Threat of Climate Change.* A report by American military officers on the likely geopolitical implications of climate change. *https://www.cna.org/cna_files/pdf/National%20Security%20and%20the%20Threat%20of%20Climate%20Change.pdf.*

→ Book: Dyer, Gwynne; 2011. *Climate Wars: the fight for survival as the world overheats.* Oneworld Publications. An imaginative description of the possible implications of climate change.

13. Margaret Thatcher's Warning
– three options for the earth

To complete our description of 'What Happens If We Do Nothing', we will quote a number of reputable organisations and individuals to emphasise the extreme gravity of the situation.

Margaret Thatcher, former British Prime Minister (and outspoken advocate of free markets) said, way back in 1988: '*For generations, we have assumed that the efforts of mankind would leave the fundamental equilibrium of the world's systems and atmosphere stable. But it is possible that with all these enormous changes – population, agricultural, use of fossil fuels – concentrated into such a short period of time, we have unwittingly begun a massive experiment with the system of this planet itself.*'[106]

A World Bank report from 2012 warns: '*we're on track for a 4 degrees Celsius warmer world marked by extreme heatwaves, declining global food stocks, loss of ecosystems and biodiversity, and life threatening sea-level rise..... there is also no certainty that adaptation to a 4°C world is possible.*'[107]

Pope Francis said in 2015: '*We may well be leaving to coming generations debris, desolation and filth. The pace of consumption, waste and environmental change has so stretched the planet's capacity that our contemporary lifestyle, unsustainable as it is, can only precipitate catastrophes, such as those which even now periodically occur in different areas of the world. The effects of the present imbalance can only be reduced by our decisive action, here and now.*'[108]

Kevin Anderson, deputy director of the Tyndall Centre for Climate Change Research, says: '*there is a widespread view that a 4°C future is incompatible with any reasonable characterisation of an organized, equitable and civilised global community.*'[109]

Given these grave words, we have a clear choice: we can accept the warnings and act to rapidly decrease our carbon emissions; or ignore the scientists, and go on burning carbon as if there's no problem.

---

* These quotes talk of 4°C warming. If the commitments made in Paris (see Chapter 24) are met, then warming may be limited to 2.5-3°C. However if they are not met, then warming may reach 4°C or more.

Part C: Clear and Present Danger – what happens if we do nothing?

There is theoretically a risk in taking the first choice – to transition to a low-carbon economy. There is a tiny possibility that we could spend considerable money and effort making the changes suggested in Parts F and G, only to learn that climate change wouldn't have been that bad after all. What, then, will we have lost? Many of the changes that will be required in the struggle against climate change – generating energy renewably, negotiating fair international agreements, consuming more responsibly – will be largely beneficial for all of us. These changes will also help counter other environmental issues, such as deforestation and pollution.

Editorial Cartoon used with the permission of Joel Pett and the Cartoonist Group. All rights reserved.

By contrast, the risk of taking the second choice – doing nothing – and being wrong is catastrophic. The magnitude of that risk has been laid out in this Part. To gamble millions of human lives, and millions of species, on the chance that climate change might not be as bad as we think, is foolish and unethical in the extreme.

Many people, and countries, want to choose a third option – do a little bit now and wait to see how things pan out before committing to any course of action. In many situations, this compromise is prudent. Unfortunately, it is not so with climate change. If doctors told you that you were virtually certain to have cancer, would you 'wait and see' or begin treatment immediately?

13. Margaret Thatcher's Warning - three options for the earth

We'll see in the next Part that it is those of us living in the West who have the largest carbon footprints. It is therefore only fair that we dramatically reduce our emissions in order to protect ourselves and others from the dire consequences of climate change.

Reflection Questions

- How do you feel, reading these quotes about the gravity of the situation?
- What do you think about the three options of how we might respond to these warnings?

Part D: Ruksana versus Bruce – who is responsible?

14. Our Carbon Budget
– the ultimate overspend

For years we have lived in slums to experience something of what life is like for the poor. We have suffered electricity outages, filled water from public taps and lived in cramped spaces. However, we will never know what it is really like to be poor: to not know where your next meal is coming from or to be unable to afford basic education and medical expenses. However several years ago, we did conduct an experiment to experience a little more of what it's like to live on a meagre budget, by limiting our month's spending to Rs5,000 (AUD$100). While we shrewdly chose February, a couple of fewer days didn't save us from feeling the pinch once our favourite snacks started running out!

This Part uses another type of budget – a carbon budget – to consider who is responsible for climate change. In this chapter we introduce the idea of a carbon budget and show that the world's carbon budget is severely strained. Chapter 15 shows that this is because Australians, and most people in the 'developed' world, use far more than our fair share of the budget. Our excessive flying, driving, shopping, and meat-eating, has a large carbon footprint. Chapter 16 shows, by contrast, that many Indians – and others in the developing world – lead relatively sustainable lives.

In Paris in December 2015, the global community finally came to a substantive agreement about climate change. The Paris accord aims to keep global temperature rise to 2°C above 1800s levels, with an 'aspirational' (hoped for) target of 1.5°C.

Where did these figures for acceptable temperature rise come from? As we've seen, global average air temperature has already risen by about 1°C. If we continue with our current emissions trajectory it will probably result in 3-5°C warming, with catastrophic results. Most climate scientists agree that there will be enormous danger with even 2°C increase, in terms of extreme weather events, species loss, reduced food production, and sea level rise. Many Pacific island

14. Our Carbon Budget - the ultimate overspend

states will become unliveable with the sea level rise caused by even 2°C of warming. The 1.5°C target was a last-minute addition in Paris to give some recognition to the extreme vulnerability of the Pacific states, who raised the slogan '1.5 to stay alive'.[110] However, many political leaders seem to believe that the 1.5°C target is unattainable and are instead aiming for 2°C, believing the damage caused by that target to be manageable.

Once we decide on a temperature target, the next question is how much we need to limit our emissions to achieve that goal. *Illustration 12* shows the correlation between emissions levels and temperatures. The horizontal axis shows the total amount of CO_2 that has been or will be emitted since 1870. The vertical axis shows the corresponding likely temperature rise. You'll see that there is a roughly linear relationship[111] (the shaded area) between human-caused CO_2 emissions and temperature rise.*

By 2011, about 1,900 Gt CO_2 had already been emitted,[112] corresponding to a temperature increase of about 1°C (the solid line). The IPCC estimates that to

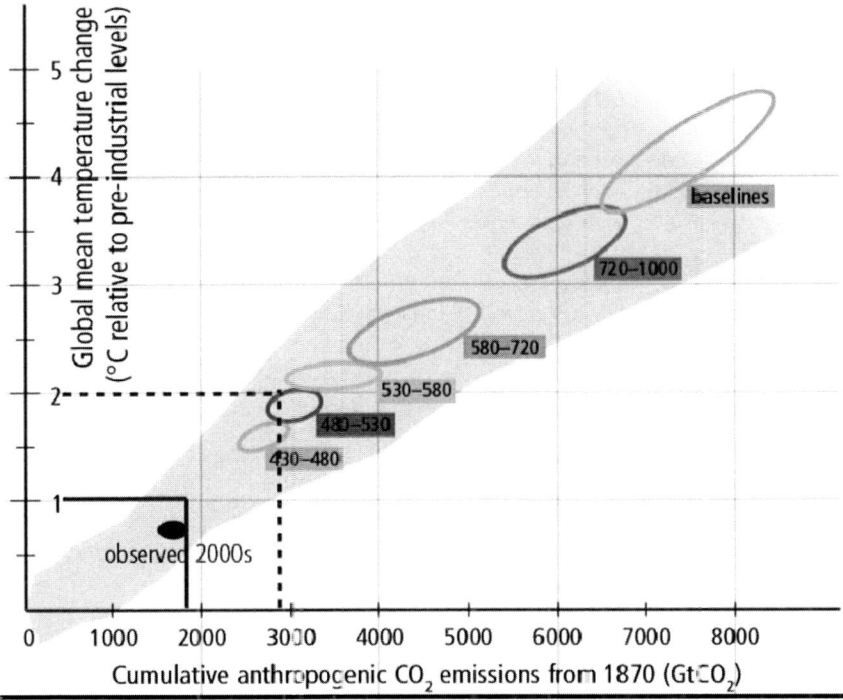

Illustration 12: Warming and human-caused cumulative CO_2 emissions   Credit: IPCC

* The ovals with numbers refer to the concentration of CO_2 in the atmosphere in that scenario. The concentration of CO_2 is now 400 ppm and going up by 2.5 ppm per year.

Part D: Ruksana versus Bruce - who is responsible?

have a 66% chance of keeping temperature increase to 2°C we need to restrict our future total emissions to another 1,000 Gt CO_2[113] (total 2,900 Gt – the dashed line).*[114] We could understand this as a global 'carbon budget'.

Our budget of 1,000 Gt CO_2 to stay under 2°C might sound like a lot, but in the six years between the IPCC's figures (2011) and the writing of this book (2017), we have already burnt through almost a quarter of this budget, leaving about 800 Gt.†[115] Fortunately, there is some evidence that global emissions have now peaked.[116] Without substantial reductions, though, we will likely hit the threshold for 2°C by 2040.‡[117]

There are some important differences between this carbon 'budget' and national or household budgets:

- A family or even a national budget is for a short, fixed period: often a month or a year. However, the global carbon budget needs to last for the remainder of the century. That's because about 1/3 of carbon emissions remain in the atmosphere 100 years after they are emitted, and 1/5 remain 1000 years on! Thus the consequences of our emissions now will be felt well into the future.[118]

- In our family budget, if we overspend, the consequences are normally manageable: a nasty credit card debt, or at worst bankruptcy, after which you can start again. However, if we overspend the world's carbon budget by continuing to emit at the current rate, we are into the realm of 3-5°C warming, with calamitous results.

- We have reasonable control over our family budget and our government has reasonable control over the national budget. However, the global carbon budget is outside individual or even national control. The amount of carbon emitted depends on the actions of governments, corporations and individuals across the globe.

The bad news is that fossil fuel companies' existing projects (coal mines, oil wells and gas fields) contain enough carbon (942 Gt CO_2) to blow our entire 'budget' for the rest of the century.[119] So even if we don't open any new mines or oil wells, but simply dig up and burn the fossil fuels in existing ones, we may well exceed 2°C *(see Illustration 13)*.

---

* If we are aiming for 1.5°C, then our carbon budget (with a 66% chance of success) is only 400 Gt CO_2.

† At 36 Gt per year, over 6 years, we've emitted about 6 x 36 = 216 Gt. Budget of 1,000 Gt – 216 Gt used = 784 Gt remaining.

‡ (1000-216)/36 Gt/yr = 22 years. This doesn't mean that the world will warm this much over the next one/two decades; rather that we will pass tipping points making it inevitable that the world will warm that much in the future.

14. Our Carbon Budget - the ultimate overspend

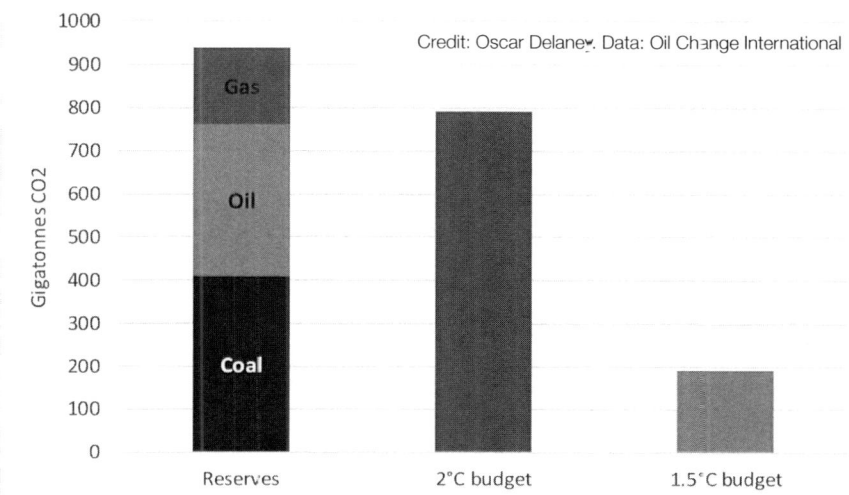

Illustration 13: Developed reserves of fossil fuels, compared to carbon budgets

The news gets worse. In addition to existing coal, oil and gas reserves in operational projects, countries and companies have discovered far more fossil fuels (1,920 Gt CO_2 worth) in other, as yet unexploited areas.[120] Despite these resources containing far more carbon than our global budget, corporations and governments are still exploring for even *more* fossil fuels.

We can also view our carbon budget on an individual level. If we divide the total remaining carbon budget of about 800 Gt CO_2 by the number of people in the world (7.4 billion), we get a budget for every individual on the planet of about 105 tonnes CO_2. A more relevant figure to use is 150 tonnes CO_2e (carbon dioxide equivalent), taking into account warming from other greenhouse gases, like methane and nitrous oxide.[121]

SCIENCE GEEK 6

Other greenhouse gases and CO_2e

Carbon dioxide (CO_2) emissions account for about ¾ of human-caused greenhouse gases, with the remainder being made up of methane (CH_4), nitrous oxide (N_2O), and other gases, like hydrofluorocarbons (HFCs). From this point on, we'll primarily talk about 'carbon dioxide equivalent' (CO_2e), which quantifies the warming effect of a mixture of gases by multiplying each by their potency relative to CO_2. In 2010, total global emissions were 49 Gt CO_2e. This consisted of:

- 36 Gt CO_2 = 36 Gt CO_2e

Part D: Ruksana versus Bruce - who is responsible?

- 0.31 Gt methane x 25 (times worse than CO_2) = 8 Gt CO_2e
- 0.01 Gt nitrous oxide x 300 (times worse than CO_2) = 3 Gt CO_2e
- smaller amounts of other gases like HFCs = 2 Gt CO_2e[122]

Emissions have increased only marginally between 2010 and 2017.[123]

This equates to a sustainable fair share of about 2 tonnes CO_2e per person per year.* As seen in *Illustration 14*, the average citizen of the world emits about 6.6 tonnes CO_2e per year.† On average, Australians annually emit 23 tonnes CO_2e, North Americans 20.5, New Zealanders 17.5 and Britons 7.9.[124] By contrast, the average Indian emits 2.3 tonnes CO_2e per year. How can it be that in the West we emit 3-10 times as much as Indians (and many others in the developing world)?

In the next two chapters, we will put flesh on these figures, by considering the different lifestyles that result in such divergent carbon footprints.

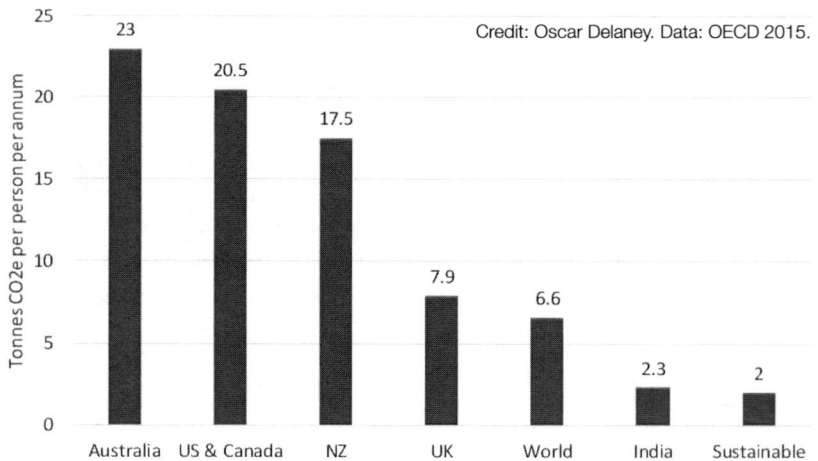

Illustration 14: Who is responsible? Relative carbon emissions

* The figure of 2 tonnes CO_2e per person per year can be derived in several ways. Firstly, by estimating the amount of CO_2 the world's oceans and forests can absorb (about 18 Gt as seen in *Illustration 2* in Chapter 4) and dividing that by the world's population of 7.4 billion gives 2.5 tonnes CO_2 per person per year. This method is not very reliable, as the capacity of the oceans and forests to absorb carbon decreases as emissions reduce. Secondly, we can divide the sustainable individual carbon budget of 150 tonnes CO_2e for the remainder of the century by a typical lifetime of 75 years = 2 tonnes CO_2e per head per year. Finally, taking a pathway to reducing emissions such as that proposed by Shrink that Footprint (see 'Want to Learn More?') has global emissions reducing to 2.1 tonnes CO_2e per head per year by 2050. 2 tonnes CO_2e per head per year is also the figure derived by the United Nations (see Human Development Report, 2007-8, p44-52).
† Dividing 49 tonnes CO_2e annually by a population of 7.4 billion.

Reflection Questions

- Is a carbon budget a helpful way to understand the challenge to restrict our carbon emissions?
- Why do you think governments and fossil fuel companies have continued exploring for new fossil fuel deposits, despite knowing that to extract and burn the existing reserves would warm the earth by more than 2°C?

Want To Learn More?

→ Website: *Shrink That Footprint; 2017. Carbon targets.* Discusses carbon budgets in easy to understand terms. *http://shrinkthatfootprint.com/carbon-targets-for-your-footprint*

→ Article: McKibben, Bill; 2016. *Recalculating Climate Math. New Republic.* Describes the idea of a global carbon budget and compares that to fossil fuel reserves. *https://newrepublic.com/article/136987/recalculating-climate-math*

→ Report: Oil Change International; 2016. *The Sky's Limit.* Argues against new fossil fuel projects, as the carbon content in existing ones exceeds the carbon budget. *http://priceofoil.org/2016/09/22/the-skys-limit-report/*

→ Report: IPCC; 2014. *Climate Change 2014, Synthesis Report, Summary for Policymakers.* The latest report from the world's leading body on climate change. Pages 8-10 discuss carbon budgets. *https://ipcc.ch/pdf/assessment-report/ar5/syr/AR5_SYR_FINAL_SPM.pdf*

→ Film: McKibben, Bill; n.d. *Do the Math; http://act.350.org/signup/math-movie/*

Part D: Ruksana versus Bruce - who is responsible?

15. Bruce
– high-carbon culprit

When we returned to Australia in 2014, we wanted to minimise our carbon footprint. We found, however, that many of our friends and family were doing just the opposite: driving around the country, flying around the world and purchasing all sorts of products on a whim. Rather than finding our kinsfolk attempting to reduce emissions, Australians were emitting more carbon per head than almost anyone else in the world: a whopping 23 tonnes CO_2e per head per year.[125] If everyone on the planet emitted as much carbon as Australians, we would burn through our global carbon budget for the rest of the century in just seven years.

23 tonnes a year is a hard figure to conceptualise. It is the weight of 4½ African elephants, or, in gas form, a volume equivalent to three Olympic sized swimming pools.[126] How is it that we emit so much carbon? In this chapter, we will look at Bruce*, an average Australian. We divide Bruce's carbon footprint into seven areas: buying 'stuff'; food; local travel; long-distance travel; domestic electricity and gas; housing; and government services and mining.

Buying 'stuff': Bruce loves buying new things: TVs, iPhones, clothes and gadgets. The production, transport and retail of all this 'stuff' releases significant emissions. As we'll see in Chapter 17, this is encouraged by the media, working hand in glove with industry, constantly urging Bruce to have the newest and best gadget. Purchasing all these products requires around 6 tonnes CO_2e emissions per year.[127]

Food: Bruce has a typically Aussie, meat-heavy diet, so eats around two kilograms of meat each week.[128] Livestock emit a lot of methane in farts and burps, so steak (and milk and cheese from dairy cattle) contributes significantly to his carbon footprint. Additionally, much of Bruce's food is packaged in plastic and transported long distances, producing further emissions. Bruce sometimes leaves food in the fridge for too long and has to throw it out. This adds to his emissions because it means he buys more than he eats and wasted food decomposes in landfill, releasing methane. All of this means Bruce's emissions for his diet are around 4 tonnes CO_2e.[129]

Local travel: There are 57 vehicles per hundred people in Australia, and this is rising, with about 1 million new cars being bought every year. Bruce is one of these car owners, and drives his car about 20 kilometres a day, accounting for 2 tonnes CO_2e per year.[130]

---

* Bruce is a fictional character – any semblance to a real person is purely unintentional.

15. Bruce - high-carbon culprit

Apart from the damage done in driving cars, their manufacture is also energy-intense, so requiring significant emissions. We explore the 'embodied energy' (energy that went into making something) for manufacturing a typical car in Science Geek (7). Bruce buys a new car once every 15 years or so, accounting for another one tonne of CO_2e per annum, bringing his total emissions for local travel up to 3 tonnes CO_2e.[31]

Science Geek 7

The energy required to build a car

A tremendous amount of energy goes into making a car before you even drive it. Approximately 100 gigajoules (100,000,000,000 joules)[132] goes into the manufacture of a car (depending on the model). To make this figure more understandable, 100 gigajoules is equivalent to the energy required for:[133]

- The food requirements for one person for 30 years, or
- Lifting 200 African elephants from sea level to the top of Mount Everest, or
- Driving a typical car 25,000 kilometres.

In Australia, most of this energy is ultimately released by coal combustion, so the carbon footprint of a typical car is about 15 tonnes CO_2e.[134]

Long-distance travel: Bruce and his family regularly fly thousands of kilometres domestically for business or holidays – to the Barrier Reef or the ski fields. Sadly, our emissions in getting to these pristine natural spots contribute directly to their degradation. Apart from domestic travel, Bruce also flies internationally – to Europe or Asia – every couple of years for work or pleasure. All of those flights add another 1.5 tonnes CO_2e per year to Bruce's account.[135]

Domestic electricity and gas use: Bruce emits about 2.3 tonnes CO_2e per year for his domestic electricity and gas consumption, as does every other member of his household.[136] This is partly because his house has many electrical appliances, from TVs and computers, to coffee grinders and microwaves. If Bruce's house is air-conditioned, as many in the West are, his electricity usage is significantly increased. Ironically, the carbon emissions from the electricity to run air-conditioners, in the long run, contribute to even higher temperatures, requiring even more air-conditioning!

Part D: Ruksana versus Bruce - who is responsible?

Housing: Bruce lives in a large house. The house size in Australia, at an average 89 m² per person for new houses being built, is now the largest in the world, as seen in *Illustration 15*. Interestingly, the number of people living in each house in Australia has fallen significantly over the last century to 2.6,[137] but house sizes continue to increase.

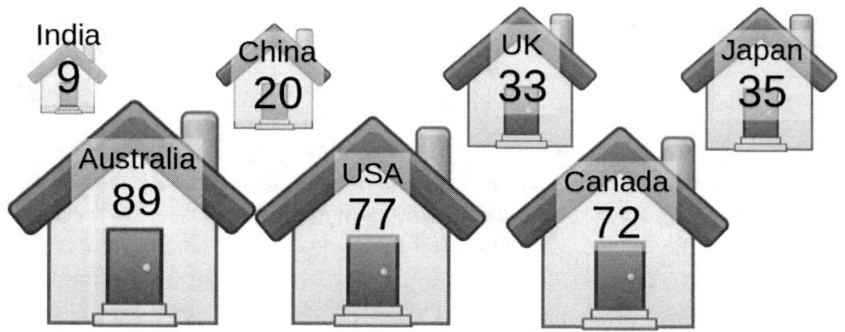

Credit: Cathy Delaney. Data: Shrink that Footprint

Illustration 15: Average house sizes (m² per person) in various countries

Why do many people in the West build such big, carbon-intensive houses when family sizes are small? One reason is that new houses and apartments these days are constructed not so much with a view to liveability, but more to resale value. So while Bruce and his partner may only have two children, they will build or purchase a large 3 or 4-bedroom house with several bathrooms and garages, as it resells for a higher price. Building such a house requires a lot of materials (cement, bricks, steel, wood and glass), the manufacture of which releases significant emissions – up to 80 tonnes CO_2e.[138] And far from being a once in a lifetime event, Bruce is encouraged to buy, build, renovate and resell his house several times in his life. If we average this out, Bruce uses around 1 tonne CO_2e per annum on his housing.

I'm told that, in coming to Australia as a toddler, one of the things which surprised me most was house size. I even got lost trying to find the toilet in my grandparent's house, which was modestly sized by Australian standards, but seemed gargantuan to a young boy used to living in one room. To this day, I have always shared a bedroom with my brother Oscar. Rather than being annoyed by a lack of privacy, we really enjoy each other's company.

Government services and mining: This final category of emissions is the most nebulous, as it attempts to account for the emissions that can't be directly attributed to any individual. We know a country's total emissions, as governments calculate it each year. From this we can calculate the per capita emissions. For Australia, this is 550 million tonnes divided by 24 million people = 23 tonnes CO_2e per head per year. We can also calculate fairly accurately, as we've done so far in this chapter, the emissions for an individual's goods purchased, food, local and long-distance travel, domestic power and housing. The gap between Bruce's carbon footprint for these six categories (17.8 tonnes CO_2e) and his share of the entire nation's carbon emissions (23 tonnes CO_2e) is basically composed of his share of public services and his share of mining emissions.

In the West, generally we have high-quality public services: good roads, well-resourced hospitals, and high-tech military hardware. All of those services require significant emissions. How much an individual is responsible for those emissions is a matter of debate. Our method is to apportion them roughly according to how much an individual uses those roads, airports and so on. So a person who drives and flies a lot is more responsible for those public service emissions.

The mining industry also contributes significantly to a country's carbon emissions. While allocations of individual responsibility are again up for debate, we do it according to who benefits most from mining industry profits. Bruce is likely to bank with one of the 'big four' Australian banks, each of which is heavily invested in fossil fuels.[139] So, though he may not know it, Bruce is partly responsible for mining industry emissions. In all, Bruce's use of government services and his share of the mining industry's emissions adds another 5.2 tonnes CO_2e to his tab.[140]

Science Geek 8

Emissions from mining

Emissions associated with mining are of three types. Scope I emissions are those on the actual mine site and include the diesel and petrol used in the mining operations as well as the 'fugitive' emissions which escape into the atmosphere when digging up the coal, oil or gas.[141] Scope II emissions are those *off* the mine site, to generate the electricity necessary to run the mine.[142] Scope III emissions are those caused when the fossil fuel that is mined, is ultimately burned.[143] Normally only Scope I and Scope II emissions are accounted for in a country's mining operations.

In total then, Bruce emits 23 tonnes CO_2e per year as seen in Table (2). So do Amanda, Sam, Julie and most people living in Australia, the US, Canada and New Zealand. Given the scale of our over-emitting, what can Bruce and the rest

Part D: Ruksana versus Bruce - who is responsible?

of us do? Part G (Small Picture Solutions) describes many concrete ways we can reduce our carbon footprints and tells the inspiring stories of people who have actually taken these low-carbon paths.

Table 2: Bruce's carbon footprint

Aspect of life	Explanation of how the emissions are caused	CO_2e emissions (tonnes per year)
Buying 'stuff'	Manufacture, transport and sale of goods.	6.0
Food	Cattle burping. Energy use on farm. Food transport and packaging.	4.0
Local travel	Burning petrol, diesel and gas in cars. Energy to build cars.	3.0
Long-distance travel	Burning jet fuel to propel planes.	1.5
Residential electricity	Burning coal to generate electricity. Gas for cooking & heating.	2.3
Housing	Manufacture of cement and other building materials.	1.0
Government services and mining	Construction and operation of roads, airports, hospitals, schools. Emissions from mining.	5.2
Total		**23**

Next we'll contrast Bruce's high-carbon life with that of our good friend in Delhi, Ruksana.

Reflection Questions

- Generally, how aware are people in the West that we emit much more than the world average?

- Use an online carbon footprint calculator (like *www.carbonfootprint.com*) to find your total carbon footprint for a year. How does that compare to the Australian average of 23 tonnes CO_2e, the world average of 6.6 tonnes CO_2e[144] and the global fair share of 2 tonnes CO_2e?

- In which areas is your lifestyle most similar to Bruce's? Where do you do better than him, and where worse?

Want To Learn More?

→ Report: *Department of Environment and Energy; 2017* Quarterly Update of Australia's National GHG Inventory. *http://www.environment.gov.au/system/files/resources/6cc33ded-14aa-4dae-b298-b6ffe42f94a1/files/nggi-quarterly-update-march-2017.pdf*

→ Books: Berners-Lee, Mike; 2010. *How Bad are Bananas? The Carbon Footprint of Everything. Green Profile.* Describes the carbon footprints of 100 different goods and services.

Part D: Ruksana versus Bruce - who is responsible?

16. Ruksana
– low-carbon champion

Mum and Dad did not set out to live as environmental radicals. When Matt Wade wrote the article (reproduced in Appendix 1) for *The Sydney Morning Herald* in 2009, we weren't exactly living like Bruce, but our overall environmental awareness on issues like climate change was limited. Even the solar panel mentioned in the article was purchased not so much for the environmental benefits, but simply because we wanted some light at night when the electricity went off, as it regularly did.

As our awareness of climate change grew, we started taking more notice of our Indian friends and neighbours' small carbon footprints. Remarkably, we found out that the average Indian is responsible for emissions of only about 2.3 tonnes[145] CO_2e per annum, ten times lower than the average Australian.

What does such a low-carbon lifestyle look like in India? In this chapter we describe a typical Indian carbon footprint, by looking at our (real) friend Ruksana's lifestyle, as well as examples from our own lives to shed some light on why emissions are so low. In reality, India's carbon emissions are distributed unequally, with many wealthy people living western lifestyles, with the associated carbon footprint, while the poor lead extremely low-carbon lives.

In our analysis, we divide Ruksana's carbon footprint into the same seven areas that we used for Bruce.

Buying 'stuff': Ruksana tends to use most of her income on food, medical costs and school fees, so she has very little 'disposable' income with which to buy consumer products. Occasionally she is given second hand things – a mobile phone or some clothes – by a friend or relative. Of what little disposable income she has, Ruksana spends most on an occasional gift for her children. Thus Ruksana's carbon emissions related to the things she buys are very low, at about 0.5 tonnes CO_2e per year.[146]

Ruksana (right) – our low-carbon champion (2008)

16. Ruksana - low-carbon champion

Food: A meat-rich diet has a considerably higher carbon footprint than a vegetarian one. Most of our neighbours in India are Muslims, for whom meat (except pork) is a much-craved part of the diet. However at Rs100 (AUD$2) per kg for chicken, Rs250 (AUD$5) per kg for buffalo and Rs400 (AUD$8) per kg for goat, meat is a luxury. Ruksana and many of our friends earn about AUD$4 a day, so they seldom eat meat – perhaps only once a week, usually reserving that for visits by guests.

Food in India is also generally less processed, not packaged, and is transported shorter distances than it is in the West. Hence, Ruksana's emissions from her diet are around 0.6 tonnes CO_2e per year.[147]

Several years after the chicken incident described in Chapter 2, I became fully vegetarian when I was confronted by Bakra Eid (Festival of the Goat). In this celebration, Muslim families save up or borrow money to buy a young goat, fatten it up for several weeks, and then slaughter it.* It was a hard-hitting experience for me as a ten-year-old. Having patted and played with goats in the build-up to Bakra Eid, there were no goats to be seen the day after. We were now given parcels of goat meat instead. The connection between the goats

Oscar and I with our friend on a cycle rickshaw, a great form of low-carbon transport in India (2008)

* This festival has many positive aspects too, such as distributing meat to the destitute.

Part D: Ruksana versus Bruce - who is responsible?

and their meat was too fresh in my mind. I couldn't stomach it. Mum and Dad were gracious enough to go along with me, perhaps thinking it was a phase that would soon blow over. If so, they underestimated my stubbornness, and were later 'converted' to vegetarianism themselves. Consequently, our family's dietary carbon footprint is, like Ruksana's, quite low.

Local travel: Ruksana and her neighbours generally go by foot, cycle rickshaw or bus when travelling within the city. In this conservative culture, many women stay in the house and only travel with other female friends. Ruksana is different – a feisty feminist. She was determined to provide for her children's education even if that meant going against gender norms by working outside the home. Her job – which involves helping women have safe pregnancies and deliveries – means that she travels a bit, but primarily on foot or by cycle rickshaw. Consequently, her carbon footprint for local travel is very low – only about 0.2 tonnes of CO_2e annually.[148]

Trying to identify with local residents, we have never owned a car in India. In Delhi's congested traffic, it is sometimes quicker to walk anyway. We mostly travel by foot, bike, bus, tempo* or Metro (Delhi's electric train system). Consequently, our carbon footprint from local travel is also very low. When I was 15 and starting to explore the issue of carbon footprints, I once went for a month without using any fossil-fuelled transport. Going by foot was a fascinating way to see Delhi and I gained new appreciation for the lives of the poor who can't afford any transport but walking.

Long-distance travel: Wealthy Indians now regularly fly for work or pleasure. However, when Ruksana and her family travel longer distances to visit relatives once or twice a year, they go by train or bus. Thus, Ruksana's long-distance transport emissions are only about 0.1 tonnes CO_2e annually.[149]

As a family, we travel within India quite a bit for work and holidays. We have many fond memories of reading and playing cards on long train trips. We feel good about emitting little carbon in normal life, however, our return flights to Australia every couple of years emit two tonnes of CO_2e per person – our fair share for a whole year! That's why we try to keep flights to a minimum. Once, when Mum and Dad were going to a conference in Thailand, Oscar and I decided to stay with friends in India instead, to avoid unnecessary flights.

Electricity and gas: Ruksana and her family have no air-conditioning in summer and no heating in winter. North India gets quite cold in winter, sometimes below 5°C overnight. With no heating, Ruksana, her husband and four children rely on quilts and body heat to stay warm at night. During the long, hot, summer months, they sleep under the ceiling fan, or on their flat roof to catch any breeze. She and her family live in a single room, in which there are several lights and

---

* Small jeep-like public transport seating 10 people.

sockets to charge their mobile phones and run their TV. She uses a gas stove to cook meals. With all this, Ruksana's domestic electricity and gas consumption requires around 0.3 tonnes CO_2e per year.[150]

We also try to live like locals, so have no air-conditioning. Electricity outages, which occur several times a week, are tough. Once, in the middle of summer, we had no electricity for a week. That was a long week! Electricity outages are alleviated a little for us by our solar lights. Many of our neighbours have no choice but to use kerosene lamps or candles.

Housing: The carbon cost of building a house depends on its size and the type of materials used to construct it. In Delhi, Ruksana and our family lived in what must have been one of the most densely populated places in the world. Janta Colony, built on a piece of land the size of a large sports stadium, is home to about 60,000 people. Ruksana's house consists of one tiny room and a kitchen/bathroom. Such a small house requires very little building material, equating to about 0.3 tonnes CO_2e per annum.[151]

(L to R) **Tom, Ruksana, Cathy and Mark in Ruksana's room (2017)**

While our current room is a little bigger than Ruksana's, it still feels crowded at times. The introverts in our family, particularly Oscar and Dad, sometimes need to retreat to the flat roof or a little 'hutch' storage area to read or work.

Part D: Ruksana versus Bruce - who is responsible?

Government services and mining: Ruksana does rely heavily on government health and education services. Unfortunately, these services are usually understaffed, poorly equipped, very crowded and often difficult for the poor to access.

As described in Chapter 2, Mark's work in India involved helping the poor access government services. While these government services aren't great, they are better than nothing. And they do require carbon emissions to provide the schools, hospitals and roads. Ruksana's share of the carbon footprint of these public goods and services is only about 0.2 tonnes CO_2e per year.[152] India also has substantial mining operations, adding another 0.1 tonnes to Ruksana's emissions.[153]

When we add these seven areas of Ruksana's emissions, it totals 2.3 tonnes CO_2e per year as seen in Table (3).

Table 3: Ruksana's carbon footprint

Aspect of life	Explanation of how the emissions are caused	CO_2e emissions (tonnes per year)
Buying 'stuff'	Manufacture, transport and sale of goods.	0.5
Food	Cattle farting and burping. Decay in rice fields.	0.6
Local travel	Burning petrol and diesel to propel motor-bikes, cars and buses.	0.2
Long-distance travel	Burning petrol and diesel to propel buses, trains and planes.	0.1
Residential electricity and gas	Burning coal to generate electricity. Burning gas, wood or dung for cooking, lighting or heating.	0.3
Housing	Manufacture of cement and other building materials.	0.3
Government services and mining	Construction and operation of roads, hospitals, schools. Mining operations.	0.3
Total		**2.3**

Our own family's slowly evolving low-carbon lifestyle is not in any way remarkable to our neighbours. They do it all the time by necessity. The only difference is that ours is a choice.

In this chapter, we've described how millions of the poor in India, and throughout the developing world, live very low-carbon lives. However, let me be clear that we are not espousing poverty. The lives of Ruksana, Kaneez, Kallu and our other friends are tough. They are often in debt, lack job security and struggle to balance food, education and medical costs. While they live environmentally sustainable lives, I would not wish their difficult circumstances upon anybody. What we do argue is that it is possible to maintain the high quality of life many westerners enjoy, while having a small environmental footprint, like most Indians. Indeed, it is through reducing our own consumption of the world's resources that we provide the 'ecological space' for developing nations like India – and people like Ruksana – to bring their consumption up to the bare basics of food, healthcare, education and housing.[154]

There are several reasons why westerners, despite our high-carbon lives and the clear correlation with climate change and its devastating consequences, have not changed our lifestyles much until now. To complete our description of the *problem* of climate change, we will unpack some of those reasons for inaction in the next Part.

Reflection Questions

- Are you more grateful, jealous or annoyed that the average Indian's carbon footprint is so low?

- What might Bruce and Ruksana think of each other's lifestyles?

Part E: Head in the Sand – why have we done so little?

17. Desire. Consume. Repeat.
– corporate and media manipulation

A TV advertisement I once saw in Australia has stuck with me. It showed beautiful trees, pristine oceans and a man gently handling plants and animals. Anyone would have been forgiven for thinking it was a David Attenborough documentary. But it turned out this was an advertisement for a fossil fuel corporation, arguably the group most responsible for climate change. How could there be such a disconnect between the lovely images on our TV and the reality outside our living rooms?

Credit: David Nagai

For some of you, our description of the science of climate change, its consequences, and our responsibility for it, will have already spurred you on towards a lower-carbon lifestyle. If so, hooray! However, there are many reasons most people go on living as they do. This Part examines four broad reasons for most people's climate inaction.

First, this chapter explores how various corporations and media outlets bombard us with advertising designed to stoke our consumption, while the costs to the climate are inadequately discussed. Chapter 18 examines our over-confidence that the government or scientists will fix climate change without us having to do anything. Chapter 19 then looks at that classic human tendency, when things are going badly – to blame someone else. Finally, Chapter 20 explores a range of other psychological tricks we play on ourselves to avoid feeling the need to change.

Corporations exist to make profits. For the corporate media, profits come from selling advertising to other corporations, who in turn want to sell us their products. Advertising is a massive industry, worth over US$500 billion worldwide.[155] A brief look at recent history reveals why advertising has become so central.

In the 1950s, major corporations in the US realised they had a problem. Consumers basically had everything they needed. Most families had a house, a car, a washing machine, a vacuum cleaner and so on. What could corporations do to keep the profits rolling in? The answer was 'planned obsolescence'* - deliberately manufacturing goods to break or become useless within a couple of years, thereby forcing the consumer to get a replacement.[156] This is easiest to see with computers. Within a few years of buying a new computer, the hard drive will be too small, the RAM too slow or the software incompatible.

In the last few decades, even planned obsolescence hasn't kept the profits rolling in quickly enough. This is where advertising comes in. 'Ads' are essentially attempts to convince people to buy stuff they don't need. Ads work primarily through seductive imagery implying: *'If you buy this, you will be happy, successful and cool.'* A stark indicator of the success of advertising is the bottled water industry. It's crazy that US$150 billion dollars a year globally is spent on something freely available from the tap.†[157]

Many advertisements aim to differentiate between products that are essentially the same, making us want to purchase the new one. This 'product differentiation' is clearly seen in the mobile phone industry. Though planned obsolescence will require us to purchase a new phone every three years or so, that's not quick enough for the industry, so every year there is a new version with slightly different characteristics: more mega-pixels in the camera, a better selection of games, or even just a different colour. Who, after all, is willing to have a boring old phone, TV, or computer, when everyone else has the newest one? The mantra for our consumerist world could be: *'Desire. Consume. Repeat.'*

---

* The term 'planned obsolescence' was first used in the 1920s in the car industry, but was popularised in the 1950s.
† At least in the West, where most tap water is drinkable. That is not the case for many developing world countries.

Part E: Head in the Sand - why have we done so little?

Our advertisement-driven, throw-away culture is working well for corporations, but it's disastrous for the environment. Every year, trillions of pieces of plastic end up in landfill. Even worse, an estimated 4-12 million tonnes of plastic end up in our oceans each year.[158] We see the results of this throw-away culture every day in India. The alleys and streets are strewn with discarded plastic bags and wrappers. When Cathy and I save plastic bags to reuse while shopping, our friends and shopkeepers often laugh at us. *'Throw that old bag away. Here, take a new one – they're free!'* Before we become too judgemental, though, we need to remember that while those of us in the West may have more sophisticated rubbish disposal mechanisms, we also produce far greater quantities of waste (2 tonnes per person year for Australians).[159] Even worse, our visible waste is dwarfed by the ten times greater invisible greenhouse gas emissions, much of which is released in the manufacture of all those new things.

Credit: David Nagai

The direct effect of advertising – fuelling consumerism and hence emissions – is obviously problematic. However, the corporate media's reliance on revenue from advertisements also leads indirectly to patchy coverage of climate change.[160]

Commercial media outlets generally only show us stories that they think will keep our interest long enough to view the next advertisement. Climate change, unfortunately, is often regarded as a dry and boring subject. This is a nasty positive feedback cycle: the media doesn't cover much on climate change, so the public doesn't care about it, so the media doesn't cover it.

This is the case for our neighbours in India. Many of them are illiterate, so don't read newspapers or magazines. The main media to which they are exposed is cable TV, which tends to be a solid diet of soap operas, Bollywood movies and cricket. Unsurprisingly, many of our neighbours have never heard of climate change. There's not even an easily understandable way to say *'climate change'* in Hindi. The media has deemed climate change to not be entertaining enough, dooming our neighbours to live in ignorance of an issue which will – and already does – affect their food, health and homes.

These warped priorities were well illustrated by the Australian media coverage of the 2015 global climate summit in Paris. I remember that the final agreement was achieved after frantic last-minute negotiations. As we'll see in Chapter 24 (Winning and Losing in Paris), it is probably one of the most important international agreements ever made, as it attempts to safeguard the future of humanity. Surely that was headline news! But no. While the Paris agreement was *almost* the lead story on the commercial TV news that day, it was beaten for that honour by a high-speed car chase – much more exciting and more likely to keep us watching through to the next ad break than some boring climate meeting.

My friends tell me that since we were last in Australia in 2016, the media coverage of climate change has begun to increase. That is great news. I hope it's a sign that we've finally turned the corner to start giving climate change the media attention it desperately needs.

The damage the media does by *not* covering climate change is exacerbated when, on the occasions climate change is discussed, its seriousness is sometimes doubted or downplayed. The logic is straightforward: if the public accepts that climate change is happening, it will lead people to living more simply and buying fewer products. That will harm profits. A study several years ago found that 97% percent of articles in the Herald-Sun, a major Australian newspaper, either doubted or rejected the scientific consensus on climate change. This is a remarkable reversal, given that in reality, 97% of climate scientists concur that climate change *is* human-caused.[161]

Coverage of climate scepticism is to be contrasted with journalistic balance: an important principle by which journalists attempt to give equal coverage to both sides of a contentious issue. For example, when the government is considering whether to increase taxes on cigarettes, it *is* good practice for the media to give some airtime to those promoting the increase, and similar airtime to those arguing against it. However, in areas in which there is strong scientific consensus among the experts, giving airtime to denialist views leads the public to the false understanding that there is genuine scientific debate. In the discussion on cigarette taxes, giving media-time to a doctor claiming no link between tobacco and cancer is irresponsible.

Some sources of news that cast doubt on climate change can be traced back to organisations funded by fossil fuel corporations and large industrialists.[162] 'Think tanks' with nice-sounding names such as *Americans for Prosperity Foundation, Heartland Institute,* and *Institute for Energy Research* seek to sow doubt in people's minds about climate science, even though, as we've seen, the science is now beyond debate.[163]

There are strong parallels between the techniques used by the fossil fuel industry to create doubt over climate science and the tobacco industry's attempt, several decades ago, to create doubt about the link between tobacco and cancer. The tobacco industry muddied the facts for years to keep people smoking before the truth finally won, and people (at least in the West) started to smoke less. In India, however, smoking and chewing tobacco are still widespread and incredibly damaging. In the neighbourhood we now live in, many people are addicted to chewing tobacco, a habit which substantially increases their chance of throat cancer, and also chews through much of their meagre income. Unfortunately, multinational corporations have a lot of sway in India, and are relatively free to peddle these deadly products.

Given the bias of many corporate media outlets *against* reporting on climate change, it is very important to find alternative sources of news. In Australia, we've found the ABC and SBS to be generally responsible TV and radio outlets, while *The Guardian, The Age* and *The Sydney Morning Herald* newspapers report well on the climate. In the US, our friends recommend *National Public Radio, The Atlantic* and *The New York Times*. In the UK, the BBC and *The Guardian* are well-regarded. Internationally, *Al Jazeera* offers a good independent perspective.

Many corporate media outlets adversely affect the environment by promoting consumerism. Further, due to inadequate or inaccurate coverage of climate change in the media, many people don't care enough about it to change their lives. In the next chapter, we examine a second reason for our inaction: overconfidence in governments and scientists.

Reflection Questions

- 🔍 When one of your 'things' is clearly older or shabbier than your friend's, how do you resist the temptation to buy a new one?

- 🔍 How often is climate change discussed in the media sources you use? What view of climate change is presented there?

- 🔍 Search the Guardian website (*www.theguardian.com*) for a climate change related article. Compare that with an article from Fox News (*www.foxnews.com*). What is the difference in flavour?

Want To Learn More?

→ Short Film: *The Story of Stuff*. A short video that comically shows the environmental cost of our 'stuff'. *http://storyofstuff.org/movies/story-of-stuff/*

→ Blog: *DeSmog*. A Canada-focused blog seeking to cut through the political 'smog' and provide current news and analysis dealing directly with climate change. *www.desmog.ca*

→ Website: *Carbon brief*. Articles explaining up-to-date news about climate change. It is UK-oriented, but relevant worldwide. *https://www.carbonbrief.org/*

Part E: Head in the Sand - why have we done so little?

18. Someone Else Will Fix It
– over-confidence in science and politics

Many readers will remember the hole in the ozone layer in the 1980s. Scientists figured out that the problem was a group of chemicals known as chlorofluorocarbons (CFCs), a component in our air-conditioning, refrigeration and spray cans. Once the chemical culprit was known, an international agreement was reached in 1987 to ban CFCs.[164] The ozone layer has now almost recovered. Science and politics worked together to avert a crisis. However, with climate change, science and politics are struggling.

Some people hope that scientists will come up with a technology that will magically fix climate change. Others believe that government laws and regulations will take care of it. If we can just leave it to the scientists or the politicians, the reasoning goes, we can go on living our high-carbon lives without worrying about it.

Tom and I love science and take a keen interest in politics. Clearly, both scientists and politicians do have a major role to play in tackling climate change. As we'll describe in Part F, the science of renewable energy, coupled with sensible political measures, *can* lead to a lower-carbon society. However, these 'big picture' solutions will not be implemented at the rate or scale needed until enough individuals change their own lifestyles. Our hope that scientists and politicians will change the world cannot be used as an excuse to avoid changing ourselves.

The scientists will fix it

Greenhouse gases in our atmosphere cause the planet to warm. Since we already know the problem, surely scientists can figure out how to fix it – can't they? Scientific solutions to climate change can be roughly divided into three categories:

- Attempts to stop putting greenhouse gases (GHGs) *into* the atmosphere,
- Attempts to get the extra carbon *out* of the atmosphere, and
- Attempts to reduce the amount of solar radiation getting to us.

Attempts to stop putting GHGs into the atmosphere: We'll see in Part F that scientists have already found ways to do this. They have invented technologies to generate energy without burning carbon-emitting fossil fuels. You'll already be familiar with many of these renewable technologies: solar, wind and hydro. It's not the technology that's lacking, rather it is the lack of political and popular will to roll out these technologies on a massive scale.

Another technology to stop putting carbon into the atmosphere is Carbon Capture and Storage (CCS). This involves continuing to burn fossil fuels, but capturing the CO_2 as it is emitted and storing it in the ground or deep ocean, rather than releasing it into the atmosphere. In 2014 the world's first CCS electricity generating station was opened at Boundary Dam in Canada. While CCS has potential, a major disadvantage is its expense, at around US$100 per tonne of CO_2 captured.[165] Another disadvantage is uncertainty over how long the captured carbon can safely be stored underground. The most significant disadvantage, however, is the limited capacity at present. All the CCS currently being planned and constructed would only capture 0.1% of the world's emissions. Unless there are rapid improvements in CCS to make it much less expensive, it will be considerably cheaper to develop and scale up renewable energy. CCS could still play a role, though, in capturing emissions from industrial processes, like cement production, which aren't amenable to renewable energy solutions.[166] We'll explore this further in Chapter 23 (Farts, Forestry and Fugitives).

Attempts to take carbon out of the atmosphere: With high levels of CO_2 in the atmosphere already (407 ppm compared to 280 ppm in the pre-industrial era) and the likelihood that human emissions will continue for some time, scientists are also working on ways to draw carbon out of the atmosphere.

The obvious solution is to use nature's way - photosynthesis. Since plants absorb carbon dioxide as they grow, this involves planting more trees. While we welcome any reforestation, there are several problems with large-scale tree planting.[167] A number of such programmes I've heard of in India start with great fanfare, but unless they are planned and managed together with local residents, they often fail.[168]

The most significant issue with tree planting is one of scale. We're currently pumping 36 Gt of CO_2 into the atmosphere each year. As we saw in *Illustration 2* in Chapter 4, all the forests and plants in the world are extracting net 11 Gt

CO_2 from the atmosphere each year. So we would need to plant about three times the world's existing forests to deal with our carbon emissions. We've spent the last two centuries doing exactly the opposite: cutting down trees so that we can build and farm more. In fact, land use change (the technical term for deforestation) causes about 11% of the extra carbon in the atmosphere.[169] To stop cutting down forests, and instead plant millions of hectares of trees, would take an enormous effort.

Which country is going to give up their agricultural land to plant billions of trees? In an experiment of this sort, Ecuador recently offered to *not* cut down sections of its forests if the international community compensated it for the loss of income it would suffer by *not* extracting the oil reserves under the forest floor. Only a fraction of the amount required was raised, so Ecuador did what any self-interested government would do: it prioritised its own budget above the needs of the planet, cut down the trees, and dug up the oil.[170]

One idea to address the lack of land for growing trees, is to grow algae in the oceans. This geoengineering (engineering the earth's biosphere) would involve pumping huge amounts of iron into the oceans, changing the chemical composition of the water to make it more amenable to algal growth.[171] That sounds pretty scary to me. What happens to marine life? What if it has unforeseen consequences? How do we reverse it if it goes wrong? The difficulty with geoengineering is that we can't use trial and error. In most scientific endeavours, all variables are carefully controlled in the laboratory. But we simply can't perform a controlled experiment with the world's oceans. Given the number of well-intentioned scientific misadventures in the past (such as the introduction of cane toads into Australia or mongooses into Hawaii), I'm just not prepared to sign off on that type of experiment with the only oceans we have.

Attempts to lower the amount of radiation reaching us: Another geoengineering 'solution' is Solar Radiation Management (SRM) *(see Illustration 16)*. Some of these techniques are benign, like making buildings more reflective. However some, like spraying sulphates into the upper atmosphere, are much riskier.

Volcanoes spew sulphates into the atmosphere. These sulphates reflect some of the sun's radiation before it reaches the earth's surface. This causes global temperatures to drop. The eruption of Mt Tambora in 1815, for example, led to 'the year without a summer' in Europe.[172] Similarly, after Pinatubo's eruption in 1991, global temperatures dropped a tiny amount.

18. Someone Else Will Fix It - over-confidence in science and politics

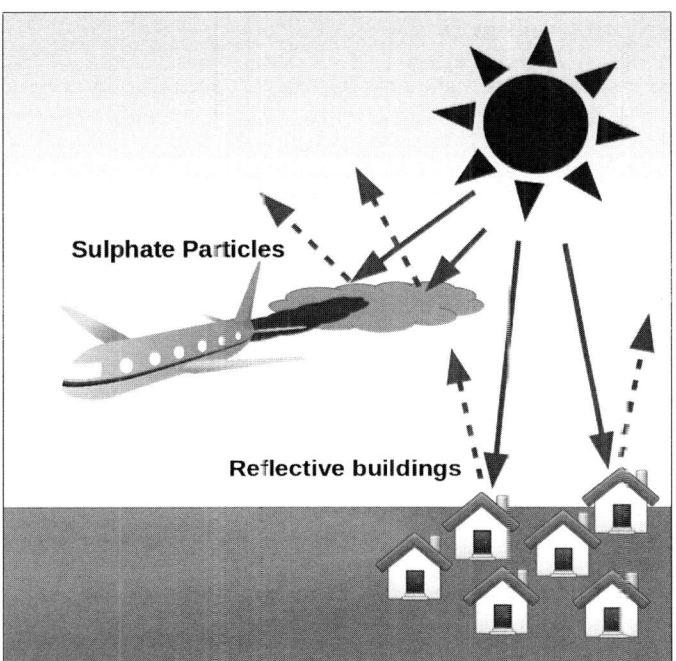

Illustration 16: Solar Radiation Management Credit: Cathy Delaney

The 'Pinatubo effect' leads some to suggest that we should copy volcanoes by releasing huge quantities of sulphates into the atmosphere to reduce the amount of solar radiation reaching earth. However, that may have negative consequences worse than the positive ones of slowing warming.[173] Even the layperson could guess that reducing the sun's radiation would impact plants' ability to photosynthesise. It also appears that the extra sulphates adversely affect rainfall.[174]

We already know the safe solution to climate change: rapidly transitioning from fossil fuel-based energy to renewables. When we compare this to the massive untestable 'solutions' of geoengineering the earth's oceans or atmosphere, I know which one I'd prefer. Kenneth Brower of *The Atlantic* sums up the situation well:

> *The notion the science will save us is the chimera that allows the present generation to consume all the resources it wants, as if no generations will follow. It is the sedative that allows civilization to march so steadfastly toward environmental catastrophe. It forestalls the real solution, which will be in the hard, non-technical work of changing human behavior.*[175]

Part E: Head in the Sand - why have we done so little?

The politicians will fix it

I described earlier how my main work in India has been helping the poor access government services. These services are often thwarted by self-serving politicians and bureaucrats. In that part of the world it is expected that politicians will act in their own interests. Political leaders regularly stoke communal tensions to gain power, corruption scandals are common, and a significant proportion of parliamentarians have serious criminal charges pending.[176] Consequently, most Indians have little faith that their politicians will act selflessly for the good of society.

I used to have more faith in Australian politicians. However, when I returned to Australia in 2014, my confidence began to crack. Australia is one of the highest per capita GHG emitters in the world at 23 tonnes CO_2e per person. It is also one of the biggest exporters of fossil fuels to other countries, including China and India. Given our vast land area and long hours of sunlight, with a different attitude from our government, Australia could become one of the biggest producers of solar energy in the world. It could also use that technology to help poorer nations bypass fossil fuels. Instead, our current government rejects both a carbon tax and an emissions trading scheme. Additionally, it grants tax concessions and loans to the fossil fuel industry.[177] These policies unambiguously encourage continued extraction and use of fossil fuels. Why would a government encourage something that was bad for the long-term welfare of society and the planet?

Our three to five-year election cycles mean that politicians are not inclined to focus on long-term issues like climate change. This point was driven home to me when I talked to my local member of state parliament about a proposed massive new coal mine. I suggested it would be appropriate, given the need to curb fossil fuel emissions, to prohibit the mine from going ahead. '*Mark,*' she said, somewhat apologetically, '*if we stop that new coal mine, we will lose the next election. It's as simple as that.*' I suggested that the viability of the planet was worth more than the next election. She didn't seem to agree.

These days, political campaigns are less a matter of debating principled policy positions than of gauging public opinion immediately before an election and targeting publicity to cater to that latest whim. If the public is concerned about

18. Someone Else Will Fix It - over-confidence in science and politics

Credit: INKCINCT. Used with artist's permission.

law and order, politicians talk about law and order. If the public is concerned about refugee numbers, politicians talk about that.

Conversely, if the public is *not* concerned about climate change, politicians will not talk about it – much less act on it. Our politicians don't lead public opinion – they follow it. We cannot rest easy, hoping that politicians will fix climate change without us needing to act; rather, politicians won't act decisively until we do. We will revisit the need for everyday people like you and me to speak out on these issues in Chapter 26 (Why Didn't You Do Something?).

The next tool in our kit for avoiding the need to change our lifestyles is that old excuse, when faced with a problem – to blame someone else.

Part E: Head in the Sand - why have we done so little?

Reflection Questions

- How much do you trust science to develop technologies that will save us from climate change?
- What do you think of the geoengineering ideas discussed in this chapter? In your view, how bad would the effects of climate change need to be to justify those geoengineering attempts?
- How much do you trust our politicians to make good decisions for the long-term sustainability of the environment? Why or why not?
- What are the main issues which determine who you vote for? Is climate change one of them?

Want To Learn More?

→ Book: Klein, Naomi; 2014. *This Changes Everything*. Simon and Schuster. See especially Chapter 8 on geoengineering.

19. It's Their Fault
– blaming others

'Yeah, climate change is happening, but the real problem is population growth.' I was talking with my relative about writing this book. His response reminded me of our classic human tendency when faced with a problem – to blame someone else.

The 'others' on whom many of us like to offload the responsibility for the climate crisis are the billions of poor people in the developing world, especially in China and India. This is often the case for right-leaning folk, like many of my extended family. On the other hand, some of our left-leaning friends find a different target to blame for climate change – multinational corporations. This chapter critiques both of these efforts to shift the blame onto external groups, and argues that there's no legitimate way to avoid our own responsibility for climate change.

Blaming the poor

In my experience, the two most often cited ways to blame the poor (minus the political correctness) are: *'If they didn't have so many children, there wouldn't be so many people in the world and we'd all be OK.'* and *'If they didn't want to drive cars and own TVs we'd be alright. Why can't they be content with what they have?'*

While these thoughts sound crass when expressed plainly, if we're honest with ourselves, many of us have thought these things at one time or another. However, Tom and I have the privilege of knowing many people who are very poor. To them, these arguments are like a slap in the face.

Population: The world cannot sustain an ever-increasing population. It is true that population growth rates are generally higher in the developing world than in the West. However, rather than blaming the poor, the only solution is to work on the factors which are major determinants of the number of children women bear: reducing poverty levels, increasing access to contraception,[178] curbing infant mortality rates,[179] and promoting women's educational and employment opportunities.[180]

97

Part E: Head in the Sand - why have we done so little?

Our own experience in India backs this up. In our neighbours' families, the older generation tended to have large families. Our friend Ruby* is a young woman, the second of twelve children, nine of whom have survived. Her parents probably didn't realise that family planning was even possible. But after migrating to Delhi, Ruby and her sisters were exposed to a more open society and government family planning campaigns, so by the time she herself married, Ruby had realised that the pill and condoms were cheaply and easily available. Consequently, Ruby has only had three children.

Another factor is infant mortality. In Ruby's mother's generation, health care was poor. Her parents knew that, in all likelihood, several of their children would not survive to adulthood. In a society where there is little by way of a social welfare net, children are, in effect, the parents' old age pension. So having only two or three children, when it is likely one or more of them will die, is a recipe for vulnerability when you get older and are unable to work yourself. As healthcare systems improve and infant mortality decreases, people tend to have fewer children.

Women's literacy and empowerment is another powerful predictor of the number of children women bear. The more educated and able to earn an income a woman is, the less likely she is to have many children. This is true for some of Ruby's younger sisters, several of whom have completed school and even gone to college. Many young women now hope to work for some time, marry in their mid-twenties, and then only have one or two children.

We need to address these issues by working towards better healthcare, education and women's empowerment. This will not only decrease population growth rates, but also markedly improve the quality of life for the world's poor.

Population growth rates are declining around the world, and India is no exception. Indeed, its latest figures are actually lower than Australia's (1.1% vs 1.4%).[181] However, barring some catastrophe, population stabilisation will still take several decades. In that time, it is imperative to reduce emissions per capita. As we saw in Part D (Ruksana vs Bruce), Australians, New Zealanders and North Americans emit much more carbon than the average Indian. Few would openly say: '*I deserve a greater share of our collective carbon budget than someone in India.*' Yet we continue to act as if we do.

---

* Name changed for confidentiality.

19. It's Their Fault - blaming others

While it is easy for my relative and many like him to implicitly criticise families like Ruby's, it is only the coldest-hearted who could look Ruby's mother in the eye and say: '*Climate change is your fault for having too many children,*' or look at Ruby herself and say: '*You shouldn't exist.*' The world has 7.4 billion human inhabitants at present, each of whom has equal right to be here.

Car usage: Vehicles are a major source of carbon emissions, both from the actual production of the car and from driving. Growth in car ownership is a major problem in some poorer countries. Owning a car is a status symbol in India, so anyone who can afford a car will buy one to show their neighbours they have 'made it'. Consequently Delhi, with a population of 15 million and 3 million cars on the road,[182] suffers terribly from traffic jams and its air has become some of the most polluted in the world.[183]

'They shouldn't want cars' — traffic in India
Credit: Wikimedia Commons

In this context, it would be wise for developing world governments to create efficient public transport systems and discourage car ownership. However it would be hypocritical in the extreme for people in the West to say to those in poorer countries: '*We got our car before climate change became an issue, but now that it is a problem, YOU can't own a car.*'

Along with car usage, the wealthy in India and other developing nations are rapidly adopting many aspects of high-carbon western lifestyles. From air-conditioning to air travel, meat-eating to mega-houses, India's wealthy are pursuing western lifestyles. Environmentally, this is a catastrophe. The world cannot sustain another billion people adopting the high-carbon lives that westerners are accustomed to. However, wealthy Indians are, understandably, often outraged when westerners tell them what they can or can't have. Until we move away from our own high-carbon lives, we have no right to blame others for theirs.

Part E: Head in the Sand - why have we done so little?

Blaming the multinational corporations

While conservatives often blame the poor overseas for climate change, many progressives blame multinational corporations. Though the target of the blame is very different, the implicit effect is the same – to absolve myself of responsibility to reduce my own carbon footprint.

Credit: David Nagai

Multinational corporations do bear massive responsibility for climate change. Their production of the 'stuff' we consume releases huge amounts of emissions and some fossil fuel corporations use their financial clout to spread doubt about climate change. Consequently, many of the environmental protests Tom and I have been involved with target fossil fuel corporations.

The problem arises, however, when our own consumption choices are viewed as disconnected from the damage corporations do to produce our 'stuff'. Of course we need to challenge the fossil fuel industry – but how can we do that while simultaneously buying more oil? We need to curb the meat industry – but that won't happen until we're willing to eat less meat. Whenever we blame corporations for climate change, we also need to accept our own responsibility for buying their products. If we didn't buy them, they wouldn't produce them.

The right-wing of politics is correct to be concerned about population growth, but wrong to blame the poor for climate change. To deal with climate change, we must address material poverty, not by blaming the poor, but instead by promoting health-care, education and women's empowerment. Left-wing activists are correct in calling for corporate environmental responsibility,[184] but unless activists change their own lifestyles, they don't have the credibility to push for corporate change. We must address corporate power, not by demonising corporations, but by changing our own consumption habits, which give corporations their power. Until we change ourselves, blaming the 'other' for causing climate change is unfair, ineffective and hypocritical.

Our final chapter in this Part considers the various psychological excuses we employ to justify our inaction on climate change.

Reflection Questions

- We often tend to blame people on the margins (refugees, homeless people, Muslims) for the state of the world. Have you ever met and talked to a refugee, a homeless person or a Muslim? Did meeting that person confirm or change your views?
- Have you (even within your own mind) ever laid the blame for climate change on the poor?
- Is it reasonable to criticise a company if you continue buying its products?

Part E: Head in the Sand - why have we done so little?

20. What Can I Do?
– psychological excuses for inaction

'I'm doing my bit – by turning off lights. That's enough isn't it?' How many times have you heard (or made) excuses like that for not doing more about climate change?

Many of us still have several psychological tricks up our sleeve to avoid the need to change. In this chapter we'll examine four of those tricks:
- *'I'm doing my share – by turning the lights off when I'm not using them.'*
- *'At least my choice is better than that!'* (another high-carbon choice)
- *'What can I do about climate change – it's such a huge issue.'*
- *'No one else is doing much – why should I?'*

'I'm doing my share – I turn the lights off.' This message is a classic piece of tokenism, assuaging our guilt for not taking more substantive action. Electricity generation causes 35% of Australia's emissions.[185] Of that electricity, only 28% is used for domestic purposes.[186] Of domestic purposes, only 6% is for lighting.[187] Suppose turning off lights regularly saves 15% of our lighting usage. Simple maths (35% x 28% x 6% x 15%) tells us that regularly turning lights off will only save one thousandth of our emissions.

That is not to say that turning off lights is useless. If it helps others around us turn off lights too, that's good. Even better, our turning off lights may birth a broader realisation of our huge carbon footprint, which may lead to more substantive action like driving less or eating less meat. If that's the result, then turning off lights has been a very worthwhile thing to do. However if turning lights off is the full extent of our action on climate change, then it is tokenistic.

'At least my choice is better than that!' When there are only two options to consider, we often feel justified if we do the better one. For instance, it is better to eat meat once a day than for every meal, and it is better to buy a second-hand car than a new one (as it doesn't require the emissions of manufacturing a new car). In real life, though, there are seldom just two options. Ignoring the other options, and only doing a comparison which shows our preference in a favourable light, is deceptive. In reality, there usually *are* other options. Thus, a third option is to not eat meat *at all* and not buy another car at all.

Ultimately, we can make any environmentally destructive choice seem reasonable by comparing it with another option that's even worse, while ignoring ways to leave a lighter impact. This is the fundamental driver of that oxymoron, 'green consumerism'. While an energy-saving, 5 star-rated, eco-friendly device might be better than an alternative product, it's probably even better to buy *neither* of them.

'What can I do anyway?' Many of you know the story of a woman walking along the beach after a storm has washed up thousands of starfish. She bends down, picks up one starfish and throws it back into the sea, where it will survive. Then she does it again, and again, one starfish at a time. A bemused onlooker asks her: '*What's the point? There are thousands of them. What you are doing makes no difference.*' The rescuer bends down, picks up yet another starfish and says to her accuser: '*It makes a difference to this one*,' throws the starfish into the ocean, and proceeds on her rescue mission.

The story is a simple one, but beautifully challenges the inertia we all feel when faced with an overwhelming problem. My small action may not make *much* difference, but it does make *some* difference. Lots of people making a small difference in their own lives will cumulatively make a huge difference. It is exactly that hope which has led to this book.

What is the alternative to doing something about the problem of climate change? To resign ourselves to the fact that our grandchildren will never see the Great Barrier Reef? To give in to our lives being dictated by corporations, advertisers and the media? To lie down and accept that the world as we know it is ending? Doing *something*, even if it seems insignificant, is much better than that.

Astute readers may object that this argument is the opposite of the first one in this chapter. Is a small thing like turning off lights tokenistic, or *is* it valuable? The answer depends on both the motivation and the other options available. If doing one small thing is an excuse *not* to take more significant action, then it is tokenistic. However, if it is done as part of broader action by you and others, then it can bring about valuable change.

'No one else is doing much – why should I?' Most of us would like to believe that our behaviour is based on ethical principles. We have various voices in our head, perhaps learnt in childhood or from our faith: '*Do good to others*', '*Be honest*',

Part E: Head in the Sand - why have we done so little?

'Treat others as you'd wish to be treated yourself', *'Stand up for what's right'*. But in reality, many of us live our lives less according to ethical principles, and more according to what people around us are doing.

In the days after the Brexit vote, a few people took the 'Exit' victory as licence to torment non-British people living in the UK.[188] As other people began to observe that behaviour, they too took licence to behave badly. Even though the perpetrators may have felt bad as they crossed their own line of ethical behaviour, such feelings of guilt are often overridden by seeing others behave that way. When people see their leaders, and more importantly their friends, behaving badly, they feel permission to do likewise, despite the conflict with their own ethical framework. The same dynamic plays out in climate change inaction. When we see our friends driving, flying and purchasing products, we tend to do likewise.

It takes courage to behave differently from the crowd, but it is possible. In Chapter 37 we recount stories of hope in which ordinary individuals like you and me have made different choices from the crowd, and as a result have made a *big* difference. Rather than following the crowd, the crowd started following them.

So far in *Low-Carbon and Loving It* we've come to understand the *problem* of climate change. We looked at the science of how climate change is affecting our earth and its inhabitants. We also saw what the world will look like for the next generation if we go on with 'business as usual', emitting unsustainable levels of greenhouse gases. Extreme weather events, rising sea levels, species extinction, lower food production and geopolitical strife will make the world a much harsher place to live. We then considered just how much we, as everyday people in the West, are contributing to the problem, compared to the average citizen of the world and compared to Ruksana in India. Finally, we looked at some of the reasons why we have kept our head in the sand on climate change for so long. With this understanding of the *problem* of climate change we're now in a good position to look at *solutions* to the climate crisis.

Reflection Questions

- Which of the excuses discussed in this chapter do you tend to use most often? How effective are these excuses at easing the pressure to change?

- As you start to take substantive action to reduce your own carbon footprint, even if no one else around you is doing so, how will you gain the courage to behave differently from the crowd?

CLIMATE
SOLUTIONS

Part F: Big Picture Solutions
– how can science and politics help?

21. Cars, Planes and Trains
– alternative fuel solutions

I went to a local Indian school up to grade 5, before home-schooling for several years, and then finishing high school by Australian distance education. I remember doing my homework by the light of kerosene lamps and candles when the electricity went out, as it often did. Their dim and flickering light was annoying to read by. Candles can create a nice atmosphere, but not if you're trying to study, or finish a suspense-filled Agatha Christie mystery. So when we got our solar light, it improved life considerably, not to mention saving carbon.

We now come to *solutions* to climate change: ways in which we can transition to a low-carbon society. This Part offers hope that 'big-picture' technological and political solutions for climate change are possible. While these solutions are crucial, we'll see that they won't happen quickly enough, unless ordinary people like you and me change our attitudes and lifestyles. At the end of the day, political and business leaders will only change when they are motivated to do so by public opinion and consumer pressure. So in Part G we will consider concrete changes that everyday people like you and I can make to lead lower-carbon lives. We'll find that a more sustainable life is not only doable, but can be very fulfilling and even fun. Finally, in Part H, we'll look at the most essential ingredients in this recipe for a low-carbon world: gathering the motivation, courage, and tools to get started.

In this Part we'll divide 'Big Picture Solutions' into scientific (Chapters 21-23) and political (Chapters 24-26). In exploring scientific solutions, it's useful to understand the source of emissions, the purpose of those emissions and the type of greenhouse gas emitted. We summarise these in Table (4).

Part F: Big Picture Solutions - how can science and politics help?

Table 4: Source, purpose and type of GHG[189]

Source of GHG		Purpose	Main greenhouse gas (GHG) emitted	%	%	Chapter
Burning fossil fuels	Direct combustion	Transport: cars, trucks, planes Household: cooking, heating, lighting Manufacturing and mining	Carbon dioxide (CO_2)	35	60	21
	Electricity generation	Coal and gas-fired power stations	CO_2	25		22
Non-fossil fuel	Agriculture	Clearing land (deforestation)	CO_2	11	28	23
		Food production: especially meat and dairy	Methane (CH_4)	8		
		Fertiliser application	Nitrous oxide (N_2O)	6		
		Rotting waste	CH_4	3		
	Manufacturing and mining	Fugitive emissions from mining	CH_4	5	12	
		Cement and steel production	CO_2	5		
		Air-conditioners and refrigeration	Hydrofluorocarbons	2		
				100%	100%	

Fossil fuel combustion accounts for about 60% of human-caused GHGs. Fossil fuels are burnt both to release energy directly, and to generate electricity. In this chapter, we'll examine how we might replace direct combustion of fossil fuels for transport and household purposes, while Chapter 22 discusses ways to generate our electricity from renewable sources. The other 40% of GHGs are from *non*-fossil fuel sources, mainly from agriculture, manufacturing and mining. Chapter 23 (Farts, Forestry and Fugitives) considers ways to reduce those emissions.

In each of these areas we argue that scientific solutions to climate change do exist, but that the primary ingredient lacking is the political and public will to implement them quickly enough and on a large enough scale to save us from catastrophic climate change. We'll explore possible political solutions in Chapters 24-26.

21 Cars, Planes and Trains - alternative fuel solutions

Fossil fuels are burnt to release energy to power a whole range of activities. We're familiar with many of these applications from our own lives: filling our car with petrol, cooking with gas, and heating our houses with gas (in some colder climates). Fossil fuels are also burnt to power a range of manufacturing and mining processes. To combat climate change, we will need to reduce emissions from all these uses.[*]

As seen in *Illustration 17*, there are two main ways we can replace transport and household uses of fossil fuels: we can use a renewable energy source, such as biofuels, to *directly power* the transport, lighting, heating or cooking; or we can use *renewably-generated electricity* to power those uses.

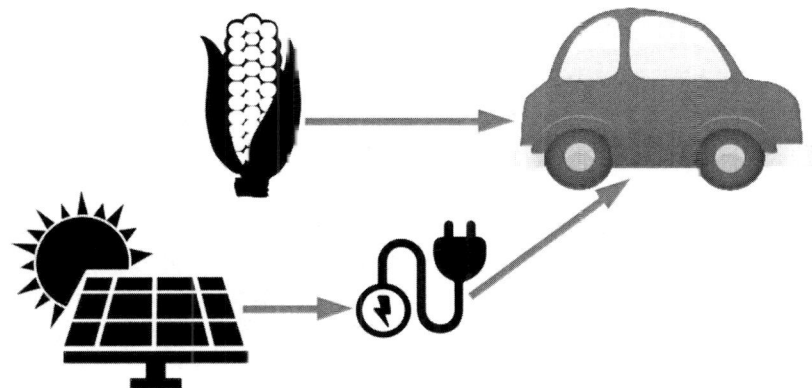

Illustration 17: Alternative methods of replacing fossil fuels Credit: Cathy Delaney

The first option – direct use of a renewable source – is simpler and sometimes more efficient. Some energy is lost in each transformation it goes through. Imagine using a wind farm to generate electricity in order to operate a clothes drier. Why not just hang the clothes out in the wind in the first place? An example of a direct use of renewables in transport is biofuel. Biofuels are made from plants, which capture energy from the sun through photosynthesis. The process is carbon neutral if we grew the plants in order to burn them, as the plant's growth captured as much carbon dioxide from the atmosphere as is released by burning them. Biofuels can be used to run cars, and even cargo ships, which currently burn much dirtier oil. However, a deeply problematic aspect of conventional biofuels is the land required to grow them. This is land which could

---

[*] This chapter primarily considers the transport and household-level processes that we're familiar with. However, the emission reduction ideas discussed in this chapter can be applied in similar fashion to reduce fossil fuel consumption from manufacturing and mining.

Part F: Big Picture Solutions - how can science and politics help?

otherwise be used to grow food. Each year the US converts 140 megatonnes of corn – enough to feed about 400 million people for a year – into ethanol for biofuel.[190] However biofuels could still play a role, especially if they're produced from by-products of agriculture, which would otherwise go to waste.[191]

The second option – replacing the direct combustion of fossil fuels with renewably-sourced electricity – is attractive because of the flexibility and control it affords. Electricity can be turned on and off easily and we can use it to generate heat, light or motion. There are many examples of the transition from fossil fuels to electricity which both reduce emissions and improve quality of life. Here we'll consider four such transitions: petrol, diesel or gas-run vehicles to electric vehicles; flights to high-speed electric rail; wood stoves to electric stoves; and kerosene lights to solar lights.

Petrol or gas-driven cars to electric vehicles: In Australia, cars release almost 2 tonnes CO_2e per person per year.[192] Electric vehicles are an excellent replacement for petrol, diesel and gas-run cars, *if* sufficient renewable electricity is generated. While electric cars are more expensive to buy, their cost is rapidly decreasing, and they're much cheaper to maintain.[193] Additionally, they are improving in efficiency and in the distance they can cover. Of course they also run much more quietly.

Flights to high-speed rail: Aeroplanes run on jet fuel, which is much lighter, per unit of energy stored, than batteries. Low weight is vital to flight, so this means long-distance electric planes will not be commercially viable in the foreseeable future.[194] Instead, high-speed rail offers a slightly slower, but much more environmentally-friendly form of long-distance transport for routes over land.

High-speed rail in Taiwan
Credit: Wikimedia Commons

High-speed rail can operate from electricity sourced from renewable energy, through an overhead cable, rather than needing to carry heavy batteries. *Beyond Zero Emissions* advocates a high-speed rail link between Brisbane, Sydney and Melbourne.[195] Sydney to Melbourne is the fifth most frequently flown route in the world, so a high-speed rail link between those cities would save huge amounts of CO_2 – about four megatonnes per year.[196] The high-speed rail trip between Sydney and Melbourne would be three hours – not much longer than the flight when you factor in airport check-in procedures. Other frequently flown overland routes like Washington DC to New York and Delhi to Mumbai would reap similar benefits.

21 Cars, Planes and Trains - alternative fuel solutions

Wood stoves to electric stoves: Hundreds of millions of people in the developing world cook on stoves that burn wood, charcoal or dried dung. These stoves often burn inefficiently, release carbon emissions, and emit noxious smoke, resulting in millions of deaths each year.[197]

My work in India is teaching basic literacy to children and young adults who either aren't going to school, or aren't learning much there. This involves visiting a lot of homes in our community, where I witness the smoke as mothers cook the evening meal. The fumes are uncomfortable for me to experience occasionally, but it's awful to think what the smoke is doing to my friends' health every day.

Gas stoves, common in many western countries, burn more cleanly and are therefore much better for health. *Ashadesh* is a social enterprise helping the poor in India transition from biomass stoves to gas ones (see 'Want To Learn More?' in Chapter 30 for details). However gas stoves still do release some carbon emissions. Ultimately, once we have a 100% renewable supply of electricity, electric stoves, especially induction stoves, will be able to bring cooking emissions to zero.

Kerosene lamps to solar lights: Thankfully, during my later childhood, I did have a solar light to use when the electricity went off. For many people in the developing world, though, adequate lighting remains inaccessible. They are forced to use kerosene lamps or even just candles. Much like some of our political debate, this is inefficient: it produces more heat than light! If everyone had access to solar lighting it would substantially improve the quality of life for tens of millions of people who are currently without electricity. It would also save the carbon emissions from burning kerosene and other fuels for lighting. *Pollinate Energy* is one group in India helping the poor to transition away from kerosene lamps to solar lights (see 'Want To Learn More?' for details).

There are a variety of solutions which will enable us to phase out the use of fossil fuels for transport and household purposes. However, much will hinge on whether we can produce cheap, abundant renewable electricity. We'll consider that next.

Part F: Big Picture Solutions - how can science and politics help?

Reflection Questions

🔍 Have you travelled in an electric car or by high-speed rail? How was that experience?

🔍 In your country, which route would be most suitable for a high-speed rail link?

Want To Learn More?

→ Report: *Beyond Zero Emissions: Electric Vehicles report.* Analysis of the potential for electric vehicles in Australia. *http://bze.org.au/electric-vehicles-report/*

→ Report: *Beyond Zero Emissions: High-speed Rail Plan.* Proposal for a high-speed rail link between Brisbane, Sydney and Melbourne. *http://bze.org.au/high-speed-rail-plan/*

→ Website: *Pollinate Energy.* An organisation that sells solar lights and other products to families living in India's slum communities who don't have regular electricity connections. *https://pollinateenergy.org/*

22. Nature's Power
– renewable energy solutions

Dad has a soft spot for the tiny European country of Denmark. When he was 18, just after finishing high school, he took a 'gap year' there. In 1985, Dad was struck by the gender equality and impressive level of political awareness. More recently, the Danes have shown the way environmentally. One day in 2015, they gave the world hope for the struggle against climate change. Denmark produced all the electricity it needed for the 9th of July 2015, entirely from renewable sources.[198]

In this chapter, we examine the science of generating electricity renewably. This is one of our most urgent challenges if we are to prevent devastating climate change, as generating electricity with fossil fuels is currently responsible for 25% of our total emissions. If we produce renewable energy cheaply and abundantly, it will also enable us to replace direct combustion of fossil fuels (as we saw in the previous chapter), accounting for another 35% of emissions.

The world annually consumes 22 petawatt (PW*) hours of electricity,[199] of which about 2/3 is generated by fossil fuels and 1/3 by renewables. The major renewable energy technologies are seen in Table (5). In this chapter we explore the potential for these technologies to supply the world's electricity needs.

Hydro: The most appropriate renewable technology for a country will depend on its terrain and climate. Nations in mountainous regions with high rainfall and major rivers, such as Nepal and New Zealand, are well suited to hydro-power. This is the oldest of the renewable technologies and has already been used extensively. The concept is simple enough: damming a river and releasing water to run a turbine, generating electricity. Hydro-power is by far the largest source of renewable energy in the world, generating half of all renewable energy and 18% of the world's total electricity.

---

* 1,000 = kilo; 1000 x kilo = million (mega); 1000 x million = billion (giga); 1000 x billion = tera; 1000 x tera = peta. A petawatt is thus a million billion watts. A watt-hour is the amount of energy it takes to run a one watt appliance for an hour.

Part F: Big Picture Solutions - how can science and politics help?

Table 5: Global electricity generation from renewable sources[200]

Renewable technology	% of global electricity needs	Growth rate per year	Approximate price (USc/kWh)	Advantages	Disadvantages
Hydro	18%	3%	6	Good energy storage. Flexible (can generate when we want it).	Flooding by dams. Indigenous people displaced.
Nuclear	11%	-1%	10	Reliable (barring natural disasters).	Shortage of uranium. Nuclear waste. Security.
Wind	4%	17%	6	Cheap (if onshore).	Not as flexible, as requires wind.
Biomass	2%	8%	6	Flexible (generates 24/7). Disposal of waste.	Lots of land required to grow the biomass.
Solar PV	1%	42%	8	Abundant. Can work at small or large scale.	Not as flexible, as requires sunlight.
Tidal, wave, geothermal	<1%	4%	8	Cheap in places with appropriate geography.	Untested at large-scale.
Concentrated Solar Thermal	<1%	35%	24	Good energy storage. Flexible: generates 24/7.	Still expensive. Only viable in very sunny environments.

22. Nature's power - renewable energy solutions

However hydro-power also suffers from serious drawbacks. Damming has caused all sorts of disasters: forests are flooded, indigenous people lose their land, and farmers lose their livelihoods.[201] Additionally, dams prevent fish migration and have a major impact on freshwater ecosystems.[202] The flooding from dams also results in vegetation rotting underwater*, releasing methane, a potent GHG.[203] However, hydro-power is likely to remain a major source of renewable energy for decades.

Nuclear: The second largest form of non-fossil fuel energy is highly controversial. Can nuclear waste be stored safely? Can we be sure dangerous technologies won't fall into the wrong hands? What about human error like Chernobyl in 1986? Natural disasters can cause problems too, as highlighted in 2011 when a tsunami severely damaged the Fukushima nuclear plant in Japan, causing a major radiation leakage. Nuclear can also be critiqued as not truly renewable, since the uranium it uses is limited. Nuclear power will continue to be a significant source of low-carbon energy for some time. However, it is unlikely, and in my opinion undesirable, for it to grow.

Hydro: Gordon Dam, Tasmania, Australia
Credit: Wikimedia Commons

Wind: This is one of the cheapest forms of renewable energy and is now the third largest source globally. Wind power is growing rapidly as its costs decline. Wind power has few downsides, but it isn't a flexible and controllable power source like hydro and nuclear. Some European countries with less land have offshore wind stations.

Biomass: Biomass (also called biofuels) can be burnt to generate steam and turn a turbine. An advantage of biomass is that it affords more flexible power generation than wind or solar. Without relying on the presence of wind or sunshine, we can turn biomass power stations on or off according to the demand. However biomass probably can't provide the bulk of renewable energy required, unless much of the world's agricultural land is turned over to growing energy crops. This prospect has unacceptable implications for food production.

---

* Why does vegetation rotting underwater release methane, rather than result in fossil fuels being formed (as detailed in Chapter 4)? Anaerobic bacteria (bacteria which live without oxygen) break down biological matter to release methane (CH_4). It is only on the rare occasions when bacteria are not present to decompose the organism, that the long process of fossil fuel formation takes place.

115

Part F: Big Picture Solutions - how can science and politics help?

Solar Photo-Voltaic (PV): This technology converts light from the sun into electricity. It has huge potential: the amount of solar energy hitting the earth in 15 minutes is equal to humanity's total electricity needs for a year![204] Solar PV, while not yet as widespread as wind, has increased five-fold in the last five years. Of all the renewable energy technologies, solar PV is the one most suited to small-scale generation, with solar panels usually sitting on your roof (more on this in Chapter 31). There are also increasing numbers of 'solar farms': large areas with thousands of solar panels, generating electricity for whole districts.

Solar PV is sometimes criticised for the amount of energy used to make the panels. However, with solar cells having a life-span of 20 years, they will typically produce over 10 times more energy in their lifetimes than was taken to manufacture them.[205]

Concentrated Solar Thermal (CST): This is the newest mainstream technology. Being so new, it is still quite expensive. Its most common form involves hectares of mirrors concentrating solar energy onto a central tower.[206] Inside the tower, salt is heated to over 600°C, melting it. Water is channelled past the molten salt, producing steam, to drive a turbine. An advantage of CST over solar PV is that it is cheaper to manufacture mirrors than solar panels. A further advantage is its ability to generate power 24/7, since the heat stored in the salt is sufficient to generate steam throughout the night. CST is already being used successfully in the US and Spain and the world's biggest facility is being planned for Port Augusta in Australia.[207]

The world's first CST plant, Spain   Credit: Wikimedia Commons

22. Nature's power - renewable energy solutions

Geothermal: Countries that are geologically active, like Iceland, are well suited to the use of geothermal technology. Water is run down to the molten rock below the earth's crust and converted to steam, which in turn runs a turbine to generate power.[208] Geothermal power will continue to provide cheap energy for a few countries, but cannot be scaled up much globally.[209]

Ocean energy: These technologies harness the power of moving water in waves and tides to run turbines. While ocean power currently generates only a small amount of power, they have great potential for a few countries, including Australia, with its massive coastline.[210]

With the renewable technologies outlined above there is already enough know-how to generate all the world's electricity needs with few or no carbon emissions. The major hurdle is for governments and corporations to make the big infrastructure expenditures necessary to unlock this enormous potential. In this regard, it is very encouraging that Sweden recently announced its intention to become the world's first fossil-fuel-free country.[211]

Unfortunately, many other governments are looking only towards the next election, rather than toward the long-term sustainability of their country or the globe. So the big question is, how we can generate the political will and economic impetus to make this transition as quickly as possible? We'll consider those issues later in this Part.

But first, 40% of GHG emissions are *not* caused by fossil fuels at all. It is to them we turn next.

Reflection Questions

- Which renewable technology is most suited to your country? Why?
- Why do you think we haven't moved towards widespread use of renewable power generation more quickly?

Want To Learn More?

→ Report: *BZE Stationary Energy Plan.* A detailed proposal for how Australia could generate all its electricity renewably. *http://bze.org.au/stationary-energy-plan/*

→ Book: MacKay, David, JC; 2009. *Sustainable Energy – Without the Hot Air.* UIT Cambridge Ltd. Examines renewable energy generation potential in Britain.

Part F: Big Picture Solutions - how can science and politics help?

23. Farts, Forestry and Fugitives
– agricultural and industrial solutions

I've been a vegetarian since I was a boy. While my move away from meat began with 'the chicken incident' (described in Chapter 2), I was strengthened in my resolve when I learnt how much damage animal agriculture does to the environment.

Fossil fuels are often portrayed as the villain in the climate change story, and rightly so, as their combustion releases 60% of human-caused GHG emissions. Less talked about, however, are the 40% of greenhouse gas emissions from other sources, as seen in Table (4) in Chapter 21. Non-fossil fuel emissions are caused by agriculture, manufacturing and mining. These emissions are not very amenable to technological solutions. Instead, we will need to change our own lifestyles: eating less meat and dairy, buying less 'stuff', and living more simply.

Methane is the second most problematic greenhouse gas, after carbon dioxide, and accounts for 16% of total emissions. One of its main sources is cattle. Cattle are endowed with a remarkable digestive system, in which microbes in the gut are able to break down tough plant matter anaerobically (without oxygen).[212] Unfortunately, in doing so, they produce significant amounts of methane, which they burp and fart into the atmosphere.

It is difficult to envisage technological solutions that would significantly reduce these emissions. Scientists are working on the problem, primarily by experimenting with different forms of cattle feed.[213] However progress is slow, and most of the initiatives have only shown emissions reductions of 10-20%. Therefore, it is likely that the only way methane emissions will come down is for everyday people like you and me to eat less meat and dairy. Another significant source of methane is food rotting in bins and landfill. Again, while scientific and political initiatives may help, the onus is on us to reduce how much food we waste. We'll consider these issues further in Chapter 28 (Waists and Wastes).

After fossil fuels, the next biggest source of CO_2 emissions is 'Land Use Change and Forestry'. This is a technical way to describe what is primarily deforestation, undertaken to make space for more agriculture. Land Use Change is significant, accounting for 11% of total GHG emissions. Logging the Amazon to make way for cattle and soyabean (much of which is fed to cattle)[214] is the most widely known example. Deforestation in Indonesia is another significant contributor, especially to make room for palm plantations.[215] Palm oil is used extensively in cooking oil, margarine and ice-cream. We recently saw graphic images of this forest clearance in Leonardo DiCaprio's powerful documentary *Before the*

23. Farts, Forestry and Fugitives - agricultural and industrial solutions

Deforestation Credit: Boundless Biology

Flood. If we reduce our consumption of meat, dairy and palm oil products, the need to clear forests to make space for such agriculture will be substantially reduced.

Nitrous oxide (N_2O) is another potent greenhouse gas which accounts for 6% of emissions. Nitrogen is applied as fertiliser to many crops. Unfortunately, some of this nitrogen is oxidised (reacts with oxygen to become N_2O) and enters the atmosphere.[216] This is particularly so if excess fertiliser is washed off by rain. Manure from livestock is another significant source of N_2O. Therefore the main avenues for reducing nitrous oxide emissions are better agricultural practices and – surprise, surprise – eating less meat.

We saw in the previous two chapters that fossil fuel combustion causes about 60% of emissions. But before the fossil fuels are burnt, their extraction process releases significant amounts of methane. Deposits of coal and oil typically have natural gas (methane) in the same geological formation.[217] When the coal, oil and natural gas are extracted, some methane also leaks out. The main way to reduce these 'fugitive emissions' is, quite simply, to extract less coal, oil and gas.

Industrial processes, especially cement and steel production are also major GHG contributors. We use cement and steel primarily in the construction of buildings, houses and other infrastructure. As seen in Science Geek (9), it's difficult to reduce the GHG emissions from these processes, so the only way to deal with the problem currently is to consume less of the product. We'll explore this further in Chapter 32 (A Castle or a Home?)

SCIENCE GEEK 9

Industrial processes

It will be difficult to find zero-emission ways of running key industrial processes, such as cement production and steel-making. This is because the very chemical processes involved release CO_2.[218]

- A major ingredient of cement is lime (CaO). This is generated by breaking down limestone ($CaCO_3$). The reaction is: $CaCO_3 \rightarrow CaO + CO_2$
- Steel is produced by reacting iron oxides like haematite (Fe_2O_3), with carbon. The overall reaction is: $2Fe_2O_3 + 3C \rightarrow 4Fe + 3CO_2$.[219]

Currently, there are no viable alternatives to replace cement or steel on a large scale. Researchers are working on ways to produce these vital construction materials without releasing CO_2, but it will take time for new technologies to be proven, and then widely utilised. The main hope, at least at this stage, is to live more simply, using less cement and steel.

A final contributor to GHG emissions are hydrofluorocarbons (HFCs). These extremely potent gases are used primarily in air-conditioning and refrigeration. In October 2016, an international agreement was reached in Kigali, Rwanda, to progressively phase out the use of HFCs from 2019 onwards.[220] While HFCs are only a small component (2%) of greenhouse gases, the agreement, like that in Paris in 2015, does give hope that political agreements can be reached to implement the scientific solutions we've just discussed. It is to these political avenues we now turn.

Reflection Questions

🔍 Have you ever considered the link between climate change and your consumption of meat, ice-cream and margarine?

🔍 How do you feel about the idea that it will require lifestyle change, rather than a scientific solution, to tackle many of the sources of emissions discussed in this chapter?

Want To Learn More?

→ Report: *Zero Carbon Industry Plan: Rethinking Cement.* Outlines emerging low-carbon cement technologies. *http://bze.org.au/rethinking-cement-plan/*

→ Report: *Zero Carbon Australia: Land Use: Agriculture and Forestry.* Describes how Australia's agricultural emissions can be brought to net zero. *http://bze.org.au/land-use-agriculture-and-forestry/*

→ Film: *Before the Flood.* *https://www.beforetheflood.com/about/*

Part F: Big Picture Solutions - how can science and politics help?

24. Winning and Losing in Paris
– international political solutions

I remember waiting anxiously in December 2015 to see whether the Paris climate conference would result in an agreement. It felt like one of those pivotal moments in history, with an enormous amount at stake. I remember thinking that if negotiators failed to strike a deal, then our planet was in deep, deep trouble. Thankfully, an agreement was reached. In this chapter, we'll examine that deal and consider whether it's enough to save us from catastrophic climate change.

In over 20 years of international negotiations on climate change, there had been little to inspire confidence that a comprehensive global agreement would be possible. The negotiations began in Rio de Janeiro in 1992. It took five years, until Kyoto in 1997, for negotiators to come up with legally binding emissions targets. However, it was a hollow accord: Canada pulled out, the US never ratified it, and Australia set itself an unambitious target of an 8% *increase* in emissions.[221] Negotiations continued every year with very little progress. Particularly low points were Bali in 2007 and Copenhagen in 2009. Their failure led many to wonder whether a genuine global agreement would ever be possible.

Credit: INKCINCT. Used with artist's permission.

There was a massive obstacle to international agreement: a division between the interests of the 'developed' (rich) and 'developing' (poor) countries. Rich countries like the US, Japan and European nations, which have released the vast majority of emissions until now (see *Illustration 10* in Chapter 11), are primarily responsible for the climate change we are experiencing today. And those of us in rich countries are *still* emitting much more per capita than people in poorer countries. However, many poorer countries are experiencing rapid economic growth and with it, rapid growth in GHG emissions. So tackling climate change effectively will be impossible without curbing emissions from both rich *and* poor countries. The impasse, then, is that rich countries don't want to significantly reduce their emissions until poorer nations agree to curb theirs. On the other hand, poorer nations, understandably, feel that they have a right to grow and 'catch up' to the West economically, so believe rich nations should be the first to significantly reduce emissions.

The first real breakthrough came in 2014, when China and the US signed a deal. These two superpowers are the biggest emitters in the 'developing' and the 'developed' world respectively, together accounting for 45% of the world's emissions.[222] The US promised to cut emissions by 26-28% (or 2005 levels) by 2025. In return, China agreed to peak its emissions by 2030 and to reduce them thereafter.[223] In effect, this will mean that by 2030, the US and China will have the same per capita emissions. This landmark agreement demonstrated that cooperation on climate change between the developed and the developing worlds was possible. There is a major hitch, however. According to this deal, the emissions of Americans and Chinese will converge in 2030 at 12-14 tonnes CO_2e per person, per year. This is far more than their fair share of the global carbon budget (2 tonnes CO_2e per person, per year).[224]

The US-China deal laid the groundwork for both the great success, and failure, of climate negotiations a year later. The Paris agreement in 2015 was truly historic, in that it involved all nations[*] agreeing to concrete emissions targets. The key to all countries agreeing at Paris, however, was that each country set its *own* target, and the commitments are entirely voluntary. There are no sanctions should countries fail to meet their own self-imposed targets, nor any way to keep countries bound to the agreement. In June 2017, the US signalled its intent to pull out of the accord. Thankfully, many other countries immediately reaffirmed their commitment to Paris, and criticised President Trump for his decision.

Also problematic is that the targets set at Paris are not nearly ambitious enough. Even if all countries meet their targets (which is far from certain) we would still have global warming of about 2.7°C, well above the stated target of 2°C and far beyond the aspirational goal of 1.5°C.[225]

---

[*] 195 nations signed. The only ones to not sign were Syria (which didn't attend due to its civil war) and Nicaragua (which felt the agreement was not strong enough). However, both countries have since signed.

Part F: Big Picture Solutions - how can science and politics help?

Optimists hope that the five-yearly reviews written into the Paris agreement will allow countries to revise targets to be more ambitious, as the dire consequences of climate change become clearer. Pessimists believe that these reviews will mean little without a way to arm-twist countries into adopting, and then meeting, more ambitious targets.

In a sense, then, the Paris agreement was a hollow victory: a win, but at a terrible cost. It is remarkable that a truly global agreement was reached, but the only way such an accord was possible was by sacrificing its ambition and enforceability. Each country has agreed to limit itself to a particular sized slice of the carbon budget 'cake', but the cake is just too small to accommodate everyone's wishes.

So, what would a better agreement look like? Ideally, a global agreement would be binding and achieve sufficient emissions reductions to keep us under 2°C warming, in a manner that is fair to all countries. This may best be achieved through a global, country-based carbon trading scheme as described in Science Geek (10).

SCIENCE GEEK 10

A possible carbon trading scheme

1. A committee, consisting of representatives from many countries, as well as climate scientists, decides on a global emissions reduction pathway which will keep us within our global carbon budget. For instance, they might decide to reduce global emissions by two gigatonnes CO_2e per year: from 49 Gt in 2018 (see Science Geek (6) in Chapter 14), to 47 Gt in 2019, 45 Gt in 2020 and so on down to zero by 2043. This would keep us under our global carbon budget of 800Gt, giving us a good chance to stay under 2°C warming and the possibility of meeting the 1.5°C target.

2. Each country's share of the global carbon allowance for any given year is calculated using their proportion of the global population in the first year.* For instance, Australia's population of 23.8 million out of the world's 7.4 billion, gives it a share of 0.32% of the carbon budget. This means that, in 2018 Australia would receive an allowance of 157 Mt.

---

* This system would be controversial for at least two reasons. Firstly, some countries might object to equal per-capita carbon allowances. Countries that are sparsely populated, like Australia, might argue that they are entitled to a bigger share of the budget because of the need to travel over long distances, while countries with cold climates, like Canada, might demand a larger share of the carbon budget because of the need for heating. However, working out a formula to take these factors into consideration would be extremely controversial. Secondly, countries with high population growth rates may object to their share being tied to their population in a base year. However, tying a country's share to their population each year may inadvertently encourage population growth.

24. Winning and Losing in Paris - international political solutions

3. Countries can trade carbon permits to make up the difference between their allowance and their actual emissions. For instance, suppose Australia emits 557 Mt of CO_2e in 2018. It would be required to purchase 400 Mt (557-157) of permits, from other countries, like India, whose allowances are greater than their actual emissions.

Of course, it is unlikely that such an agreement will be made in the foreseeable future. It would probably be blocked by rich countries, which want to pollute way above their fair share without having to pay for it.

In lieu of an enforceable, ambitious and just global agreement on climate change, we must capitalise on what we have – the Paris accord. As we've seen, this relies on voluntary targets in which there is no accountability 'from above' to ensure governments fulfil their commitments. Instead, it is imperative that we keep our national leaders accountable 'from below'. It is up to us to pressure our governments to increase the ambition of their targets. Whether this pressure involves petitions, meeting your member of parliament, legal challenges, or even peaceful protests, it is vital that we become more politically active. We'll explore this further in Chapter 26 (Why Didn't You Do Something?) For the Paris agreement to save us, we must first save the Paris agreement.

International political agreements are vital, but so too are national policies to implement them. It is these national political solutions to which we turn in the next chapter.

Part F: Big Picture Solutions - how can science and politics help?

Reflection Questions

🔍 Find your country's emissions reduction target submitted at Paris at the Climate Action Tracker website (*www.climateactiontracker.org*) and read the analysis. Do you think your country's target is reasonable?

🔍 How much hope do you have that the Paris agreement will be adequate to save us from runaway climate change? Why?

Want To Learn More?

→ Report: *Adoption of the Paris Agreement.* A dense, 30-page document with an excellent summary of the fuller agreement. *https://unfccc.int/resource/docs/2015/cop21/eng/l09.pdf*

→ Film: *An Inconvenient Sequel: Truth to Power.* Al Gore's follow up to his original Oscar-winning film, *'An Inconvenient Truth'*. The sequel focuses on the Paris agreement.

25. Incentives for Good
– national political solutions

Talking with people about climate change can be tricky. Trickier still is suggesting that the government should play a significant role. Many people believe: *'the market will solve it – no need for government intervention.'* In this chapter we will see that it *is* still necessary for national governments to assist in the transition to a renewables based economy.

Why government intervention?

As Chapter 22 (Nature's Power) described, there are many renewable energy technologies which together have the capacity to replace fossil fuels. The costs of wind and solar have been rapidly decreasing, such that, in many parts of the world, they already make sense from a strictly economic point of view, without the need for government intervention. We saw in Table (5) in Chapter 22 that wind generation is increasing at 17% a year, while solar PV is growing even faster (42% a year). While I'm optimistic about the spread of these technologies, I'd argue that we still need national governments to intervene in the market to enable the transition to a renewables-based economy to happen safely, fairly and rapidly. There are several reasons for this:

Regulating harm: Just as chemicals pollute our waterways and plastics clog our oceans, fossil fuel emissions pollute our atmosphere. Greenhouse gases being invisible doesn't make them any less dangerous. Corporations and individuals responsible for the pollution generally act to maximise profit or enjoyment, rather than maximising the welfare of society as a whole, so it is entirely appropriate for governments to regulate GHG emissions, just as they regulate chemical or plastic pollution.

Ensuring a fair transition: The growth of renewable energy has contributed to a significant drop in the price of coal over recent years, causing many coal mines to shut.[226] While this is a cause for celebration environmentally, it often isn't celebrated locally, as regional communities where mines shut are left with a polluted environment and a lack of jobs – in a hole, so to speak. The government should ensure fossil fuel companies clean up after themselves, and could provide funding to help retrain workers for a renewables-based economy.

Speeding up the transition: The transition from fossil fuels to renewables needs to happen very quickly if we are to keep temperature rise to under 2°C. Renewables are growing under the market system, but given the short time

Part F: Big Picture Solutions - how can science and politics help?

frames involved, and the risks of not transitioning quickly enough, governments should subsidise renewables to accelerate the transition.

Assisting to develop large infrastructure: Some of the large infrastructure investments we discussed earlier in this Part may be too expensive for private industry alone. Projects like high-speed rail links and concentrated solar thermal plants may need government investment to supplement that by private industry.

How can governments intervene?

If we accept that government intervention is necessary to drive the transition to a low-carbon economy, then how best should this be done? Many economists argue that putting a price on carbon would be the easiest and most sensible way. Indeed, about 40 countries already have a carbon price, including members of the EU, and the UK.[227] However carbon taxes are still very controversial in many political environments, including Australia's, so it is important to clarify the advantages of putting a price on carbon.[*]

The idea behind a carbon tax is simple. Carbon emissions, if unpriced are a 'negative externality'. This economic term means that even though the benefit of purchasing a particular product is limited to the consumer, some of the negative consequences of manufacturing the product (such as the emissions to make it) are spread over the whole world. In other words, only a proportion of the total cost of a carbon-intensive product, like a flight, is paid by the consumer – the rest is borne by society as a whole. The idea then, is that by taxing carbon emissions, the price of the carbon-based product more accurately reflects its social and environmental cost. An advantage of accurately pricing carbon-intensive products is that, with an increased price, the quantity of the product consumed will fall, while the quantity of low-carbon products, now more competitively priced, will increase.

One argument against a carbon tax is that it will push up the cost of many goods and services, including electricity. Indeed, in most cases it will.[†228] In fact, the whole point of a carbon tax is to ensure products are priced to reflect their true costs. It is likely that this will disproportionately impact the poor, who can ill-afford to pay more. The revenue raised from a carbon tax, however, could be partially used to increase the income-tax-free threshold, or reduce any goods

---

[*] I use the term 'carbon tax' and 'price on carbon' interchangeably here, although there are other ways to put a price on carbon, like an emission trading scheme (ETS). See http://www.abc.net.au/news/2011-07-07/explained-carbon-tax-es-emissions-trading-and/2785736. The differences between a carbon tax and an ETS are often debated by environmentalist nerds (like me). For a pro-tax view, consider https://www.carbontax.org/cap-and-trade-problems/.

[†] Although, in Australia's case, most proposed carbon taxes wouldn't have a major impact on the price of electricity. For instance, a carbon price of AUD$20 per tonne would raise electricity prices by about 2c/kWh. With an average Australia consuming 6kWh/day, this equates to less than AUD$50 per year increase. In reality, rising electricity costs in Australia have more to do with the costs of maintaining and expanding the grid.

25. Incentives for Good - national political solutions

and services tax in place, or even be directly paid to low-income households – thereby offsetting the effects on the poor.[229]

The limits of growth

Finally, in our discussion of national and economic solutions, we need to consider the goal of almost every government in the world – perpetual economic growth. Many fossil fuel projects are justified as contributing to economic growth, while environmental regulations are taboo if they will impede growth.

The quest for unending growth is unnatural.[230] Human beings, plants and animals don't continue to grow indefinitely. Growth is needed to start with, physically for a child, and economically for developing world countries, to get to a healthy maturity, but no one needs infinite growth. In medicine, there is a term for rapid, uncontrolled growth of cells: cancer. Sadly, cancer is a reasonable analogy for what we humans are doing to the earth in our quest for limitless growth.

As climate change worsens, we will inevitably have to face the truth that the earth is finite. Its resources are limited and its forests and oceans have a finite ability to absorb carbon. We simply can't continue to grow infinitely, at least not with growth based on the extraction and processing of resources.

Given these environmental considerations, why is economic growth still seen to be the ultimate goal by many politicians? The economy grows when more goods

Credit: Felix Schaad, Tages Anzeiger

and services are produced, sold and consumed. The assumption is that the more people consume, the happier they will be. However, most people realise that once we have our basic physical needs met, we derive most pleasure and meaning from things that the economy cannot price: time with friends and family, being awed by the ocean, or listening to beautiful music. It is when these deeper needs are frustrated, that we turn to the false hope that consumer goods will buy us love, purpose and belonging.[231]

This questioning of growth as the ultimate goal is beginning to gain some support from research that shows economic growth, beyond a certain point, is *not* actually the key to a healthy society.[232] Wilkinson and Pickett, in their book *The Spirit Level,* show that reducing inequality has a much greater effect on the physical and emotional health of a society than its economic growth.

So the deepest shift that must take place – in our governments, our homes and our hearts – is a realisation that more money and more growth should not be our aim in and of itself. Instead, a better aim is a joyful, sustainable and meaningful life. In Part G we explore ideas for creating that type of life.

National political solutions to climate change are possible. Some national governments, like Sweden's, are moving quickly in this direction. Unfortunately, most of our governments are moving far too slowly. In that context, it is important for people like you and me to encourage our politicians and CEOs to design responsible environmental policies and products. In the last chapter of this Part, we'll consider the role of peaceful protest in making these solutions a reality.

Reflection Questions

🔎 What role do you think national governments should play in the transition to a renewables based economy?

🔎 How do you feel about the critique of economic growth offered in this chapter?

🔎 How would you describe the most important goals of your life? To what extent are they related to having more money?

Want To Learn More?

→ Documentary: Australian Broadcasting Commission; 2015. *The End of Coal.* The decline of the coal industry in Australia. *http://www.abc.net.au/4corners/stories/2015/06/15/4253096.htm*

→ Book: Wilkinson and Pickett; 2009. *The Spirit Level – Why More Equal Societies Almost Always Do Better.* Allen Lane. Argues equality is more important to happiness than wealth.

Part F: Big Picture Solutions - how can science and politics help?

26. Why Didn't You Do Something?
– protest solutions

'Are you ready to be arrested?' The question was confronting. I'm a law-abiding guy. I play by the rules. I have never even had a speeding ticket! The notion of being arrested was disturbing, but for climate change, I was seriously considering it.

In a sense, protest is the intersection between the 'big picture' solutions of this Part and the 'small picture' solutions of Part G. It's a way that people like us can call on the 'big boys' to make the big changes necessary. While we can't *force* anyone to change, if enough everyday people protest poor political or corporate behaviour, then it becomes much more likely that our leaders *will* change. In this chapter, we'll consider three types of protest: protest against governments for harmful environmental policies, protest against private enterprise for irresponsible business practices, and legal challenges against governments or corporations.

Protest against governments: On 11 September 2015, Peter Dutton, a senior minister in the Australian government, was caught on microphone joking with then Prime Minister Abbott about 'Cape York time': *'Time doesn't mean anything when you're about to have water lapping at your door.'* [233]

Couched in a cultural criticism of the more fluid approach to time in northern Australia and the Pacific islands, the comment was apparently meant to be a joke aimed at the future viability of Pacific states. It seems the 'joke' indicated Mr Dutton did accept that climate change is real and affecting the viability of whole nations. Astonishingly, however, it also indicated that he thought it was funny!

It was in this context that, together with about twenty other activists, I'd agreed to do a sit-in at Peter Dutton's office in Brisbane. The 2016 national election was looming and the battle for Mr Dutton's electorate was expected to be closely fought. We divided into several sub groups, depending on the level of protest we were comfortable with. One group would attempt to gain entry to Mr Dutton's office by legal means and then 'sit-in'. If requested by police to leave the office, they were planning not to do so, thereby precipitating an arrest,

26. Why Didn't You Do Something? - protest solutions

which was more likely to gain media attention and take the message to a wider audience. I'd resolved that government ministers joking about climate change was an important enough issue that I was willing to sit-in and be arrested if necessary.

Together our group had also resolved to behave peacefully and respectfully, not to impede others who wanted to access the minister's office and to go peacefully should the police opt to arrest us. We had nothing against everyday members of the public, or indeed the police, who were only doing their job.

Being a follow-the-rules kind of guy, my resolution meant a nervous week leading up to the protest. A couple of calls to activist friends helped ease my nerves. Andy, my Catholic Worker friend and seasoned activist responded: *'Great, good on you. And don't worry. No one ever does 'time' for that.'* Mary, an older Mennonite friend, who had been arrested for a similar protest, also thought there was little possibility of being imprisoned. *'And even if you do some 'time', imagine the great conversations you can have inside.'* (I wish she had stopped before saying that last bit.) I was also heartened to find the two other men willing to sit inside the office and be arrested were not dread-locked hippies, but thoughtful, compassionate grandfathers. We each felt that we owed it to future generations to take action. We didn't want our grandchildren, in twenty years, facing a world of runaway climate change, to ask in disgust: *'Why didn't you do something?'*

Mark at the Peter Dutton protest (2016) Credit: 350.org

Part F: Big Picture Solutions - how can science and politics help?

Our attempt to gain entry to the office was blocked by two police officers. Apparently, such political actions are often monitored by police on social media, so they are aware of the action before it takes place. The officers politely declined to allow us entry to Mr Dutton's office, but did allow us to do our protest on the footpath where we were soon joined by about 50 others. Over the next couple of hours, we sang, waved placards and heard impassioned speeches.

Of course, I was relieved not to be arrested. I'm happy too that I dealt with some of my fear of 'breaking the rules'. Given the respectful interaction with the police, I now feel a little less scared of 'arrestable' actions in the future. It was very disappointing though, that two weeks later, despite a 5% swing against him, Mr Dutton narrowly won the election for his seat. My hope is that in the next election, Mr Dutton and other politicians who don't take climate change seriously will *not* retain office.

Protest against corporate behaviour: As well as criticising government behaviour, we can also challenge the way fossil fuel corporations and financial institutions do business, by 'divesting' from those which ignore environmental concerns, and instead investing in those that behave more responsibly. That may involve not only selling our shares in Exxon-Mobil or BP, but also shifting away from superannuation, pension funds and banks which finance fossil fuel projects.

The divest movement began on American college campuses in 2012. Its critics suggest that a few people selling their shares or withdrawing their savings won't make any difference, but like most of these issues, if enough people *do* divest, it will send a clear message to corporations. In recent years, the divestment movement has gained considerable momentum. As of 2016, 688 institutions and nearly 60,000 individuals in 76 countries have divested US$5 trillion from fossil fuel assets.[234] High profile 'divestors' include Norway's Sovereign Wealth Fund,[235] the Church of England, Rockefeller Brothers Fund and the British Medical Association.[236]

The thinking behind divestment is simple enough. If enough people choose *not* to invest in institutions which lend to the fossil fuel industry, then it will no longer be profitable for those institutions to continue such financing. If the fossil fuel companies can't finance their projects, they can't go ahead. Divestment 'puts your money where your mouth is': if you're opposed to the destruction of the planet, then you shouldn't be profiting from it through interest and dividends.

Arguably it is also becoming more *financially* prudent for individual investors to divest from fossil fuels. If the world's governments *do* take climate change seriously, as the Paris agreement indicates is beginning to happen, then governments will be more reticent to approve new fossil fuel projects. Thus, those new projects are at risk of becoming 'stranded' – that is, they cannot be converted into actual profit-making projects.[237]

The litmus test for the divestment movement in Australia since 2015 has been the financing of the massive Carmichael coal mine in my home state of Queensland, being built by the Indian corporate giant, Adani. If built, this mine will extract coal with embedded emissions of 4.6 Gt of carbon dioxide over its lifetime.[238] As we saw in Chapter 14, fossil fuel companies already have proven reserves, which, if burnt, would exceed our 800 Gt CO_2 carbon budget. One would think, given this simple maths, that our political leaders would put a halt to approvals of all new fossil fuel projects. Instead, the state government not only approved the mine but granted it 'critical infrastructure' status.[239]

Even though Adani had government approval for the mine, it still needed to finance the project. It was in that context that I did a 'flash mob'* dance outside a branch of the Commonwealth Bank. We were trying to build pressure on the bank to not invest in the Adani project. The dance went off well, although I did feel a little out of place, being 30 years older than most of the dancers!

Thankfully, the Commonwealth Bank is distancing itself from the Carmichael mine.[240] Now all of the 'big four' banks in Australia have indicated that they won't finance the project.[241]

If we 'divest' our money from fossil fuel companies and the banks that finance them, where do we invest it instead? Some financial groups use 'negative filters' by which they filter out any investment which is proven to be harmful. Hence, they won't invest in industries like tobacco or armaments. Other financial groups go a step further and use a 'positive filter' to actively seek investment opportunities that bring good to society and the environment. Groups like *Australian Ethical Investment* (see 'Want To Learn More') use this positive filter to find, among other things, renewable energy projects. Investors can therefore be assured that their money is going to help, rather than harm, the environment.

---

* Protest in which activists mill around looking normal and then, at an appointed sign, perform a choreographed dance.

Part F: Big Picture Solutions - how can science and politics help?

Legal protest: Some ordinary citizens who are adversely affected by poor environmental policies and practices may be able to legally challenge the government or corporation at fault. Such challenges have been successful in many situations around the world. A group of Dutch citizens sued their own government for not taking climate change seriously enough. They won, forcing the Dutch government to cut emissions by 25% within five years.[242] In other contexts, indigenous groups have also been able to use legal avenues to challenge mining on their land.[243]

Big picture solutions do exist for climate change. However, most political and business leaders won't act quickly enough of their own accord. It is only when individuals like you and me speak out in protest, as well as changing our *own* consumption patterns, that big picture solutions will occur quickly enough. In Part G we take a closer a look at the 'small picture' changes we can make to our own lifestyles.

Reflection Questions

🔍 Have you ever been involved in a political protest? How was that experience for you?

🔍 Do you think protests are useful? Why or why not?

🔍 Which financial institution do you bank with? Find the level to which your bank invests in fossil fuels:
If you live in Australia, go to the Market Forces website: *www.marketforces.org.au*
If you live in the UK, go to the Ethical Investment Association: *http://ethicalinvestment.org.uk/*
Does that level of investment surprise you? If your bank does not rate well, find a bank with better environmental credentials.

Want To Learn More?

→ Website: *Australian Ethical Investment.* Financial group which uses a positive filter to find investments. *https://www.australianethical.com.au/*

→ Website: *350.org.* Climate change action group. *www.350.org*

→ Website: *Environmental Defenders Office.* Group assisting with legal challenges on environmental issues in Australia. *http://www.edo.org.au/*

→ Website: *Rising Tide North America.* US grass-roots climate group. *https://risingtidenorthamerica.org/*

→ Documentary: *Digging into Adani. An exposé of Adani's environmental record. http://www.abc.net.au/4corners/digging-into-adani/9608500*

Part G: Small Picture Solutions – what can you and I do?

27. The 5 R's
– low-carbon 'stuff'

Growing up in a poor neighbourhood in north India, Tom and Oscar didn't have a lot of stuff, including not having (or wanting) a TV. Instead, we we spent a lot of our spare time as a family playing sport, reading and enjoying board games. When Tom's birthday was approaching a few years ago, we asked him what he'd like for a present. After a moment's thought he said, quite honestly and without pretence: *'Nothing really, I've got everything I want.'* That statement was wonderful for Cathy and me to hear, not because it saved us buying a present, but because it indicated that Tom had, at least for now, avoided being infected by the consumerism 'bug' that is so pervasive in our society today.

In Part F we looked at 'big picture' solutions to climate change, both scientific and political. As important as those solutions are, Tom and I would argue that everyday people like you and me need to make changes in our own lifestyles in order to create the impetus for the politicians and CEOs to implement those big picture solutions quickly enough.[244] Throughout history, most big changes have not been won 'top down', but primarily from the 'bottom up'. Gandhi's leadership of the Indian independence movement would have achieved little without a groundswell of support from millions of ordinary Indians. World War II was not won by Churchill, Roosevelt or Stalin – but by millions of ordinary citizens' sacrifices. In the same way, climate change will not be solved solely in the big picture by scientists, politicians and CEOs. It will also require each of us to act in our own lives and, in doing so, to catalyse a broader movement for change.

In this Part, we'll set out the concrete changes we can make to our own lifestyles. We'll describe what we as a family have done to attempt to keep our carbon

27. The 5 R's - low-carbon 'stuff'

emissions down, and we'll introduce you to some inspiring friends who have taken similar steps. The good news is that this transition to a low-carbon life is doable. Those of us who are already doing it are not only tolerating it, but largely enjoying it. My hope is that you and millions of others can join us, and together we can turn this mess around.

In Part D we examined seven sources of our carbon footprint: buying products; diet; local travel; long-distance travel; domestic electricity and gas; housing; and government services and mining. This Part looks at all but the last of these categories to show how we, as individuals, can substantially reduce our carbon footprint and become people who really are 'low-carbon and loving it'. Initially we'll consider the biggest part of our carbon footprint – 'stuff'.

As we've seen, the manufacture of goods releases significant emissions. There is, however, an environmentally responsible alternative to buying a new item every time an existing one breaks or goes out of fashion. It can be summarised as the 5R's:

- **Running** items until they wear out.
- **Repairing** broken items when possible.
- **Recycling** items when they can't be repaired.
- **Re-using** items unwanted by others.
- **Responsibly** purchasing new goods when re-used ones are not available.

A well-used Settlers of Catan game – played by a much younger Oscar and Tom (2011)

Running items until they wear out:

There are good feelings associated with running an item through to the end of its life. This is often the case with our clothes. We become attached to our favourite clothes. We feel comfortable in them and somehow, they feel like 'us'. Sometimes there is even a sense of sadness when we finally need to throw away

Part G: Small Picture Solutions - what can you and I do?

something that's been dear to us. For me, this happens with my running shoes. I love running, so I grow attached to my shoes. When I finally wear them out, I feel a sense of loss. So too with our favourite board game, Settlers of Catan. For years we played it almost every week, such that the images are wearing off the cards!

Repairing: Fixing broken items can be fun. Patching our favourite clothes, gluing the sole back on our joggers, and putting a new grip on our tennis racquet, all bring warm feelings of responsibly using the things we're privileged enough to have. Our table fan is a good example. When temperatures are in the 30s and 40s, as they often are in north India, fans are essential equipment. Our fan recently stopped oscillating, but I was able to pull it apart, find the oscillation mechanism, and fix it with a simple screw.

Repairing is admittedly harder for items that require more expertise to fix. It is often cheaper to buy a new one than pay someone to repair it. The battery in my old iPhone 3 is almost dead. I've found that I can buy a new battery for $50. But the phone is not designed for an ordinary person to be able to replace the battery, so I need to go to a specialist who will charge another $50 for labour. It turns out it's as cheap to buy a new smartphone for $100 (although *not* an iPhone) as it is to repair the old one. However, if enough people do choose the financially 'silly' option and repair, rather than buy new, then eventually the price of repairing will come down.

Recycling: When we've run an item through to the end of its life and it can't be repaired any more, we will need to throw it away. At this point, it's important to recycle the materials where possible, so that the discarded item can be remade into another product without using extra resources. Glass, plastic, metal and paper are easily recycled in most western cities. Recycling other items can be trickier, but with a little effort you can do it for many things. For example, in Australia, old mobile phones can be recycled at Officeworks, batteries at Battery World and tyres at Beaurepaires.[245] In India, there is a thriving recycling industry in which people even go door-to-door buying your old things.

Re-using: Once our favourite things have run their course and can't be repaired, we may need to buy another one. At this point many people will just go to the shop and buy a new one, especially given that the price of many consumer goods is so low. This is certainly the case for electronics. The price of computers, for example, just keeps coming down. However, as cheap as they seem, we

27. The 5 R's - low-carbon 'stuff'

need to recognise that all new products require resources and greenhouse gas emissions to manufacture. The environmentally better way is to re-use what others no longer want. Most products can be purchased second-hand (or 'pre-loved' as some call it). Cars and houses are obvious, but many other second-hand consumer goods are readily available on e-Bay or similar websites for a fraction of the price of a new one and, most importantly, without the resources and emissions required to manufacture it. In recent years, we've purchased many items online, second-hand, including camping gear, a smartphone, a camera and a musical instrument. All are still working well.

Many used items are also available at thrift shops. Purchasing from thrift shops has the bonus of our money going to a good cause, since many are run by charities. When living in Australia for several years recently, we got almost all our furniture, clothes, kitchen gear, and bicycle from thrift shops.

Credit: John Atkinson. Used with artist's permission

Responsible purchasing: It's better to buy something new only when you need it, not because your friend has a better one. Even when purchasing new, we can do so responsibly by using an ethical buying guide, which tells us which manufacturers have the best environmental records, are fairest in their treatment

Part G: Small Picture Solutions - what can you and I do?

of workers, use ethical marketing practices and so on (see 'Want To Learn More?').

Once, when Cathy asked our very poor friend Kaneez* if we could buy anything for her, she replied: *'No thanks, I've got everything I need.'* This from a woman who lives in a shack with a sum-total of possessions that would fit in most people's pantry! That response redefined responsible purchasing for me. The pleasure derived from owning and consuming things is temporary. We've been sold a lie that the latest gadget or experience is necessary to be content. It is not. As many of us know deep down, true joy comes not from consumer goods, but from the simple things in life: friendships, nature, music, creativity. Our own experience of living very simply for many years confirms this. While aspects of living so simply have certainly been difficult, overall it's been very fulfilling.

If we follow these 5R's guidelines, it will be relatively easy to bring our emissions associated with buying 'stuff' to under one tonne CO_2e per year.

Finally, it is also worth briefly discussing our consumption of services. Our consumption falls into two categories: goods and services. It is primarily the consumption of goods which is problematic for the planet, since goods require physical resources and carbon emissions to manufacture. It's generally better for the environment to buy a service.[246] So if you're thinking of a birthday gift for your friend and have a choice between a new TV or a ticket to her/his favourite music band or sports team – go for the latter. The TV took considerable resources and emissions to make, whereas generally the music or sporting show requires fewer resources (when averaged over the whole crowd at the event). We also tend to derive more pleasure from experiences than we do from goods. I'm likely to remember my recent birthday trip to the Great Barrier Reef much longer than I would a new iPhone.

The next biggest part of our carbon footprint is diet. We'll chew on that next.

---

* Who you met in Chapter 2.

Reflection Questions

- Have you recently tried to repair anything that broke? How was that experience?
- Have you purchased any re-used goods from the web or a thrift shop? How did that go?
- Think of one product and one service/experience you've purchased recently. Which gave you greater pleasure?

Want To Learn More?

→ Booklet: (Australian) *Ethical Buyer's Guide.* http://www.ethical.org.au/know-the-score-in-the-store/
The mobile App version is: http://www.ethical.org.au/get-involved/resources/shop-ethical-app/
The UK equivalent is *Ethical Consumer:* www.ethicalconsumer.org

→ Website: *Repair Café.* A UK initiative to get together with others to repair broken items. https://www.thegoodlifecentre.co.uk/events/repair-cafe-a-community-project-to-repair-reuse-recycle-1/ and https://therestartproject.org/

→ Documentary: *ABC. War on Waste.* Discusses the large quantities of waste produced in suburban Australia. http://www.abc.net.au/tv/programs/war-on-waste/

28. Waists and Wastes
– low-carbon diets

A couple of years ago, my nephew Angus became vegetarian. What got Angus away from his carnivorous tendencies was a documentary called *Cowspiracy*. The documentary argues, correctly, that a significant proportion of harmful greenhouse gases are produced by animal agriculture.[247] It helped Angus make a big change in his lifestyle.

For most people in the West, a significant proportion of our carbon footprint is caused by our diet. This is because we eat a lot of animal products and waste a lot of food. There is considerable scope to reduce these emissions – although doing so will require some changes to our lifestyles.

Animal agriculture is an inefficient way to produce food. Plants grow using nutrients and water from the soil, CO_2 from the atmosphere and energy from sunlight. Cattle, sheep, pigs and chickens get their energy and nutrients from eating plants. By eating animals, rather than plants, we add an extra link to the food chain. The world has plenty of grain to feed everyone,[248] yet millions of people in Asia and Africa remain hungry, in part because so much grain is fed to animals. Curbing our consumption of meat, eggs and dairy products would reduce not only emissions, but also global hunger. Many of our Indian friends complain of inflation in food prices. They struggle to feed their families, as the cost of staples – wheat, rice, vegetables – rises more quickly than their meagre wages. The disturbing reality is that western consumption of grain-fed, resource-intensive animal products keeps the price of food staples high, as land that could otherwise be feeding human stomachs is diverted for animal agriculture. An astonishing 77% of global farm land is devoted to animal agriculture, even though its products provide only 17% of human calorific intake and 33% of protein.[249]

Quite apart from the environmental impacts of a meat-based diet are significant concerns around the harsh conditions in which livestock are raised, fed and slaughtered. The great Indian thinker and activist Mahatma Gandhi, raised as a vegetarian, was considering eating meat as a young man. His father took him to a slaughterhouse and invited him to eat meat, *if* he were willing to kill the animal himself. I wonder how many of us would become vegetarian if we had to personally kill each animal we ate?

Westerners (particularly Australians[250]) are big meat-eaters. There are historical reasons for this. Most Australian, Canadian, US and New Zealander families would only need to go back a few generations to find farming ancestors. On the farm, meat was a readily available food source. It's not surprising then that meat eating has become a part of our culture. Until my parent's generation, the standard Australian evening meal was 'meat and three veg'. More recently, diet has changed a lot, with Asian, European and Latin-American cuisine becoming mainstream. Nowadays the average western family might eat 'meat and three veg' only once or twice a week, the other nights perhaps being a Chinese stir fry, an Italian pizza or Mexican burritos. Nevertheless, westerners still consume a lot of meat, even if that's chicken in your stir fry, ham on your pizza or mince in your burritos.

According to *Shrink That Footprint,* the emissions associated with the average diet in the US are over 2.5 tonnes CO_2e per person per year.[*251] A meat lover's diet is even more, at 3.3 tonnes. Their analysis, shown in *Illustration 18,* suggests

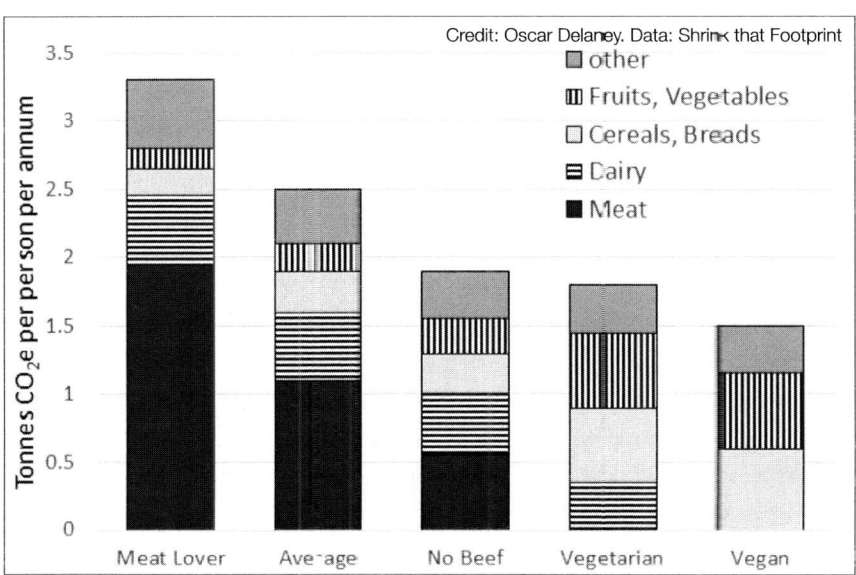

Illustration 18: Carbon footprint of different diets

* Note that this analysis assumes a consumption of 2600 kcal/person/day. However, once food that is wasted (that is, not consumed) is taken into account, the average footprint rises to closer to our 4 tonnes figure. (see Chapter 15)

that simply replacing red meat with chicken (less methane burps), reduces emissions substantially to 1.9 tonnes CO_2e. Replacing meat altogether with other forms of protein in a vegetarian diet (no meat, but using other animal products like eggs and milk), reduces the footprint to 1.8 tonnes CO_2e, going down to 1.5 tonnes CO_2e for a vegan diet (no animal products at all).

But what about the health implications? If you're like me, you may have been told since childhood that red meat is vital for protein and iron. However, there are relatively easy ways to obtain the protein and iron we need without red meat.[252] In our family, we get our protein from chickpeas, lentils, soy milk, eggs and peanut butter, while our iron comes from green leafy vegetables. In addition, there is a growing body of evidence that the levels of red meat, particularly processed meats, consumed in the West are unhealthy.[253]

It is difficult to change diet. Certain foods are a part of our culture. Just as red meat may be a part of Australian culture, so too whale meat is part of Japanese culture, and pork a part of south-east Asian cultures. However, while some aspects of culture may be ethically neutral, other aspects are unethical. Some cultures condone violence against women, and some divide society into castes and classes. Most people would emphatically agree with changing these aspects of 'culture'. Similarly, I'd suggest that some aspects of our diet, like eating large quantities of red meat, are, because of climate change, ethically unjustifiable.

Our journey to vegetarianism began a long time ago when Tom felt sad about a chicken dying for his birthday lunch and goats being killed on Bakra Eid. In the years we've been vegetarian, I hardly miss eating meat. Admittedly it's very easy in India, where most people don't eat meat and there are delicious lentils and vegetable curries in abundance. It's a little harder in the West, where it's still common to go to an eatery and find only one (or none) of the dozen things on the menu to be vegetarian.

All of us can reduce our consumption of animal products to more moderate levels. An ideal solution would be for everyone to take a step or two along the continuum from meat-lover to vegan. So if you're a meat-lover, then a helpful step would be to eat red meat only a few times a week rather than every day. After a seminar Tom ran recently, we were encouraged when one participant committed to changing from eating beef to pork. Terrific. Or if you don't eat much meat anyway, you might want to consider, like my nephew Angus, becoming vegetarian. Finally, if you're largely vegetarian, you might want to consider becoming vegan.

Food waste is another significant part of our diet's carbon footprint. Our friend, Andy, who regularly 'dumpster dives' (foraging through retailers' trash) can attest to the extent of food waste. He tells us that, contrary to popular opinion, much of the food thrown out by supermarkets is not rotting, mouldy, bad or even beyond its use-by date. Much is thrown out simply because the container is slightly marked or the fruit is not visually appealing. In all his years of 'dumpstering' Andy reports never once getting sick.[*] Lately, the amount of food thrown out by retailers has made it into the mainstream media, to the extent that some governments have begun regulating it.[254]

It's not only supermarkets that waste food, it's families like yours and mine. In a combination of over-buying and not going through the fridge and pantry regularly, we often let food go off, or even throw out what's perfectly edible. *Foodwise* suggests that Australian households throw out up to 20% of food purchased – that's AUD$8 billion worth, an average of $1,000 per household per year.[255]

Food miles are also an important aspect of our diet's carbon footprint. In general, it's preferable to buy locally produced food, because transport by aeroplane, truck or ship entails considerable emissions from the fuel used. Air transport is about 10 times more emissions-intensive than trucking, and 50 times worse than shipping.[256] So it's environmentally much better to buy locally produced, rather than imported food – especially for perishable fruits and vegetables, which, if they're from another country, would have been air-freighted. So rethink those Californian oranges or kiwi fruit from New Zealand (unless you live in California or New Zealand). They may be cheaper, but for the environment, they're very expensive. In addition to the environmental aspects, there are many other benefits of buying locally produced food: supporting your own community, knowing where your food is coming from, and less packaging. Our friends, Phil and Julie, are trying to eliminate plastic packaging completely from their food purchases, something made considerably easier by buying locally.

If we adopt a largely vegetarian diet, we will relatively easily be able to reduce the carbon footprint of our diet to under 2 tonnes CO_2e per year. If we make a significant effort to buy locally, reduce food wastage and minimise packaging, we could bring that down to 0.5 tonnes CO_2e.

---

[*] In case you're judging Andy as a lazy drain on society, I'd quickly add that he works, earns income, pays his rent and gives generously to others.

Part G: Small Picture Solutions - what can you and I do?

The next biggest part of our carbon footprint is our local travel. We'll cycle on to that next.

Reflection Questions

- Are you, or is anyone in your family, vegetarian? What caused that person to make their decision: taste, environment, animal rights, or some other reason?

- How is vegetarianism seen in your family – as a smart move, or as a bit weird? Why?

- What is one way that you could cut down your meat and dairy intake?

- What are some ways people you know have attempted to reduce food wastage and packaging?

Want To Learn More?

→ Website: *Shrink that Footprint.* A website that gives suggestions for reducing our carbon footprint in a range of areas, including diet. *http://shrinkthatfootprint.com/food-carbon-footprint-diet*

→ Website: *Foodwise.* An Australian website assisting ordinary people to eat more ethically. *http://www.foodwise.com.au/foodwaste/food-waste-fast-facts/*

29. Cycle to Freedom
– low-carbon local travel

Tom with fully loaded bike (2015)

At the age of 21, I can honestly say that I intend to never own a car, nor learn to drive. Far from restricting my freedom, it's been an enriching experience.

It's much easier to not use a car if you don't own one. For our family, not owning a car provides a strong incentive to find other ways to get around. For trips of up to about 10 kilometres we all use bikes. When we're in Australia, Mum rides the 9 kilometres to work and back each day; my brother Oscar the 6 kilometres to school and back. We also do our shopping by bike using a crate or panniers hanging from the rack. Sure, it's sometimes inconvenient – like when I need to ride up a hill with a crate full of soy milk! Overall though, riding is a great way to stay fit, and over short distances, is as quick as a car. For longer distances, we use public transport extensively. Public transport has the bonus of providing the opportunity to read, play games, chat or relax, rather than needing to concentrate on the road.

In many European cities, cycling is part of mainstream life. In Copenhagen and Amsterdam, many people cycle as their normal mode of transport.[257] This is made much easier when the city authorities build dedicated bike lanes, and employers provide bike lock-up and shower facilities. If enough people cycle to work in other cities, those city planners will start providing similar facilities. In Brisbane, things aren't as good as Copenhagen yet, but the network of bike-ways and facilities is growing. People like my friend Darren now regularly cycle to work, finding it considerably cheaper than paying the parking fee every day.

Cars are admittedly useful in a range of contexts, from daily commuting in cities, to travelling interstate. The speed, flexibility, and comfort they offer

Part G: Small Picture Solutions - what can you and I do?

are compelling. People love the convenience of jumping in the car and going wherever they want, whenever they want. It could even be said that Australians, and perhaps North Americans, are addicted to driving. There are certainly geographical reasons for that addiction. The distances between cities and even within cities are large compared to, say, Europe. However, as we saw in Chapter 15, the environmental cost of our addiction to cars is enormous, with the emissions required to build a car being around 15 tonnes CO_2e, and every kilometre driven requiring about 250 g CO_2e.

Electric cars have many advantages over petrol or diesel ones – not least that they don't contribute directly to CO_2 emissions, nor to the urban air pollution which claims the lives of around 1500 Australians each year.[258] They run silently, helping our cities be quieter, calmer places to live. However, the manufacturing impact of electric cars is similar to that of normal cars.[259] The power to run an electric car, if it is taken from the grid (government electricity supply), also has a significant carbon footprint. In Australia, where grid electricity is relatively carbon intensive due to the reliance on coal, a typical electric car would indirectly release about 210 g CO_2e/km – similar to a conventional vehicle.[260] In other words, if you run an electric car without using electricity that has been generated renewably, there is little benefit – at least from a climate change perspective.

Several years ago, our friends, Helen and Rob, purchased an electric car. They also installed substantial solar capacity on their roof and buy 100% 'Greenpower' for the power they can't produce themselves. In Australia, when buying Greenpower, the electricity provider is obliged to buy the equivalent amount of electricity from renewable sources.[261] Helen and Rob can now drive their car with a very low-carbon footprint.[262]

Other friends, Greg and Katie, had two cars for many years, but recently gave their second one away. They now both ride to work and, if they both (or their adult children) need the car at the same time, they car pool with others or catch a bus or taxi. They are happy to have made the move to one car and report that it's working well for them.

When I (Mark) think of low-carbon travel, I think of our Indian friend and colleague, Anthony. I first met Anthony as I was looking around a poor neighbourhood in Delhi, considering whether we might move in. I happened across a signboard for a social welfare group helping the poor. Intrigued, I knocked on the door and entered. There was Anthony. He greeted me with his lovely smile and we proceeded to have a fascinating conversation (in perfect English) about living with and serving the poor.

Over the next 10 years, Anthony became a dear friend to me, Cathy, Tom and

29. Cycle to Freedom - low-carbon local travel

Oscar. We would often visit each other to chat about various neighbours, the difficulties they were having and what might be done about it.

Anthony was from a lower middle class south Indian business family. It would have been entirely normal, and indeed expected of him, to go into the family business or into a professional career. His

Mark and Anthony – at home in India (2006)

salary would have allowed him to live in a comfortable air-conditioned house, own a car and take the occasional international flight. Instead, Anthony chose to spend his life serving the poor. As a result, Anthony was known and loved in the neighbourhood where he worked. Attempting to live like the poor people he loved, Anthony chose to walk many places locally and to travel by train when he had to go a long way. In 2016, Anthony tragically died of cancer. We miss him dearly. This book is dedicated to him.

Given the environmental cost of manufacturing and driving cars significantly reducing our car usage is vital. However, very few groups are interested in spelling out the environmental costs of driving – certainly not the car industry, the fossil fuel industry, or the insurance industry, each of which relies on us buying more cars and driving them more often. So we will have to encourage each other to make these changes and vote with our feet (or our bike).

If people do own a car but drive only when necessary, or use an electric vehicle, carbon emissions for local travel will be substantially cut to around one tonne CO_2e per year. If we don't own or use a car, then our emissions for local travel can be under 0.5 tonnes.

But what about our longer-distance travel? We'll take that trip next.

Part G: Small Picture Solutions - what can you and I do?

Reflection Questions

- 🔍 Are there routes you regularly drive that you could travel as easily and cheaply by public transport, cycling or walking?

- 🔍 Do you know anyone who doesn't own a car? How do they get around?

30. Rail and Sail
– low-carbon long-distance travel

In 2015, I needed to travel 2,000 kilometres from my home in Brisbane, to Adelaide. Wanting to keep my carbon emissions down I opted not to fly, but instead took the train from Brisbane to Sydney (16 hours), another train from Sydney to Melbourne (11 hours) and then a bus from Melbourne to Adelaide (another 11 hours).[263] After several days in Adelaide, I did it all in reverse to come home. It was far more expensive and took perhaps 10 times longer than flying directly from Brisbane to Adelaide. To many readers that may sound like the trip from hell, but on the contrary, I found it enjoyable! I got to catch up with friends in Sydney and Melbourne, who I wouldn't have seen otherwise. I also saw some beautiful countryside, watched movies and had some good self-time (lovely for an introvert like me). Another bonus I hadn't expected was an opportunity to understand more about the lives of some of the other passengers. Of the six legs on that return trip, I had significant conversations during five of them, hearing of people's marriage break-ups, custody battles for children, struggles with alcohol and motorcycle gangs. It was eye-opening. Rarely do I have such conversations on a flight!

How do the various forms of long-distance transport compare in terms of emissions per kilometre? Driving a typical car emits around 250 g CO_2e per km, and flights have a similar impact per passenger km.[264] Thus, when the alternative is one person driving a large, inefficient car, flying may be better than

Credit: David Nagai

driving. However as soon as a reasonably efficient car is being used, or there's more than one person in the car, driving is definitely preferable to flying. Buses and trains are between 3 and 100 times more efficient than cars, depending on the number of passengers.[265] Trains are particularly good, as they have proportionally little friction against the tracks and air. Trains and buses also have the benefit of being used many hours a day for many years, so that the emissions from manufacturing the vehicle are quite small compared to the distance they travel.

Flying frequently is a hugely environmentally damaging way to travel. While it feels very smooth and efficient when you're inside the plane, it takes an enormous amount of fuel to get all those tonnes of metal into the air and to keep them there. A typical domestic flight from Brisbane to Melbourne return, for example, will cause emissions of about 400 kilograms per person.[266]

I can hear many readers objecting, saying that flying is now such an integral part of life that we can't do without it. A globalised world means often our family members live overseas and much of our business is conducted internationally – all of which requires air-travel. And in terms of travel for pleasure – who is willing to holiday locally, when many of our friends are having exotic experiences in San Francisco, Spain and Sri Lanka?

I've learnt to raise the issue of excessive flying only with friends I know reasonably well and even then, very sensitively, as people are often quite defensive about any challenge to their lifestyle. Generally, people haven't even thought about the environmental cost of flying. Hence, most people go on flying as frequently as their budget allows.

> ### ⚡ Myth-busting 12: My flight won't make a difference – will it?
> A return flight from Sydney to Tokyo releases 2.15 tonnes CO_2e per person[267] – equivalent to an individual's fair share of the global carbon budget for the whole year. This figure of 2.15 tonnes is obtained by dividing a typical aeroplane's emissions for the trip, by the average number of passengers on it. One climate myth suggests that it makes no difference whether or not you fly, because the aeroplane was going anyway, and if you didn't fly, there would have been an empty seat. This is a logical fallacy, since airlines do in fact decide flight routes and frequencies on the basis of passenger choices. If people stopped taking flights, airlines would cancel those flights.[268]

30. Rail and Sail - low-carbon long distance travel

Another justification for flying often is that international travel is a relatively small component of total global emissions (2-3%), so it doesn't make any difference. While this may be true at the global level, at an individual level, one international flight may be 10% or more of a person's total carbon emissions for the year, so it is a very significant part of our individual carbon footprint. Our good New Zealander friends the Mathiases lead very simple lives. Their family of six had a total carbon footprint of 18 tonnes CO_2e in 2016 (3 tonnes each). Of that 18 tonnes, 11 tonnes were in flights! Another New Zealander we spoke to recently told us that she budgets her flights to two hours per year, meaning that she needs to 'save up' for several years before flying home to New Zealand, since the flight from Australia takes three hours.

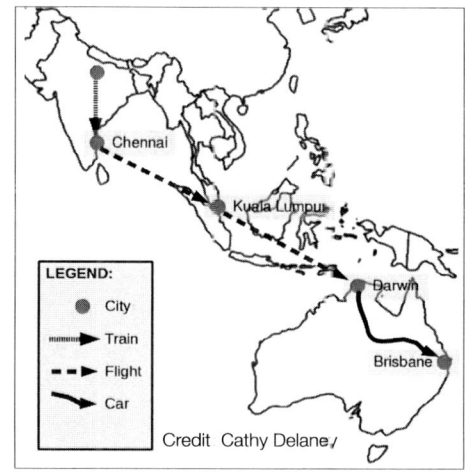

Illustration 19: The long way home

Another friend, Tim (also a New Zealander), has taken not flying even more seriously. He is attempting to not fly at all. So when he came to Australia, he took a position as a crew member on a sailing boat. It was, according to Tim, a 'hairy' trip, but he made it OK. I sometimes wonder, looking at the adventure sports that people do these days (hang-gliding, bungee jumping, jet-skiing), whether we could put more of our 'adventure' energy into trips like Tim's, which not only provide adventure, but save emissions as well.

When our family needs to fly, we attempt to reduce the environmental damage. The best way is to minimise the air-miles flown. So if you can cover some of the distance on land by train or bus then that's great. The next consideration is to keep the number of flights to a minimum, as significant fuel is used in take-off and landing. So it's better to take a trip with one or two legs, than a cheaper one with three or four legs.[269]

Given these factors, when we returned to Australia in 2014, initially we took a 36-hour train trip to south India. Then we took a flight from Chennai to Kuala Lumpur and from there a second flight to Darwin. Finally, we drove for 4 days from Darwin to Brisbane, with our friend Rob, who happened to be going to Brisbane anyway. The whole trip took us six days compared to 24 hours if we'd flown from Delhi to Brisbane. It was also considerably more expensive. But it was much lower-carbon and it was actually helpful to slow down the transition from the chaos of India to the suburbs of Brisbane.

How can we enjoy holidays without flying internationally? You might be surprised at the many wonderful destinations within your own borders. Cathy, Tom and Oscar recently organised a surprise holiday for me to celebrate my 50th birthday. They took me to the Great Barrier Reef. We travelled entirely by public transport, taking the train, bus and then ferry to Great Keppel Island. It was a wonderful holiday, all with a very minimal carbon footprint.

Once we know our carbon footprint from long-distance travel, it's a good discipline to 'offset' that amount of carbon. Carbon offsetting involves paying an accredited organisation to reduce or absorb carbon emissions, often through planting trees or investing in energy efficiency. Some offsetting programmes are more credible than others,[270] so it's a good idea to choose carefully which group you offset with. We've given two offsetting options in 'Want To Learn More?'. If you are offsetting your long-distance travel, you might want to consider offsetting the rest of your carbon footprint too. However, offsetting doesn't relieve us of the responsibility to reduce our carbon emissions as much as we can.

We realise, all too well, the difficulties and dilemmas involved in reducing our carbon footprint from flying. In spending more money and time on slower travel and missing opportunities to spend time with friends and family, the decision *not* to fly can be difficult. However, as we've sought to show, there are also surprising benefits.

If we do all or most of our long-distance travel by train or bus, with perhaps only one domestic flight a year and restrict international air travel to once every four years, we can bring our carbon emissions from long-distance travel down to under one tonne CO_2e. And maybe, like our sailing friend Tim, you'll have had a good dose of adventure doing it.

One of the easiest ways for us to reduce carbon emissions is to produce our own electricity cleanly. Let's power on to that next.

30. Rail and Sail - low-carbon long distance travel

Reflection Questions

- How many international holidays did your grandparents take? Did that make their holidays any less memorable?

- Think of some beautiful destinations within your own country that you haven't seen yet. How could you travel there by public transport, or at least by sharing a car with friends?

Want To Learn More?

→ Offsetting option #1: *Ashadesh* – helping families in India cook with clean-burning gas. *http://www.ashadesh.com.au/*

→ Offsetting option #2: *A Rocha** – Environmental group working on conservation issues around the world. *http://www.arocha.org/en/*
Their carbon-offset arm is Climate Stewards *http://www.arocha.org/en/climate-stewards/*

*No payment or benefit was received from these or any other organisation mentioned in this book.

Part G: Small Picture Solutions - what can you and I do?

31. Produce on Your Roof
– low-carbon electricity

When our friends Greg and Katie got their first electricity 'bill' after having their solar panels installed, the notion of being paid to produce electricity on their own roof was exciting.*

As we saw in Chapter 22, the technology is available for most countries to produce *all* their electricity renewably, whether that be by wind in Denmark, hydro in Nepal, or solar in Australia. However, many large renewable energy schemes, like Concentrated Solar Thermal plants, require significant government investment. It is here that short-sighted politicians play to our fears, saying: '*No, no, no – if we move away from cheap, coal-fired power generation, your electricity bills will be higher.*' Rather than be victim to that fear-mongering, we can take our electricity generation and consumption into our own hands. One thing that is not under debate is that most homes in the West can relatively easily install their own solar panels and generate much of their own electricity, without the need for massive government infrastructure, nor the political debate that goes with it.[271] All that's necessary is to have reasonable sunshine fall on your roof. Rooftop solar generation is, in a sense, the 'low hanging fruit' of climate change solutions – the easiest one to do that most of us should be plucking and eating!

How expensive is installing solar these days? At the time of writing (2017), you could buy a fully installed 5 kW system in Australia, enough for a normal household, for about AUD$6,500 (including the government rebate).[272] With electricity bills averaging $425 per quarter ($1,690 a year), this would lead to a financial 'payback time' of five to ten years – not a bad investment, given that solar panels operate for 20 years.[273]

Even people who don't own their own home can invest in solar generation for other community buildings through groups like *Clear Sky Solar* (see 'Want To Learn More?'). These schemes involve members of the public investing money to enable relatively large-scale solar power generation on community buildings such as libraries and supermarkets. There is also a tool for renters and landlords

---

* Greg and Katie installed solar panels at a time when the government offered a generous 50c/kWh for feeding electricity into the grid. They were paid about AUD$220 a quarter, just more than their consumption of $200 a quarter, so were therefore actually being paid by the power company. However the power company has since increased the charge to be connected to the grid, so Greg and Katie now pay about $120 a quarter.

31. Produce on Your Roof - low-carbon electricity

Rooftop Solar   Credit: Wikipedia

to collaborate to put solar on a rental property. *Digital Solar* helps landlords sell solar electricity to their tenants at lower-than-grid prices. If you're a tenant or a landlord, you might want to look at the website in 'Want To Learn More?'

Until *all* of our country's electricity is generated renewably, we also need to curb our electricity usage. Reducing consumption cuts both our bills and our carbon footprints, and can be surprisingly simple for many households. Some small changes are as easy as not leaving appliances on standby. Some changes, however, require a little more 'sweat'. For many households, a substantial amount of electricity is consumed in air-conditioning for cooling (in warmer parts of the world) or for heating (in cooler parts). To reduce consumption in this realm requires us to install better ventilation and fans (in hot environments) or insulation (in cold environments). It also involves a willingness to dress according to the weather, rather than change the 'weather' according to our dress. The tragic irony of air-conditioning is that, in controlling the climate in our own house, we contribute to the world's climate going out of control.

We've personally found Australia to be *too* air-conditioned. Our American friends tell us that the southern states in the US are similarly over-cooled. We regularly need to take a sweater, socks and even a scarf when we sit in air-conditioned libraries for hours (to write this book) or travel by air-conditioned public transport. We've also found it not so good for our health to be constantly moving from cool, air-conditioned environments inside to the heat outside. It seems that our rapid adoption of air-conditioning has been yet another victory

Part G: Small Picture Solutions - what can you and I do?

for corporate marketing and an indicator of the human tendency to follow the crowd. Where once, most people in the West were content with a fan in summer or an extra blanket in winter, we've become convinced by advertisers (and our friends and neighbours) that climate-controlled houses and offices are absolutely necessary.

Even if we retain some degree of air-conditioning for the hottest and coldest days, it is possible to do so in a more energy-efficient manner. In colder climates, where houses have internal heating, better insulation will decrease energy consumption. In Australia, *Beyond Zero Emissions* has produced a helpful guide, to changing our houses to become more energy efficient, including ventilation, insulation, and efficient cook-tops and water heaters (see Want to Learn More?).

If we produce most of the electricity we consume on our rooftops, and reduce our consumption of energy, we can take the emissions associated with our domestic electricity and gas to near zero. Even better, if we produce *more* electricity than we consume, then our surplus zero-carbon electricity can be used by other people who would have used coal-fired electricity. In effect, this can make our carbon footprint from electricity *negative,* thereby compensating for our footprint in other areas of life, as we'll see in Table (6) in Chapter 33.

The size of our houses is also a significant contributor to our carbon footprint. We'll open that door next.

Reflection Questions

🔍 Do you own your home (or are at least paying the bank for it)? If so, and you haven't done so already, what would stop you installing solar panels?

🔍 Did your parents or grandparents have air-conditioning in their house when they were growing up? If they didn't, how did they deal with the heat or cold?

🔍 Do you experience any negative effects of moving in and out of air-conditioning?

Want To Learn More?

→ Website: *Clear Sky Solar*. Helping people invest in rooftop solar on community buildings like libraries and supermarkets. *http://clearskysolar.com.au/index.php*

→ Website: *Digital Solar*. Helping landlords and tenants to install rooftop solar. *http://matter.solar/*

→ Booklet: *Beyond Zero Emissions. The Energy-Freedom Home Book.* *http://energyfreedom.com.au/book/*

Part G: Small Picture Solutions - what can you and I do?

32. A Castle or a Home?
– low-carbon housing

I'm from a family of house builders. Part of our family dream was for each of us children, once adults, to design and build our own house on a large block of land. My siblings have all achieved that dream, some many times over. I have not. In fact, it's with some amusement that I look back over my adult life and see that I've never built my own house, never owned my own house and for many years, have been living in a home smaller than most Australian garages. For significant periods, Cathy, Tom, Oscar and I have even shared housing with others. Despite not living up to my family dream, I'm genuinely content with the accommodation I've had during my life so far. It has been difficult at times, logistically and relationally, but overall it has been very fulfilling. It has also been low-carbon.

As we saw in *Illustration 15* in Chapter 15, Australians live in the biggest houses in the world – although Americans and Canadians aren't far behind. The carbon cost of constructing such huge houses is enormous, up to 80 tonnes CO_2e per house.[274]

Our own home in India consists of one 10 m² room which acts as our dining, lounge, play and study area at different times of the day. We also have a similar sized flat roof area (on top of the room) where we sleep during the summer, and a small 5 m² kitchen/bathing area. For our family of four, that translates to about 6 m² each. Living in a small space is challenging at times, but we've got used to it and it does help us understand our neighbours who live in similarly small houses. They feel at home when they come into our room, because it's similar to their own. (As an added advantage, our home is also very quick to clean!) While living in such a compact space won't be possible for many westerners, our experience does show us that most houses in the West are considerably oversized.

Our good friends Cheryl and Anugrah are from middle class Indian families and both work professional jobs. Yet they voluntarily chose to live for several years in a single room in the poor neighbourhood in which we lived. It took as much cultural adjustment for them to move in as it did for us, but just as for our family, the experience for them was very positive and they maintain

32. A Castle or a Home? - low-carbon housing

Our home: dining, lounge and bedroom combined (2017)

friendships in the neighbourhood to this day.

In recent years, some people in the West have also woken up to the obvious, that houses are more for *living in,* than for resale. The 'downsizing' movement is a name given to a simple idea – moving from a large house to a smaller one. This is common among retirees, for whom the upkeep of a large house has become burdensome. Additionally, the money they make by selling their large house and buying a smaller one increases the 'nest egg' for their retirement.

A more radical edge of downsizing is the tiny house movement. Tiny houses are typically 13–38 m². Proponents suggest that owners of tiny houses are freer and happier because they are less burdened by debt, enjoy living more simply, and have a lower carbon footprint. Our friends Stephen and Emma are building such a tiny house. Initially they renovated the small, run-down house on their property to be their family home. It was a modest 128 m², for a family of five (25 m² each). Then, as their boys grew up, they portioned off one end of the house to be their own tiny house, measuring 38 m² (19 m² each), leaving the boys to live in the rest of the house independently.

Another excellent way to reduce the carbon footprint of our accommodation is to share housing with others. This has an obvious financial advantage – the

163

rent is lower. There are also substantial savings to be made in sharing the grocery bill, since shopping for six or more people allows us to buy bigger quantities, which is often cheaper. There are also considerable savings of time, with each person needing to cook and wash the dishes less often. For most of 2016, we shared house with five other friends. While it had its tense moments, overall it was a very good experience and enriched our relationship with each of our house-mates. We all agreed, prior to moving in, to attempt to have open and honest communication with each other. We also attempted to resolve conflict constructively, apologising when we were at fault and adjusting our behaviour to accommodate others' preferences and vulnerabilities. This meant that we got to know each other better than if we were just friends in different households.

If you downsize your housing to under 45 m² per head and restrict yourself to building a new house only once in a lifetime, then your carbon footprint from housing can come down to only 0.5 tonnes, or even lower if you don't ever build a new house during your lifetime.

If you're not ready to downsize or live in a share house with others just yet, that's OK. We hope this chapter at least helps you think about the carbon footprint of housing, and perhaps to think twice before making that new fancy home improvement or buying that next huge house.

Now that we've considered each part of our carbon footprint, it's time to put it all together to see what a low-carbon lifestyle can look like in its entirety.

Reflection Questions

- How big is your house? Measure its length and width and do the math(s). How many metres is that per person? How does that compare to the average in your country (see *Illustration 15* in Chapter 15)?

- For you, what is the most important aspect of your house, its resale value or its liveability? Why is that?

- What would you find most difficult about downsizing your home? What is most appealing about the idea?

- Have you ever shared housing with others? How was that experience? Why do you think more people don't do that?

Want To Learn More?

→ Website: *Welcome to Your Home.* Australian government's guide to environmentally friendly housing. *http://yourhome.gov.au/introduction/welcome-your-home*

→ Website: *The Tiny Life.* More detail on the Tiny House Movement. *http://thetinylife.com/what-is-the-tiny-house-movement/*

Part G: Small Picture Solutions - what can you and I do?

33. Mel and Joe
– low-carbon living

To see what a complete low-carbon lifestyle looks like, let's now compare the life of our old mate Bruce, with his friend Mel, who, after reading this book, made some changes in her life and whose carbon footprint is now a third of what it was. As we've seen in this Part, these changes are very doable and can be fun and fulfilling. Mel will also take considerable comfort from the fact that she is now emitting only 6.6 tonnes CO_2e per year, the same as the average citizen of the world, rather than the unfair amount that most people in the West emit. We summarise the comparison between Bruce and Mel in Table (6).

For the more ambitious reader, let's also include in our analysis Joe, who resolves to go lower than the global average and only emit a sustainable share of the world's carbon budget (2 tonnes CO_2e per person per year). While Joe's lifestyle will take considerably more resolve, we've seen in this Part that it *is* doable. However, Tom and I would not recommend aiming for Joe's lifestyle just yet. First aim to achieve Mel's. If that's going well, you can aim for Joe's next year!

It's all too easy for authors to advocate one thing and do another. So to offer a little accountability for our own lifestyle, Oscar calculated the Delaney family carbon footprint. For 2016 it was 4.9 tonnes CO_2e per head – far less than the average Australian, but we still have a way to go. If you're interested in the details, you can find the calculations on our blog (see 'Want To Learn More?'). We hope that next year, by investing in a community solar project, we can get it down closer to 2 tonnes CO_2e per head.

It may be daunting to consider the many changes required to live a low-carbon life. However, in our experience, the different aspects of lifestyle change often affect each other, making each easier, in a positive feedback loop. If you don't have much stuff, you don't need a big house to keep it in. If you live in a small house, it will be easier to have lower electricity consumption. If you ride more and eat less meat, you'll probably end up consuming fewer government services like roads and hospitals. Many of these changes will save you money, meaning you have the freedom to work fewer hours – which may mean you don't feel the need to keep getting away on overseas holidays.

It's heartening for us to know that we're not the only people trying to live a very low-carbon life. We hope the examples of our friends, who we've described here, inspire you to move further along your own road to a more sustainable life.

33. Mel and Jo - low-carbon living

Table 6: Bruce, Mel and Joe Numbers in **bold** and brackets ( ) are tonnes CO_2e per year

	High-carbon Bruce	Low-carbon Mel	Sustainable Joe
Buying stuff	**6 tonnes** Spends $20,000 per year on latest stuff.[275]	**1 tonne** Spends $5,000 per year on new and second hand goods. Uses products until worn out.	**0.5 tonnes** Spends little on new goods. Buys second hand. Uses products until worn out.
Food	**4 tonnes** Eats meat 1-2 meals/day. Buys imported, highly processed, packaged food. Throws out 20% of food.	**2 tonnes** Eats meat twice a week. Buys locally produced food. Reduces wastage.	**0.5 tonnes** Eats animal products only 1-2 times per week. Buys slightly damaged fruit and veg to reduce retail wastage.
Local travel	**3 tonnes** Buys new car every 15 years (1 t). Drives 7,500 km/year (2 t).	**1 tonne** Drives a fuel-efficient second hand car, or an electric car, sparingly.[276]	**0.5 tonnes** Cycles within city (0.05 t).[277] Uses public transport (0.2 t).[278] Uses cars minimally (0.25 t).
Long distance travel	**1.5 tonnes** Flies internationally once every 2 years (1 t). Flies domestically once a year (0.5 t).	**1 tonne** Flies internationally every 4 years (0.5 t). Flies domestically once a year. (0.5 t).	**0.5 tonnes** Flies internationally once in 8 years (0.25 t). Uses train or bus for domestic travel (0.25 t).
Residential electricity and gas	**2.3 tonnes** 6 kWh/day grid electricity. 16 MJ/day gas. No solar.	**-1.7 tonnes** Installs 2 kW grid-connected solar PV system once in 20 years (0.3 t). 9 kWh/day back to grid (-3.0 t).[279] Uses 3 kWh/day electricity (1 t).	**-2 tonnes** Installs 2 kW grid-connected solar PV system once in 20 years (0.3 t). 9 kWh/day back to grid (-3.0 t). Uses 2 kWh/day electricity (U./ t).
Housing	**1 tonne** More than 90 m²/person. Builds or buys large new house twice in his life.	**0.5 tonnes** Lives in house which is 45-90 m²/person.[280] Buys new house once in lifetime.	**0.2 tonnes** Lives in house which is smaller than 45 m²/person, in a tiny house or shares house with others.
Government services/ mining	**5.2 tonnes** Lots of road/airport use. Shares in fossil fuel companies.	**2.8 tonnes** Some road and airport use. Uses a bank which doesn't invest in fossil fuels.	**1.8 tonnes** Little road or airport use. Invests in companies working on renewable energy/energy efficiency.
Total	**23 tonnes**	**6.6 tonnes**	**2.0 tonnes**

Part G: Small Picture Solutions - what can you and I do?

In the final Part of *Low-Carbon and Loving It,* we'll describe some tools and, most importantly, the mindset necessary to make these changes in our own lives and inspire others to do likewise.

Reflection Question

🔍 Are Mel's or Joe's lifestyles in any way attractive to you? Why?

🔍 Do you think Mel's or Joe's lifestyles are attainable?

Want To Learn More?

→ Video: *Shrink That Footprint.* Suggestions for how to shrink your carbon footprint. *http://shrinkthatfootprint.com/the-30-day-shrink-video-series*

→ Website: *Zero Carbon Britain.* Analysis of ways Britons can lower their carbon footprints. *http://www.zerocarbonbritain.org/en/*

→ Website: *Live on One Planet.* A challenge to raise money for an aid organisation, TEAR Australia, by pledging to reduce your consumption of resources. *https://www.liveononeplanet.com/*

→ Blog: *Low-Carbon and Loving It.* Blog for this book, including the post on the Delaney carbon footprint for 2016. *www.lowcarbonandlovingit.wordpress.com*

Part H: Building a Movement for Change
– where to begin?

34. The Middle Path
– between fatalism and fantasy

Dad and I differ somewhat in our approach to climate change. Dad tends to be a pessimist, feeling the extreme gravity of the situation and sometimes losing hope that we can claw our way out of this mess. In a way, this book is his attempt at calling his friends, his family, himself and everyone else to change. On the other hand, I tend to be more optimistic, believing that together we *can* forge a different world. Both of these perspectives are understandable, but in their extremes are unhelpful, as they can lead to passivity and inaction.

In this final Part, we'll discuss the mindset needed, and offer some tools, for you to actually start reducing your carbon footprint. Initially, in this chapter, we'll consider the balancing act in dealing with this climate crisis: not being unrealistically optimistic, nor unhelpfully pessimistic. Next, in Chapter 35 (The Rubber Hitting the Road) we offer you a very doable set of eight steps to begin changing your lifestyle. Chapter 36 (Spreading the Word) provides some tools to talk with *others* about climate change – to encourage them to join all of us in building a more sustainable society. Finally, in Chapter 37 (Kallu and a Kid), we tell some stories to give us hope that small, courageous actions can catalyse big changes. This crisis can be solved, but, quite simply, it's up to us.

First, let's examine both fatalistic pessimism and fantasising optimism, as we attempt to find the middle path to realistic and hopeful climate action.

Pessimists tend to say: 'Climate change is impossible to solve. We'll never get fossil fuel corporations to stop digging up coal and oil, nor convince the Chinese to stop burning it. Any action that I could take would require sacrificing my lifestyle, and would make no difference anyway.'

Part H: Building a Movement for Change - where to begin?

As we saw in Chapter 20, some pessimists feel that cutting a few tonnes off their own carbon footprint will make no difference in the long run. If that's you, I hope this book encourages you that, like the woman throwing starfish back into the ocean, your little bit actually *does* make a difference. Not only that, the changes you make in your own lifestyle can encourage others to make similar changes, so that together we can pressure politicians and business leaders to make the policies and products necessary for a sustainable world.

Credit: David Nagai

On the other hand, optimists tend to say: *'Climate change is easy to solve. Renewable energy is growing rapidly. In Paris, governments agreed to limit warming to 2°C. Scientists will come up with new technologies to suck carbon out of the atmosphere. It's all under control – no need for me to do anything.'*

We've already had a look at some optimists who believe that politicians have the problem in hand. However, in modern democracies, elected officials tend to be more conscious of the next election than the long-term sustainability of the planet. We also saw in Part F that while scientific solutions for climate change – like large-scale renewable energy generation – do exist, they require a supportive public and environmentally responsible governments to roll out those changes as quickly as possible.

Tom's right. I am a pessimist. Perhaps the lowest point of this journey for me was the election of Mr Trump in 2016. I knew he was a climate sceptic and, if elected, was highly likely to pull the US out of the Paris climate agreement. I remember e-mailing all my American friends, begging them to do everything they could to prevent him being elected. Many reassured me that it was almost impossible he would become President. But then the impossible happened. I experienced a very low period as I tried to come to terms with the new reality.

They say the darkest hour is just before the dawn. Mr Trump's announcement that the US would withdraw from the Paris accord immediately drew strong

34. The Middle Path - between fatalism and fantasy

condemnations from the German, French and other world leaders. They were committed to the Paris agreement, despite the American decision. Perhaps Mr Trump's disdain for the environment will also stir ordinary people to action. My American friend Amy, for example, on hearing of Mr Trump's election, immediately started becoming more engaged with environmental issues.

I will probably always be a pessimist, but the challenge for us is to maintain hope and keep going, despite what seem to be terrible setbacks. Conversely, optimists like Tom need to remember that the big-picture solutions to climate change will only happen when individuals like you and me stand up and are counted. We must walk this middle path between fatalism and fantasy.

The pessimist and the optimist agree on very little, except one thing: it's not worth doing anything ourselves. We've attempted to show the folly of both positions. We need a path between the two extremes, because the truth is more complex than either. We should neither pin all the blame, nor all our hopes, on the actions of others. Instead we must accept both the bad news (our own responsibility for climate change) and the accompanying good news (that we can do something about it).

We trust that by now, walking the path between optimism and pessimism, you're convinced of the imperative to change your own lifestyle. The next chapter gives a concrete tool for how to get started.

Reflection Questions

- How pessimistic or optimistic do you feel about the prospects of us dealing with climate change?
- Is the challenge before you to have more hope, or more realism?

Part H: Building a Movement for Change - where to begin?

35. The Rubber Hitting the Road
– 8 steps to a low-carbon life

When I experimented with veganism in an attempt to reduce my carbon footprint, I still really enjoyed eating. However, I realised that I had become a much harder person to invite for a meal. Many main courses (from lasagne to pizza) and almost all deserts (from cake to ice cream) use eggs and/or dairy products. Practical difficulties like this do create real challenges in reducing our carbon footprint.

Many of the logistical problems we encounter in leading lower-carbon lives can be overcome with a bit of creativity. Even more than practical difficulties, though, changing our lifestyles to become lower-carbon is difficult because we're often afraid of the unknown. The high-carbon path is generally convenient, comfortable, cool and, in the West, widely followed. In fact, for many of us, it's all we've ever known.

In this chapter we offer a process to overcome both the practical and emotional bonds holding us back from a lower-carbon life. There are eight steps:

Table 7: Carbon footprint 'hotspot' identifier
For each area of life, tick ✔ the one that best describes your lifestyle)

Area of life	High-carbon hotspot		Low-carbon		Sustainable	
Buying goods	Regular new purchases		Some new goods		Mostly second-hand	
Diet	Highly meat and dairy-based		No beef. Less dairy		Vegetarian or vegan	
Local travel	Drive most days		Drive occasionally		No car	
Long-distance travel	International flights		Domestic flights		All train and bus	
Domestic electricity and gas	No solar. Lots of air-conditioning		Some solar. Some air-conditioning		Full solar. No air-conditioning	
Housing	More than 90 m² per person		45-90 m² per person		Less than 45 m² per person	
Government services and mining	Heavy use of government services. Shares or investments in fossil fuels corporations.		Moderate use of government services. Banks with institutions invested in fossil fuels.		Moderate use of government services. Banks with institutions using positive filters.	

35. The Rubber Hitting the Road - 8 steps to a low-carbon life

1. **Identify** 'hotspots': the areas of your life which cause the greatest emissions. You can use a carbon footprint calculator (such as that at www.carbonfootprint.com) or alternatively use Table (7). The hotspot I identified was my consumption of dairy products. For others it might be the amount you drive or the number of new products you buy each year.

2. **Brainstorm** ideas on how to reduce your carbon footprint in your 'hottest' spot. Be creative at this stage – try not to let financial or other constraints get in the way. There were several options for me: shifting to a different breakfast (toast rather than cereal with milk), replacing dairy milk with soy milk, and using tofu instead of cheese. If your hotspot is, for example, the drive to work every day, you might brainstorm ideas from the obvious (taking a train, riding your bike or car-pooling) to the more radical (working from home one or two days a week, changing jobs, or moving house to be closer to work).

3. **Evaluate** the advantages and disadvantages of each idea For me an advantage of switching to soy milk was its easy availability at the supermarket, but disadvantages were the extra expense and making it harder for others to cater for me. For you, catching the train to work might have the disadvantage of taking longer, but carry advantages of being cheaper than parking costs, giving time to read, and being less stressful than driving.

4. **Experiment** with an idea that appeals to you by implementing that change for a short period. experimented with veganism for a month. You might catch the train to work for a week, or just on Mondays.

5. **Reflect** on your experiment. Were the advantages and disadvantages as you had expected? Find solutions which might enable you to maximise the advantages and minimise the disadvantages. For me, the advantage of the

Vegan diet – home grown cucumber (2006)

soy milk was clear: lower emissions. However, being strictly no-dairy made it more difficult to share food with others in our community house and that was a significant disadvantage. I decided to use soy milk where feasible, but not be too strict on myself. For you, suppose the train commute was really cutting into family time. Perhaps you could reduce your work hours. Maybe you could watch

Part H: Building a Movement for Change - where to begin?

your favourite TV show on the train, so that when you're at home, you could spend time with family instead.

6. **Repeat** the process until you have a way of reducing your carbon footprint that you're happy with. Start doing that regularly. When you're ready, do it all over again for the next 'hottest spot' in your life.

7. **Celebrate** your achievements by doing something you love. For me, that's playing tennis with friends or reading a good book. For you, it might be eating roast beef on board your flight to Hawaii to buy a massive holiday home... just kidding!

8. **Share** your story with others, and listen to theirs. Encourage each other in living a low-carbon life. In the next chapter, we'll offer some hints on how to do this well.

Reflection Questions

- Which of these 8 steps seem easy and which more difficult?
- Is your 'hottest spot' immediately obvious, or will it take some thought to identify?
- Have you ever changed your lifestyle for environmental reasons?

36. Spreading the Word
– talking with others about climate change

Having spent most of my life in India, I haven't had a lot of time with my uncles, aunties and cousins in Australia. Each time we return to Australia, I get to know them a little more. Being passionate about climate change, when the chance presents itself, I try to talk with my relatives and friends about the issue. One thing I've learnt, however, is to be sensitive in how I go about it.

Hopefully by now you're also passionate about climate change and have started working out ways to reduce your own carbon footprint. Almost as important is that you begin talking with others about these changes and

Credit: David Nagai

encouraging them to do likewise, as addressing climate change requires a groundswell of individuals courageous enough to live differently.

What area of climate change you talk about with someone depends on where they are up to in their environmental journey. Your role isn't to turn your friend into an environmental hero; it is to help them take the next step on their journey. If they have never heard of climate change, you could explain what it is (Part B of this book). When you're talking to someone who's apathetic about climate change, you could discuss its grave impacts (Part C). If they care about climate change, but don't see the connection with their own lives, you could talk about how much we in the West have contributed to the problem (Part D). At this stage, many people will have excuses for their inaction – you could gently debunk these (Part E). If they realise the seriousness of climate change, but are in despair, you could discuss the rapid growth of renewable energy and the landmark Paris agreement (Part F). If they don't see how they can make a difference, you can point your friend to solutions they can enact in their own lives (Part G).

Part H: Building a Movement for Change - where to begin?

Simple, right? Not always. There are several reasons talking about climate change can be daunting. Some of the fears and doubts I face include:

'Climate change is a complex issue – what if I don't get my facts straight?' It's important to know the facts, so that you can speak convincingly. To this end, you might test your understanding with the quiz in Appendix 4. We've also included a table of vital statistics in Appendix 5. You might want to remember some of those facts and figures to bring into your conversation. However, facts alone are not very persuasive. Most of us are more likely to make changes to our lives when we see those same changes modelled by others, especially our friends. A chat with a friend is worth more than a book (even this book), so don't let your lack of expertise in climate change hold you back from talking with others.

'What if my talking about our responsibility for climate change comes across as judgemental and makes people feel guilty?' Judgemental tones and criticisms are likely to turn people off, and there's no point speaking if no one is listening. So it's important to be humble and friendly in our conversations about climate change. That said, we do have a responsibility to speak honestly about our responsibility for climate change, even if it makes people uncomfortable. Speak the truth, but do so sensitively.

'I'm not living a perfect lifestyle myself – what if they turn the tables and start criticising me for my latest holiday or purchase?' None of us are perfect, but imperfection isn't a reason to *not* talk about such an urgent problem. We should be honest about our own shortcomings – this often puts people at ease to discuss high-carbon aspects of their own lives.

Based on these ideas, I've found three techniques helpful in talking about climate change:

- **Non-judgemental questions.** People generally prefer to be asked their opinion than be lectured to. A useful way to phrase questions is: *'I really enjoy (flying/driving/meat), but I realise that it causes significant emissions. This is a dilemma for me. What do you think, since you seem to like (flying/driving/meat) too?'* If the person has never thought about the carbon impact of their action, a question like this will be thought provoking, without being judgemental.

- **Personal stories.** Many people tune out when they hear facts and figures, but instead love to hear stories. Describe your own, and others', successes and failures in living a low-carbon life.

- **Humour.** Sometimes, making a joke about climate change will allow your message to get through others' defences. For instance, if you let out a burp, you might joke that you're almost as bad as a cow for methane emissions. Later, they might reflect on the joke. It's generally safe to make jokes at your own expense, as this puts people at ease.

36. Spreading the Word - talking with others about climate change

Finally, choose carefully which people to talk with. It probably won't be useful speaking to an outright climate change denier, whereas a well-intentioned, but poorly informed person will likely be more receptive.

Talking about climate change is not always easy in the current social and political climate, but it is a crucial part of enhancing our impact and building a movement. Hopefully in five years, the tide will have turned and everyone will be talking about how to reduce their carbon footprint. For now, though, we simply need to do the best we can.

In the final chapter, we tell several stories to show that ordinary people like us really can bring extraordinary changes.

Reflection Questions

- Is the prospect of talking to others about climate change energising or scary?

- List some people who you think might enjoy such a chat. List some who definitely would not.

Want To Learn More?

→ Website: *Climate for Change.* In Australia, host a dinner party in which a volunteer comes to your house to run an informal discussion about climate change. *http://www.climateforchange.org.au/about*

→ Website: *Carbon Conversations.* Groups in Britain that involve people getting together for six meetings to discuss climate change and support each other in cutting their carbon footprints. *http://www.carbonconversations.co.uk/*

Part H: Building a Movement for Change - where to begin?

37. Kallu and a Kid
– ordinary people making an extraordinary difference

Core to our identity as humans is the notion of giving the 'little person' a chance – what Australians call a 'fair go'. Many people think that notion has died – drowned in an ocean of selfishness, lost in a desert of apathy. However, every now and then, something happens to show us that the 'fair go' is doggedly holding on. Many will remember Alan Kurdi, the Syrian toddler who drowned in the Mediterranean Sea in 2015. Even though hundreds of people, including toddlers like Alan, had drowned in the months prior, somehow, seeing the photo of the limp little boy, lifeless on a beach, broke our hearts and forced us out of our self-protective mindset to become more welcoming to refugees. The Australian and Canadian governments were shocked at the turnaround in opinion. They thought they'd played to the public's preference by keeping refugees *out*, but now, all of a sudden, because of one photo, people took to the streets in their thousands demanding that refugees be let *in*. As a result, those governments adopted more generous refugee policies.[281] Change happened!

Artist's depiction of Alan Kurdi   Credit: UNHCR

37. Kallu and a Kid - ordinary people making an extraordinary difference

I wonder what the 'Alan Kurdi moment' will be for climate change. Perhaps it will be an image of a Pacific Islander family trying to canoe to Australia as their home goes underwater, or maybe an image of huge swaths of once colourful coral, now dead. We haven't found that transformative moment yet. My heartfelt hope is that you'll join Tom and me, and a growing movement of people around the world, such that together we will soon see an 'Alan Kurdi moment' for climate change.

As we saw in Chapter 20 (What Can I Do?), the human tendency to follow the crowd can be depressing when people adopt the selfish or nasty behaviour of others. However, when viewed another way, the tendency to follow is also hope-giving. It means that if one person finds the courage to behave differently – to walk instead of drive, to take the train instead of fly, to install solar panels, to become vegetarian – our friends and family are more likely to do likewise. In this small way, courageous individual actions can eventually start a movement, and ultimately become the 'new normal'. History gives us many examples of everyday people courageously speaking and acting for what is right, and ultimately catalysing much bigger changes than they could have imagined.

Telemachus was a humble monk in the 4th century Roman world. The first time Telemachus went to Rome he noticed, to his surprise, everyone walking towards a massive round building – the Colosseum. He went along with the crowd and found, to his horror, that spectators were being entertained by brutal gladiatorial battles. Telemachus felt disgusted, but before becoming immune to the brutality, as most people had, he spoke out. He climbed the barrier, entered the arena, and ran from gladiator to gladiator, appealing in the name of God to stop the violence. Initially, the crowd thought that Telemachus was comic relief, but when they realised he was trying to stop their entertainment, they stoned him. After some time, Telemachus lay dead in the arena, either a victim of the crowd's stones or a gladiator's sword. But then a strange thing happened. The crowd fell silent. One by one the spectators got up and left, feeling the shame of what they'd done. Remarkably, that was the last gladiatorial battle ever fought. One man's sacrifice had led to a change in thousands of hearts, catalysing a societal transformation.

A much more recent example of 'little' people acting to bring about big change was the Chipko movement in the 1970s in India. Poor women and men in rural north India were alarmed at the rampant deforestation around their villages.

Part H: Building a Movement for Change - where to begin?

The lack of trees was making their small-scale gathering of fodder and wood much more difficult. The tree-felling was also resulting in catastrophic landslides. Local villagers initially appealed to the government for relief. The government denied their requests and continued to award contracts to industrialists for large-scale logging. So local women took matters into their own hands, and began taking non-violent action. They stood with their arms around trees, defying the lumber men, the industrialists and the government. The women's tactics of hugging trees led to the movement being called 'Chipko', after the Hindi word for 'sticking'. Eventually, the government enacted more stringent anti-deforestation laws and indigenous rights began to be recognised. The movement has been an inspiration to environmentalists around the world.[282]

There are many other examples of everyday people courageously speaking and acting to bring about profound change to an unjust system. Rosa Parks' refusal to vacate her seat for a white passenger was a turning point in the civil rights movement. Edward Snowden's courage to speak out against US surveillance exposed extensive infringements on privacy. We'll share a final story here, one dear to our hearts – that of our friend Kallu.

Kallu was our neighbour in the Barapula slum described in Chapter 2 – 6,000 people crammed onto the bank of a drainage canal. In the winter of 2001, a notice went up on the public toilet block announcing that the slum would be 'rehabilitated' in six days. Everyone knew what that meant. It was 'government speak' for: '*We will bulldoze your slum and relocate some residents (only those with the necessary identity documents) to a piece of land on the remote outskirts of the city. All others will become homeless.*' On seeing the notice, the residents were in uproar. The slum had been there for 30 years. Most people knew that they didn't actually own their land, but had come to hope that the government would allow them to stay permanently. Even so, most people were prepared to be relocated, but six days' notice was outrageous. It was winter and temperatures were getting down to 5°C overnight, so having your house demolished and sleeping 'rough' would be awful. In addition, the children were about to do their exams and worst of all, Eid, the biggest festival in the Muslim calendar, was coming up.

We held some rapidly convened community meetings with several hundred residents. It was decided to fight the eviction in court. Having studied law in Australia, I found myself as the liaison person between the lawyers and the residents. Being a foreigner, I couldn't be a party to the case, so we needed some residents who were courageous enough to put their name on the petition against the government. Most people were too scared to do so, lest the government persecute them later. But Kallu and three other residents volunteered. Kallu was a humble man, small in stature, with little formal education and no significant standing in the community. However, he was courageous and the other residents trusted him, so he put his name forward.

In court, we initially won a delay of the demolition for a couple of weeks. Then, over the next several months, we went back and forth to court, arguing that the residents were willing to be relocated, but only within a reasonable time frame, and only if the government gave title deeds to the new land *before* the demolition. Our lawyers also asked to see the list of residents who were going to be allocated land in the relocation area, so as to identify the people who felt they were entitled, but weren't on the government list. The government refused. The court ordered a compromise: if the residents could produce a list of everyone in the slum who thought they were entitled to land, they would be allowed to compare it to the government's list. Again, Kallu volunteered to help compile the list of hundreds of names.

Bizarrely, while working tirelessly to help his community, Kallu was accused by some residents of colluding with the government to actually *instigate* the whole demolition. He was heartbroken. Nevertheless, he kept going and eventually we were able to compare our list to the government's. Through Kallu's and several other residents' efforts, we helped several families, who otherwise would have become homeless, to be allocated land. We also won the court's order that the government grant title deeds for the new land *before* the demolition.

In the end, the demolition did take place, but only after the end of winter, Eid, and the kids' exams. The residents calmly used the trucks provided to move to their new land. The government even asked us to write a brochure for how to conduct orderly relocations in the future! Through it all, Kallu became somewhat of an expert at liaising with government officers. In the relocation area, people would come to him for advice on how to get the drinking water supply improved or electricity connections installed.

Significant change often comes about when one person or a small group of people are courageous enough to stand up to an unjust system. During the demolition of Barapula, Kallu was that little guy, who was prepared to stand up

Part H: Building a Movement for Change - where to begin?

Kallu (left), family and belongings 'relocating' (2002)

for what was right. In doing so, Kallu became an everyday hero.

We hope this book has helped you come to terms with the truth about climate change, what it is and how it will adversely affect all of us within our own lifetimes, and even more so, our children's lifetimes. Our central message is simple: it is absolutely necessary, entirely possible and actually enriching for ordinary people like you and me to live low-carbon lives. That change will sometimes require courage and the willingness to act against the crowd. However, it is primarily *our* actions which will create the necessary pressure for our leaders to make the big decisions necessary to ensure a habitable planet for the coming generations.

I sometimes think that we are a bit like David battling Goliath. In our struggle against massive corporations, biased media, self-serving politicians and self-indulgent neighbours, it sometimes feels like we're very little people, battling a huge giant. But if, like David, Telemachus, the Chipko women, Rosa Parks, Edward Snowden and Kallu, we take courage and do the little things we can, then this giant can be brought down. Knowing there are thousands of others out there like us, doing their little bit, gives us hope that together we can preserve a liveable planet for ourselves and our children.

Reflection questions

- Which story in this chapter inspires you most?
- Do you know anyone who has acted courageously and by so doing, seen positive change happen?
- How will you find the strength to act for the good of the world, even if it that means going against mainstream society?

Want To Learn More?

→ Book: Andrews, Dave; 2012. *People of Compassion.* Wipf and Stock. Inspiring stories of change brought about by everyday people – including that of Telemachus.

→ Book: Hart, Deborah; 2015. *Guarding Eden.* Allen and Unwin. True stories of twelve ordinary people willing to do extraordinary things to prevent climate change.

→ Film: *Snowden.* 2016. The story of Edward Snowden's courageous revelation of NSA surveillance.

Appendices

Appendix 1: 'Australians who live on slumdog millionaire's row – and love it'

Matt Wade writing for The Sydney Morning Herald (Feb 2009)*

MARK and Cathy Delaney don't need to see the hit movie Slumdog Millionaire. The Brisbane couple experience slum life in India every day.

For 13 years they have lived in the shanty towns of the Indian capital, New Delhi, raising their children and sharing their lives with the locals. Their two sons, Tom, 12, and Oscar, 7, were born in India and have lived most of their lives in slums.

The family home, in a neighbourhood called Janta Mazdoor Colony, is about the size of a typical Australian bedroom. They have no running water, no TV, no fridge and no washing machine. Two mattresses, used to sleep on at night, double as a "lounge" during the day. Meals are eaten sitting on the floor and they share with neighbours a squat toilet in a small bathroom.

But the Delaneys are not complaining. For them, living in a slum has been deeply enriching.

"It baffles us that more people in Australia who say they are sick of their lives don't do something like we have," says Cathy Delaney, who holds a masters' degree in pure mathematics.

"The longer we have stayed here the more we can see the positive effect it has had on us as people. I feel much freer of money and possessions – these things don't define my life."

Mark Delaney, a 42-year-old lawyer, says more than a decade in Delhi's squatter settlements has been a "radical detox" from consumer society.

"For the first couple of years I thought, 'We'll do this for a while and then we'll go back to Australia, get a deposit and build a house', and so on, but I've let go of all that now," he said.

Mark works part-time for a Delhi-based medical organisation but the family's main focus is on their slum. They are strongly motivated by their Christian faith, believing that life is more about caring for others than comfort and success.

"Our main purpose is simply to experience what life is like here, to live with and learn from the poor and contribute something positive to people's lives," says Mark.

The Delaneys moved into their current neighbourhood on the eastern outskirts of Delhi in 2003. About 60,000 people are packed into the illegal settlement which is less than half a square kilometre. It is one of an estimated 1500 squatter settlements scattered across Delhi that house at least 3 million people.

The settlement started 30 years ago as a cluster of makeshift humpies in an open field but as time went by, people gradually upgraded. Flimsy walls were replaced with bricks, slab roofs were added in place of black plastic. Even so, open drains still run along the slum's maze of narrow alley ways and empty into a putrid canal not far from the Delaneys' front door.

Properties are bought and sold in the slum and there are even informal titles exchanged to

---

* Used with permission of author/journalist Matt Wade. The story can be found at The Sydney Morning Herald *http://www.smh.com.au/world/australians-who-live-on-slumdog-millionaires-row – and-love-it-20090227-8k84.html*
A similar article is at The Age: *http://www.theage.com.au/national/a-real-riches-to-rags-story-20090227-8kd9.html*

prove ownership. Although these documents would not hold up in court they give those purchasing a slum hut a sense of security. A three-level slum house in the area recently changed hands for 190,000 rupees (about $6000).

The Delaneys pay 1800 rupees ($56) a month in rent, although many small rooms in the slum are half that. Each day the family witnesses some of the vulnerability and powerlessness of the characters portrayed in the film.

Witnessing this has nurtured a strong sense of social justice in the boys.

"I have realised that the most important thing is to help other people," says Tom.

"But I have also realised that I have limits."

There is hot debate in the household about how simply they should live.

"Cathy is a bit harder line than me," says Mark

"Sometimes she says 'let's move down a bit' but I'm usually a bit resistant. Most people think we are pretty stupid already."

Once Tom asked how much income his neighbours had to live on and insisted their family do the same.

So for the experience, they cut their monthly budget from 10,000 rupees ($310) to 5000 rupees.

"First we ran out of cornflakes and then we ran out of jam. Our diet got much simpler," says Cathy. "It was a hard experience but a really good one. It gave us so much more respect for the people who live here."

Mark has been pleasantly surprised by how much their boys have benefited from the experience of living in a poor neighbourhood. Oscar is in year 2 at a local school and Tom has recently switched to home schooling.

When the boys were asked if they wanted to move back to Australia later this year or stay in the slum, they chose to stay.

"I used to think that, with the kids, we would just endure living here for a while and then go," said Mark.

"But now I'm thinking this is a good thing for them and I want to stay not for my sake, but for the sake of my kids."

Things that most families take for granted bring the Delaneys great satisfaction.

Such as electricity. The power goes off in the neighbourhood several hours each day.

To help the family cope, Cathy got a small solar panel worth about $100 for her 40th birthday that powers a lamp during the blackouts.

A striking feature of the Delaneys' lifestyle is their small environmental footprint. They use very little electricity, create only a small amount of waste and rely exclusively on public transport.

Appendix 2:   Abbreviations

CCS	Carbon Capture and Storage
CH_4	methane
CO_2	carbon dioxide
CO_2e	carbon dioxide equivalent
CST	Concentrated Solar Thermal
GHG	greenhouse gas
Gt	gigatonne (billion tonnes)
HFC	hydrofluorocarbons
IPCC	Intergovernmental Panel on Climate Change
kWh	kilowatt hour
Mt	megatonne (million tonnes)
NASA	National Aeronautics and Space Administration
ppm	parts per million (usually of CO_2 in the atmosphere)

Appendices

Appendix 3: Index of Illustrations, Science Geeks, Myth-busting and Tables

Illustrations

1	Global energy use over time	19
2	CO_2 cycling between air, land and water (in gigatonnes per year)	20
3	Correlation of CO_2 and temperature	22
4	The greenhouse effect	23
5	Global temperature and CO_2 concentration 1880 - 2014	24
6	The sceptic's 'escalator'	28
7	Reduction in Arctic sea-ice	44
8	The Netherlands with 2-metres sea level rise	47
9	Projected change in food production	55
10	Countries most responsible for historic carbon emissions	57
11	Possible mass displacements and conflicts due to climate change	61
12	Warming and human-caused cumulative CO_2 emissions	67
13	Developed reserves of fossil fuels compared to carbon budgets	69
14	Who is responsible? Relative carbon emissions	70
15	Average house sizes (m^2 per person) in various countries	74
16	Solar Radiation Management	93
17	Alternative methods of replacing fossil fuels	109
18	Carbon footprint of different diets	145
19	The long way home	155

Science Geeks

Science Geek 1	Are humans really causing an increase in CO_2 concentration?	20
Science Geek 2	How do scientists know about the history of the earth's climate?	23
Science Geek 3	Is temperature rise really caused by the greenhouse effect?	25
Science Geek 4	Rising ocean temperatures	37
Science Geek 5	Species on earth	50
Science Geek 6	Other greenhouse gases and CO_2e	69
Science Geek 7	The energy required to build a car	73
Science Geek 8	Emissions from mining	75
Science Geek 9	Industrial processes	120
Science Geek 10	A possible carbon trading scheme	124

Myth-busting

Myth-busting 1	Cherry-picking	28
Myth-busting 2	False experts	29
Myth-busting 3	Logical fallacies	29
Myth-busting 4	Oversimplification	29

Appendices

Myth-busting 5	Red herrings (irrelevant facts)	30
Myth-busting 6	Conspiracy theories	30
Myth-busting 7	The reef is fine, isn't it?	39
Myth-busting 8	Glaciers growing?	42
Myth-busting 9	Sea levels falling?	46
Myth-busting 10	Polar bears thriving?	52
Myth-busting 11	Increased food production?	56
Myth-busting 12	My flight won't make a difference – will it?	154

Tables

Table 1	Ice-sheets and associated sea level rise	42
Table 2	Bruce's carbon footprint	76
Table 3	Ruksana's carbon footprint	82
Table 4	Source, purpose and type of GHG	108
Table 5	Global electricity generation from renewable sources	114
Table 6	Bruce, Mel and Joe	167
Table 7	Carbon footprint 'hotspot' identifier	172

Appendix 4: Test Your Understanding (answers following)

Part B. Climate Science Demystified

1. What is the process in which plants use CO_2 from the atmosphere to grow?
2. What is the reverse process in which animals use oxygen and plant matter to generate energy, releasing CO_2?
3. What proportion of the CO_2 humans emit is absorbed by oceans and forests?
4. What evidence is there that humans, rather than nature, have caused the rise in CO_2 levels?
5. Between what minimum and maximum has the CO_2 concentration in the atmosphere varied over the last 400,000 years until recent centuries?
6. What is the current CO_2 concentration in the atmosphere? What is its rate of increase per year?
7. How do increased carbon levels in the atmosphere cause an increase in the temperature?
8. What percentage of climate scientists have concluded that human-caused climate change is happening?

Part C. Clear and Present Danger

1. How does climate change increase the frequency and severity of extreme weather events?
2. How does climate change lead to the degradation of coral reefs?
3. Which type of ice-melt contributes to sea level rise?
4. How much has the sea level risen already? How much is it likely to rise by the end of the century?
5. How does climate change make extinctions more likely?
6. How will climate change make it harder to grow food in some parts of the world?
7. Which continents are likely to be most adversely affected by decreased food production?
8. What are some possible sources of conflict arising from climate change?

Part D. Ruksana vs Bruce

1. What was the global carbon budget in 2011 to have a 66% chance to stay below 2°C warming?
2. How much of that budget have we already used?
3. What is a sustainable carbon footprint for each person in the world?
4. What is the average carbon footprint for: everyone in the world, an Australian, a North American, a New Zealander, a Briton?
5. What are the major greenhouse gases apart from CO_2?
6. What is CO_2e?
7. What aspects of Bruce's life create the largest part of his footprint?
8. What is the average Indian's annual carbon footprint?

Appendices

Part E. Head in the Sand

1. What is 'planned obsolescence'?
2. Why do many media outlets ignore or downplay climate change?
3. What are the three categories of scientific solutions to climate change?
4. Describe some of the limitations of Carbon Capture & Storage.
5. How might we be able to draw greenhouse gases out of the atmosphere? What are the risks of those 'solutions'?
6. What is SRM? What are the risks of that 'solution'?
7. Which groups do many people offload the blame for climate change onto?
8. What are some of the psychological tricks we play on ourselves to avoid acting on climate change?

Part F. Big Picture Solutions

1. Name five renewable technologies.
2. How much time of the sun's energy hitting the earth would it take to generate the world's electricity needs for a year, if it were all converted to electricity?
3. What proportion of greenhouse gas emissions are methane from food production? Why do cattle emit so much methane?
4. What proportion of greenhouse gas emissions are from land use change (deforestation)? What is the major cause of deforestation?
5. What are some of the factors impeding international negotiations on climate change?
6. What temperature targets did the Paris agreement set?
7. If all countries signing the Paris agreement met their targets, how much temperature increase would result?
8. What is the divestment movement?

Part G. Small Picture Solutions

1. Why is consuming a service generally more environmentally friendly than consuming a product?
2. Why does meat consumption require higher carbon emissions than a vegetarian diet?
3. What percentage of food is thrown out by the average Australian household?
4. How much carbon is emitted in the manufacture a new car?
5. What emissions are associated with a return international flight from Sydney to Tokyo?
6. How can we reduce the amount of household electricity we consume?
7. How can installing solar panels reduce our carbon footprint?
8. How can emissions associated with our housing be reduced?

Answers to 'Test Your Understanding'

Part B. Climate Science Demystified

1. The process in which plants use CO_2 from the atmosphere to grow is photosynthesis. Chapter 4
2. The opposite process, in which animals use oxygen and plant matter to make energy, releasing CO_2, is respiration. Chapter 4
3. About half the CO_2 humans emit is absorbed by oceans and forests. Chapter 4
4. The falling ratio of Carbon 13 to Carbon 12 in the atmosphere is evidence that humans have caused the rise in CO_2 levels. Chapter 4
5. The CO_2 concentration varied between 180-300 ppm over the last 400,000 years – until the last century. Chapter 5
6. The current CO_2 concentration is just over 400 ppm, increasing at 2.5 ppm per year. Chapter 5
7. Rising carbon levels in the atmosphere cause the greenhouse effect: an increase in the temperature due to lower frequency radiation from the earth having difficulty penetrating the carbon-dense atmosphere to make it back out to space, so changing the energy equilibrium. Chapter 5
8. 97% of climate scientists have concluded that human-caused climate change is happening. Chapter 6

Part C. Clear and Present Danger

1. Climate change increases the frequency and severity of extreme weather events by the extra heat altering ocean and atmospheric currents and the hotter air holding more moisture, so creating extra humidity. Chapter 7
2. Increased ocean temperature leads to bleaching, and often the death of the coral. Increased acidity in the oceans leads to weakening of the coral structure. Chapter 8
3. Melting of land-ice contributes to sea level rise. Melting of sea-ice does not (directly). Chapter 9
4. The sea level has already risen by 0.2 metres in the last 200 years. It likely to rise 0.5-1.3 metres by the end of the century. Chapter 9
5. Climate change makes extinction more likely because of: species' inability to deal with higher temperatures; reduced access to food; difficulty in finding new habitats; increased contact with humans; species migrating faster than their food sources; and mismatch of timing between pollination and pollinators. Chapter 10
6. Altered rainfall patterns, and increased frequency and severity of extreme weather events resulting from climate change will make it harder to grow food in the future. Chapter 11
7. Africa, South Asia, Latin America and Australia are likely to be adversely affected by decreased food production. Chapter 11
8. Possible sources of geopolitical conflict arising from climate change are: water; food; Arctic resources; and unilateral geoengineering. Chapter 12

Appendices

Part D. Ruksana vs Bruce

1. The global carbon budget in 2011 to stay below 2°C warming was 1,000 gigatonnes CO_2. Chapter 14
2. We've already used over 200 gigatonnes CO_2 of that budget. Chapter 14
3. A sustainable carbon footprint for each person in the world is approximately 2 tonnes CO_2e per year. Chapter 14
4. The average annual carbon footprint for everyone in the world is 6.6 tonnes CO_2e; an Australian is 23 tonnes; a North American 20.5 tonnes; a New Zealander 17.5 tonnes; and a Briton 7.9 tonnes. Chapter 14
5. The major greenhouse gases apart from CO_2 are Methane (CH_4) and Nitrous Oxide (N_2O). Chapter 14
6. CO_2e is carbon dioxide equivalent. It measures the warming effect of a mixture of greenhouse gases. Chapter 14
7. The biggest contributors to Bruce's footprint are buying products (6 tonnes CO_2e) and diet (4 tonnes CO_2e). Chapter 15
8. The average Indian's annual carbon footprint is 2.3 tonnes CO_2e. Chapter 16

Part E. Head in the Sand

1. Planned obsolescence is deliberately manufacturing a product not to last. Chapter 17
2. Many media outlets do not want people to take climate change seriously as doing so may reduce consumption levels and therefore advertising revenue. Chapter 17
3. The three categories of scientific solutions to climate change are: releasing less greenhouse gases into the atmosphere; taking carbon out of the atmosphere; and stopping radiation reaching the earth. Chapter 18
4. Some of the disadvantages of Carbon Capture and Storage are its limited capacity, uncertainty over length of storage, and its expense. Chapter 18
5. We can draw greenhouse gases out of the atmosphere by massive tree-planting or geoengineering the ocean to make them more conducive to algal growth. The risks are possible unforeseen consequences for marine life, and the irreversibility of the 'solution'. Chapter 18
6. SRM is Solar Radiation Management. The risks are that decreasing radiation may impair photosynthesis and have possible adverse effects on rainfall. Chapter 18
7. People on the right of politics tend to blame the global poor for climate change, while people on the left of politics sometimes offload the blame onto multinational corporations. Chapter 19
8. Some of the psychological tricks we play on ourselves are: 'I'm doing my share '; 'At least my choice is better than that '; 'What can I do anyway '; and 'No one else is doing much – why should I? ' Chapter 20

Appendices

Part F. Big Picture Solutions

1. Renewable technologies are: hydro, nuclear, wind, biofuels, solar PV, geothermal, ocean energy and CST. Chapter 22
2. 15 minutes of the sun's energy is enough to produce the world's electricity for a year. Chapter 22
3. 8% of greenhouse gas emissions are methane from food production, primarily from cattle. Cattle emit so much methane because their digestive systems break down carbohydrates to release energy, but in so doing produce methane. Chapter 23
4. 11% of greenhouse gas emissions are from deforestation. The major reason for deforestation is to clear land for agriculture like soyabean and palm oil. Chapter 23
5. The main factor impeding an international agreement on climate change has been the impasse between developing and developed countries. Developing countries assert that rich nations are primarily responsible for the problem, so should be most responsible for reducing their emissions quickly, while developed countries want poorer nations to cap their emissions. Chapter 24
6. Temperature targets set at Paris were 2°C, but ideally 1.5°C. Chapter 24
7. If all countries met their national targets submitted at Paris, global warming of about 2.7°C would still occur. Chapter 24
8. The divestment movement encourages individuals and institutions to take their money out of any institution which invests in fossil fuels. Chapter 26

Part G. Small Picture Solutions

1. A service typically requires fewer emissions than those to create than a good. Chapter 27
2. Meat consumption requires higher emissions because of the methane cattle emit and the deforestation required for animal agriculture. Chapter 28
3. The average Australian household throws out 20% of its food. Chapter 28
4. 15 tonnes of CO_2e emissions are required to manufacture a new car. Chapter 29
5. 2.15 tonnes of CO_2e emissions per passenger are required for a return flight from Sydney to Tokyo. Chapter 30
6. We can reduce household electricity consumption by using more insulation or ventilation and using less air-conditioning. Chapter 31
7. Using solar panels to generate more electricity than we consume can reduce our carbon footprint. Chapter 31
8. Emissions from housing can be reduced by building smaller houses, and sharing housing. Chapter 32

Appendix 5: Vital Statistics in *Low-Carbon and Loving It*

#	Units	Significance	Chapter
180-300	ppm CO_2	Range of fluctuation of CO_2 concentrations over 400,000 years.	5
407	ppm CO_2	Current (2017) concentration of CO_2 in the atmosphere.	5
2.5	ppm/year	Rate of increase of concentration of CO_2 in atmosphere.	5
97	%	Proportion of climate scientists who accept human-caused climate change is happening.	6
0.5	°C	Change in average ocean temperature in last 200 years.	8
26	%	Increase in the acidity of the world's oceans in last 200 years.	8
0.5-1.3	metres	Projected sea level rise by the end of the century.	9
3-5	metres	Projected sea level rise from the disintegration and melting of the West Antarctic ice-sheet.	9
500	million	People projected to lose their homes from sea level rise.	9
1	°C	Rise in average global surface temperatures since pre-industrial times.	14
2	°C	Target for maximum warming set at the Paris meeting.	24
2.7	°C	Warming that the world is on track for, *if* all countries meet their targets set at the Paris meeting.	24
800	Gt CO_2	Carbon budget remaining to have a 66% chance of keeping under 2°C, (as of 2017).	14
942	Gt CO_2	CO_2 emissions released if all the fossil fuels in existing mines and projects are burnt.	14
36	Gt CO_2	Global CO_2 emissions per year.	14
49	Gt CO_2e	Global CO_2e emissions per year – about 7 tonnes per person.	14
2	tonnes CO_2e	Fair share of global carbon budget, per person per year.	14
23	tonnes CO_2e	Australian carbon emissions per capita in 2015.	15
2.3	tonnes CO_2e	Indian carbon emissions per capita in 2015.	16
22.5	petawatts	Global annual electricity generation, of which ⅔ is from fossil fuels and ⅓ from renewables.	22
15	minutes	Length of time of solar energy hitting the earth needed to power the world for a year, if converted to electricity.	22
42	%	Annual global growth rate of solar PV over last 5 years.	22

Acknowledgements

Tom and I are deeply thankful to our many friends and colleagues who contributed over the long journey of this book's development.

We're especially grateful to Cathy, (my wife and Tom's mum) and Oscar (our younger son and Tom's brother). This was a family project. The book was read, debated, discussed and refined over many a mealtime! Oscar and Cathy also helped with many of the illustrations.

Our good Indian friends, Ruksana, Anthony, Kallu, Kaneez and Kamran provided inspiration and hope that low-carbon lives are possible. We dedicate this book to them, especially to our dear friend Anthony (described in Chapter 29), whose life was cut short by cancer in 2016.

Matt Wade kindly allowed us to use the article he wrote in *The Age* and *The Sydney Morning Herald* in 2009.

John Cook at the University of Queensland provided useful insights on the science of climate change and the psychology of climate science denial, especially through the online course 'Making Sense of Climate Science Denial'.

Dave Andrews, Roland Lubett, Mark Worthing, and Nick Mattiske offered helpful suggestions regarding the publishing process.

David Nagai drew many of the cartoons specifically for this book. Chris Madden, INKCINCT, John Atkinson and Felix Schaad graciously offered the use of their cartoons for free.

Alistair Craig designed a great cover and laid out the book beautifully.

Jo-Anne Bragg gave helpful legal advice.

Many friends also helped along the way with editing, proofreading and adding their own ideas and thoughts. Many thanks to Helen Beazley, Kaaren and Shanti Mathias, Steve Wilson, Sharne Winter, Elspeth Lee, Jon Hakim, Katie Manning, Helen McCall, Robyn O'Loghlin, Nick Delaney, Amy Hickman, Chris Brown, Dave Fittell, Phil Sparrow, Keron Savins, Natalie James, Andrew Shepherd, Peter Sidebotham, Charles Ringma, Ben Wildflower, Sannie Pritchard and Ewen Heathdale.

Copyright Notices

Illustrations

Illustration 1, Chapter 4. By Oscar Delaney. Data from Vaclav Smith estimates and BP Statistical data. See also *https://ourworldindata.org/energy-production-and-changing-energy-sources/*

Illustration 2, Chapter 4. Adapted from Skeptical Science's image (available at *https://www.skepticalscience.com/graphics.php?g=2*), using the US Department of Environment's figures (available at *https://scied.ucar.edu/imagecontent/carbon-cycle-diagram-doe-numbers*).

Illustration 3, Chapter 5. Adapted from Wikimedia Commons. *https://commons.wikimedia.org/wiki/File:Vostok_Petit_data.svg*

Illustration 4, Chapter 5. By Cathy Delaney. Using information from NASA Earth Observatory. *https://earthobservatory.nasa.gov/Features/EnergyBalance/page6.php*

Illustration 5, Chapter 5. Environmental Protection Agency. *https://www.epa.gov/sites/production/files/2017-01/cs_global_temp_and_co2_1880-2012_v3_1.png*

Illustration 6, Chapter 6. Skeptical Science. *https://skepticalscience.com/graphics.php?g=47*

Illustration 7, Chapter 9. Wikimedia Commons. Assembled from NASA Earth Observatory images by Jesse Allen. *https://commons.wikimedia.org/wiki/File:Arctic_Sea_Ice_Minimum_Comparison.png*

Illustration 8, Chapter 9. *http://flood.firetree.net/* © 2006-2015, Alex Tingle

Illustration 9, Chapter 11. Modified from Wikimedia Commons. *https://commons.wikimedia.org/wiki/File:Projected_impact_of_climate_change_on_agricultural_yields_by_the_2080s,_compared_to_2003_levels_%28Cline,_2007%29.png*

Illustration 10, Chapter 11. Kiln: The Carbon Map. *https://www.kiln.digital/projects/carbonmap* See *http://www.carbonmap.org/*

Illustration 11, Chapter 12. By Tom Delaney. Ideas drawn from: IPCC 2014 Synthesis report (p7); and CNA Corporation (2007) - National Security and the Threat of Climate Change.

Illustration 12, Chapter 14. Figure SPM.10 from Climate Change 2014: Synthesis Report. Contribution of Working Groups I, II and III to the Fifth Assessment Report of the Intergovernmental Panel on Climate Change. [Core Writing Team, Pachauri, R.K. and Meyer, L. (eds.)]. IPCC, Geneva, Switzerland.

Illustration 13, Chapter 14. By Oscar Delaney. Data from: Oil Change International (2016); and The Sky's Limit: Why the Paris Climate Goals Require a Managed Decline of Fossil Fuel production. *http://priceofoil.org/2016/09/22/the-skys-limit-report*

Illustration 14, Chapter 14. By Oscar Delaney. Data from: OECD. 2015. Greenhouse gas emissions per capita. *https://stats.oecd.org/Index.aspx?DataSetCode=AIR_GHG*

Illustration 15, Chapter 15. By Cathy Delaney. Based on *www.shrinkthatfootprint.com/how-big-is-a-house*

Illustration 16, Chapter 18. By Cathy Delaney. Icons from All Free Images *http://all-free-download.com/free-vector/download/alternative-energy-options-icons_311137.html*

Copyright Notices

Illustration 17, Chapter 21. By Cathy Delaney. Corn & solar panel icons from All Free Images. *http://all-free-download.com/free-vector/download/alternative-energy-options-icons_311137.html*

Illustration 18, Chapter 28. By Oscar Delaney. Based on *www.shrinkthatfootprint.com/food-carbon-footprint-diet*

Illustration 19, Chapter 30. By Cathy Delaney.

Photographs and images

1. **Our neighbourhood.** (2007). A Father, a Son and the Climate. By the Delaney family.
2. **Low-carbon and loving it.** (2006). A Father, a Son and the Climate. By the Delaney family.
3. **Friends outside their house.** (1995). Chapter 1. By the Delaney family.
4. **Barapula.** (2002). Chapter 2. By the Delaney family.
5. **Kaneez and children.** (2007). Chapter 2. By the Delaney family.
6. **Australia's natural beauty.** (2016). Chapter 3. By the Delaney family.
7. **Aftermath of Typhoon Haiyan.** Chapter 7. By Wikimedia Commons *https://commons.wikimedia.org/wiki/File:Tacloban_Typhoon_Haiyan_2013-11-14.jpg*
8. **Bleached coral.** Chapter 8. By Wikipedia *https://en.wikipedia.org/wiki/Coral_bleaching*
9. **Comparison of McCarty Glacier.** Chapter 9. By Wikimedia Commons *https://commons.wikimedia.org/wiki/File:McCarty_Glacier.jpg*
10. **Polar Bear.** Chapter 10. By Flickr. Credit: Christopher Michel *https://www.flickr.com/photos/cmichel67/19160462274*
11. **Ruksana.** (2008). Chapter 16. By the Delaney family.
12. **Cycle rickshaw.** (2008). Chapter 16. By the Delaney family.
13. **Ruksana's room.** (2017). Chapter 16. By the Delaney family.
14. **Traffic in India.** Chapter 19. By Wikimedia Commons *https://commons.wikimedia.org/wiki/File:Trafficjamdelhi.jpg*
15. **High-speed rail in Taiwan** Chapter 21. By Wikimedia Commons *https://commons.wikimedia.org/wiki/File:THSR_700T_Modern_High_Speed_Train.jpg*
16. **Hydro: Gordon Dam.** Chapter 22. By Wikimedia Commons *https://upload.wikimedia.org/wikipedia/commons/e/ee/Gordon_Dam.jpg*
17. **The world's first CST plant, Spain.** Chapter 22. By Wikimedia Commons *https://commons.wikimedia.org/wiki/File:PS10_solar_power_tower.jpg*
18. **Deforestation.** Chapter 23. By Boundless Biology *https://courses.lumenlearning.com/boundless-biology/chapter/threats-to-biodiversity*
19. **Peter Dutton protest.** (2016). Chapter 26. By 350.org. Used with permission.
20. **Settlers of Catan.** (2011). Chapter 27. By the Delaney family.

Copyright Notices

21. **Tom with fully loaded bike.** (2015). Chapter 29. By the Delaney family.
22. **Mark and Anthony.** (2006). Chapter 29. By the Delaney family.
23. **Rooftop solar.** Chapter 31. By Wikipedia *https://en.wikipedia.org/wiki/File:PV_solar_roof_mount_and_rack.jpg*
24. **Our home.** (2017). Chapter 32. By the Delaney family.
25. **Vegan diet – home grown cucumber.** (2006). Chapter 35. By the Delaney family.
26. **Alan Kurdi.** Chapter 37. By UNHCR http://data2.unhcr.org/en/news/16490
27. **Kallu family and belongings.** (2002). Chapter 37. By the Delaney family.

All photos taken by the authors were with permission (where possible) of photographic subjects.

Cartoons

1. **Life Map.** Chapter 1. By David Nagai. All David Nagai cartoons in this book were commissioned specifically for it. More of David's cartoons are available at: *www.evokepeace.com*
2. **Burying head in the sand.** Chapter 6. By Chris Madden. Used with artist's permission.
3. **Sharks and sea level rise.** Chapter 9. By *www.CartoonStock.com*. Used with artist's permission.
4. **Climate summit.** Chapter 13. By Joel Pett. Editorial Cartoon used with the permission of Joel Pett and the Cartoonist Group. All rights reserved.
5. **Saving whales.** Chapter 17. By David Nagai.
6. **Brad Pitt.** Chapter 17. By David Nagai.
7. **Scientists and politicians.** Chapter 18. By INKCINCT. Used with artist's permission.
8. **Why do you keep buying?** Chapter 19. By David Nagai. Available at: *www.evokepeace.com*
9. **Bali climate change conference.** Chapter 24. By INKCINCT. Used with artist's permission.
10. **Climate change threatening the economy.** Chapter 25. By Felix Schaad, Tages Anzeiger. Used with artist's permission.
11. **A brief history of consumption.** Chapter 27. John Atkinson. Used with artist's permission.
12. **Landfill.** Chapter 27. By David Nagai.
13. **Frequent flying.** Chapter 30. By David Nagai.
14. **Someone else can save it.** Chapter 34. By David Nagai.
15. **You seem normal.** Chapter 36. By David Nagai.

Endnotes and References

Intoduction

1. **Carrington, Damian and Safi, Michael. 2017.** How India's battle with climate change could determine all of our fates. The Guardian. *https://www.theguardian.com/environment/2017/nov/06/how-indias-battle-with-climate-change-could-determine-all-of-our-fates*

Chapter 1

2. **Economic Times. 2011.** India's middle class population to touch 267 million in 5 yrs. *http://articles.economictimes.indiatimes.com/2011-02-06/news/28424975_1_middle-class-households-applied-economic-research*

Chapter 3

3. **Anand, Anu. 2015.** Breathing poison in the world's most polluted city. BBC. *http://www.bbc.com/news/magazine-32352722*
4. **Steketee, Mike. 2016.** Climate change has dropped off the political agenda (and this is a big problem). ABC News. *http://www.abc.net.au/news/2016-04-15/steketee-climate-change-has-dropped-off-the-political-radar/7328538*

Chapter 4

5. **BBC. n.d.** Formation of Fossil Fuels. *https://www.bbc.co.uk/education/guides/z27thyc/revision*
6. **Food and Agriculture Organisation. 2012.** State of the World's Forests. p21 *http://www.fao.org/docrep/016/i3010e/i3010e.pdf*

    World Bank. 2016. World Development Indicators: Deforestation and Biodiversity. *http://wdi.worldbank.org/table/3.4*

7. We updated the figures on this diagram, to reflect the more recent figure of 36 Gt CO_2 anthropogenic emissions.

    National Centre for Atmospheric Research. n.d. Carbon Cycle Diagram from the DOE with numbers. *https://scied.ucar.edu/imagecontent/carbon-cycle-diagram-doe-numbers*

    Intergovernmental Panel on Climate Change. 2014. Synthesis Report, Summary for Policy Makers p4 *https://www.ipcc.ch/pdf/assessment-report/ar5/syr/SYR_AR5_FINAL_full.pdf*
    Hereafter referenced as: IPCC. 2014. SPM. This report has slightly different figures: 30% absorption by land, 30% absorption by ocean, and 40% staying in atmosphere.

8. **Cook, John. 2010.** The Scientific Guide to Global Warming Skepticism. p2. *https://skepticalscience.com/docs/Guide_to_Skepticism.pdf*

Chapter 5

9. **NASA. 2017.** Vital Signs: Carbon Dioxide. *http://climate.nasa.gov/vital-signs/carbon-dioxide/*
10. **Davies, Bethan. 2015.** Antarctic Glaciers: Ice Core Basics. *http://www.antarcticglaciers.org/glaciers-and-climate/ice-cores/ice-core-basics/*
11. **Miller, Brandon. 2016.** 2015 is the Warmest Year on Record, NOAA and NASA say. CNN. *http://edition.cnn.com/2016/01/20/us/noaa-2015-warmest-year/*
12. Disturbingly, almost 40% of Australians hold this 'climate change is happening but is natural' viewpoint. See: **Leviston, Zoe et al. 2015.** Australian Attitudes to Climate Change, 2010-2014. CSIRO. *https://publications.csiro.au/rpr/download?pid=csiro:EP158008andisid=DS2*

Endnotes and References

13. Cook, John. 2010. The Scientific Guide to Global Warming Skepticism. *p10*. *https://skepticalscience.com/docs/Guide_to_Skepticism.pdf*
14. Cook, John. 2010. The Scientific Guide to Global Warming Skepticism. pp5 & 9. *https://skepticalscience.com/docs/Guide_to_Skepticism.pdf*
15. Cook, John. 2010. The Scientific Guide to Global Warming Skepticism. p7. *https://skepticalscience.com/docs/Guide_to_Skepticism.pdf*

Chapter 6

16. Funk, Cary & Kennedy, Brian. 2016. Public Views on Climate Change and Climate Scientists. Pew Research Centre. *http://www.pewinternet.org/2016/10/04/public-views-on-climate-change-and-climate-scientists/*
17. Leviston, Zoe et al. 2015. Australian Attitudes to Climate Change, 2010-2014. CSIRO. *https://publications.csiro.au/rpr/download?pid=csiro:EP158008anddsid=DS2*

    The Guardian Essential Report. 2017. 19 September. *https://www.theguardian.com/australia-news/ng-interactive/2017/sep/19/the-guardian-essential-report-19-september-results#table2*
18. IPCC. 1995. Working Group 1: The Scientific Basis. *https://www.ipcc.ch/ipccreports/tar/wg1/440.htm*
19. IPCC. 2013. Press release: Human influence on Climate Clear, IPCC report says. *http://www.ipcc.ch/news_and_events/docs/ar5/press_release_ar5_wgi_en.pdf*
20. NASA. 2016. Scientific Consensus: Earth's Climate is Warming. *https://climate.nasa.gov/scientific-consensus/*

    Cook, John et al, 2016 Consensus on consensus: a synthesis of consensus estimates on human-caused global warming, Environmental Research Letters Vol. 11 No. 4, 13 April; DOI:10.1088/1748-9326/11/4/048002
21. Skeptical Science. 2017. The 97% on Global Warming. *https://www.skepticalscience.com/global-warming-scientific-consensus-intermediate.htm*
22. Orsekes, Naomi. 2007. The Scientific Consensus on Climate Change: How We Know We're Not Wrong. MIT Press. p73. *http://www.project2061.org/events/meetings/climate2010/includes/media/NotwrongClimateChange.MITPress.2007.pdf* (human-caused) added to original quote.
23. Bump, Philip, 2015. Jim Inhofe's snowball has disproven climate change once and for all. The Washington Post. *https://www.washingtonpost.com/news/the-fix/wp/2015/02/26/jim-inhofes-snowball-has-disproven-climate-change-once-and-for-all/?utm_term=.3651828d68e2*
24. For an explanation of the weather phenomenon resulting in extreme cold temperatures, see:

    Cohen, Judah et al. 2014. Recent Arctic amplification and extreme mid-latitude weather. Nature geoscience, 7(9), 627-637. *https://www.nature.com/ngeo/journal/v7/n9/full/ngeo2234.html?cmpid=newscred*
25. Matthews, Dylan. 2017 Donald Trump has tweeted climate change skepticism 115 times. Vox. *https://www.vox.com/policy-and-politics/2017/6/1/15726472/trump-tweets-global-warming-paris-climate-agreement*
26. Thompson, Lonnie. G. 2010. Climate Change: The Evidence and Our Options. Association for Behaviour Analysis International. *https://www.ncbi.nlm.nih.gov/pmc/articles/PMC2995507/*
27. Gillis, Justin & Schwatz, Hohn. 2015. Deeper ties to corporate cash for doubtful climate researcher. New York Times. *https://www.nytimes.com/2015/02/22/us/ties-to-corporate-cash-for-climate-change-researcher-Wei-Hock-Soon.html*

Goldenberg, Suzanne. 2013. Secret Funding Helped Build Vast Network of Climate Denial Thinktanks. The Guardian *https://www.theguardian.com/environment/2013/feb/14/funding-climate-change-denial-thinktanks-network.*

Union of Concerned Scientists. n.d. Global Warming Skeptic Organizations. *http://www.ucsusa.org/global_warming/solutions/fight-misinformation/global-warming-skeptic.html#.WHQ1L4VOLIU*

28. Mann, Michael. 2016. I'm a scientist who has gotten death threats. I fear what may happen under Trump. Washington Post. *https://www.washingtonpost.com/opinions/this-is-what-the-coming-attack-on-climate-science-could-look-like/2016/12/16/e015cc24-bd8c-11e6-94ac-3d324840106c_story.html?utm_term=.9394f45278fd*

Kurtz, Lauren. 2016. Climate Scientists are under attack from frivolous lawsuits. The Guardian. *https://www.theguardian.com/environment/climate-consensus-97-per-cent/2016/jul/07/climate-scientists-are-under-attack-from-frivolous-lawsuits*

Chapter 7

29. IPCC. 2014. SPM. p8.
30. Robine, Jeanmarie et al. 2008. Death toll exceeded 70,000 in Europe summer of 2003. PubMed Commons. *https://www.ncbi.nlm.nih.gov/pubmed/18241810*
31. Nature International Weekly Journal of Science. 2009. Australian Bushfires Rage. *http://www.nature.com/news/2009/090209/full/news.2009.89.html*
32. Carrington, Damian. 2011. Deadly heatwaves will be more frequent in coming decades, say scientists. The Guardian. *https://www.theguardian.com/environment/2011/mar/17/deadly-heatwaves-europe*
33. World Meteorological Organisation. 2010. A snapshot of some extreme events over the past decade. *http://indiaenvironmentportal.org.in/files/extremes.pdf*
34. ABC News. 2013. World's Worst Recent SuperStorms. *http://www.abc.net.au/news/2013-11-09/major-global-storms-since-2007/5080952*
35. CNN. 2013. Typhoon Haiyan death toll tops 6,000 in the Philippines. *http://edition.cnn.com/2013/12/13/world/asia/philippines-typhoon-haiyan/index.html*
36. Watkins, Kevin. 2017. Famine warning signs were clear – so why are 20 million lives now at risk? The Guardian. *https://www.theguardian.com/global-development/2017/mar/07/famine-warning-signs-were-clear-so-why-are-20-million-lives-now-at-risk*
37. Allen, Nick et al. 2017. Hurricane Irma: Trail of Devastation Across Caribbean as Strongest Ever Atlantic Storm Wreaks Havoc. The Telegraph. *http://www.telegraph.co.uk/news/2017/09/06/hurricane-irma-latest-live-news-strongest-ever-atlantic-storm/*
38. Skeptical Science. 2015. Is Extreme Weather Caused By Global Warming? *http://www.skepticalscience.com/extreme-weather-global-warming-intermediate.htm*
39. Wikipedia. n.d. List of Natural Disasters by Death Toll. *https://en.wikipedia.org/wiki/List_of_natural_disasters_by_death_toll*
40. National Centre for Environmental Information. 2017. US billion-dollar weather and climate disasters, 1980-2017. *http://www.ncdc.noaa.gov/billions/events.pdf*
41. IPCC SPM. 2014. p8.
42. Meehl, Gerald & Tebaldi, Claudia. 2004. More Intense, More Frequent and Longer Lasting Heatwaves in the 21st century. Science Magazine. Vol 305, Issue 5635, pp994-997. *http://science.sciencemag.org/content/305/5686/994.full*

Endnotes and References

43. Chulov, Martin. 2017. Iraq sends workers home as 'ungodly' heat grips Middle East. The Guardian. *https://www.theguardian.com/world/2017/aug/10/iraq-sends-workers-home-as-ungodly-heat-grips-middle-east*
44. IPCC. 2014. SPM. p17-19.
45. World Health Organisation. 2017. Fact Sheet: Climate Change and Health. *http://www.who.int/mediacentre/factsheets/fs266/en/*
46. World Health Organisation. 2017. Fact Sheet: Climate Change and Health. *http://www.who.int/mediacentre/factsheets/fs266/en/*
47. Chen, Han. 2015. Paris Climate Agreement Explained: Climate Finance. National Resources Defence Council *https://www.nrdc.org/experts/han-chen/paris-climate-agreement-explained-climate-finance*
48. StatisticsTimes.com. 2017. List of Countries by projected GDP. *http://statisticstimes.com/economy/countries-by-projected-gdp.php*
49. Taylor, Lenore & Goldenberg, Suzanne. 2014. Green Climate Fund will get AUD$200 million from Australia after Tony Abbott's about-turn.The Guardian. *https://www.theguardian.com/environment/2014/dec/10/green-climate-fund-200m-australia-tony-abbott-about-turn*
    The AUD$200 million is spread over a 4 year period.
50. IPCC 2014. SPM. p17.

Chapter 8

51. Moore, Tony. 2016. 'Godfather of coral' warns of Great Barrier Reef 'mass extinction'. Brisbane Times. *http://www.brisbanetimes.com.au/queensland/godfather-of-coral-warns-of-great-barrier-reef-mass-extinction-20160306-gnbsj5.html*
52. Milman, Oliver. 2016. World's Oceans Warming at Increasingly Faster Rate, Study Finds. The Guardian. *https://www.theguardian.com/environment/2016/jan/18/world-oceans-warming-faster-rate-new-study-fossil-fuels*
53. Great Barrier Reef Marine Park Authority. 2017. Climate Change Impacts on Corals. *http://www.gbrmpa.gov.au/managing-the-reef/threats-to-the-reef/climate-change/what-does-this-mean-for-species/corals*
54. Australian Institute of Marine Science. 2016. Coral Bleaching Events. *http://aims.gov.au/docs/research/climate-change/coral-bleaching/bleaching-events.html*
55. National Geographic. 2017. Ocean acidification. *http://ocean.nationalgeographic.com/ocean/explore/pristine-seas/critical-issues-ocean-acidification/*
    IPCC. 2014. SPM. p4.
56. World Wildlife Foundation. n.d. Coral Reefs. *http://wwf.panda.org/about_our_earth/blue_planet/coasts/coral_reefs/*
57. Sydney Morning Herald. 2016. Pauline Hanson lands in hot water over Great Barrier Reef dive. *http://www.smh.com.au/environment/conservation/pauline-hanson-lands-in-hot-water-over-great-barrier-reef-dive-20161126-gsy4wm.html*
58. Australian Broadcasting Corporation. 2016. The Great Barrier Reef. *http://www.abc.net.au/tv/programs/david-attenboroughs-great-barrier-reef/*

Chapter 9

59. Intergovernmental Panel on Climate Change. 2014. Synthesis Report. p42. *http://www.ipcc.ch/pdf/assessment-report/ar5/syr/AR5_SYR_FINAL_All_Topics.pdf* Hereafter referenced as: IPCC. 2014. SR

60 Carbon Brief. 2013. Extra water or more heat: what's driving sea-level rise? *https://www.carbonbrief.org/extra-water-or-more-heat-whats-driving-sea-level-rise*

    IPCC. 2007. WG1 Sea-level *http://www.ipcc.ch/publications_and_data/ar4/wg1/en/ch10s10-es-8-sea-level.html*

61 Davies, Bethan. 2014. West Antarctic Ice-sheet. Antarctic Glaciers. *http://www.antarcticglaciers.org/antarctica/west-antarctic-ice-sheet/*

62 Data in table drawn from: National Snow and Ice Data Centre. 2017. Quick Facts on Ice-sheets. *https://nsidc.org/cryosphere/quickfacts/icesheets.html*

    Davies, Bethan. 2017. Calculating Glacier Ice Volumes and Sea Level Equivalents. Antarctic Glaciers. *http://www.antarcticglaciers.org/glaciers-and-climate/estimating-glacier-contribution-to-sea-level-rise/*

    Oskin, Becky. 2012. World's Glaciers have new size estimate. Live Science. *http://www.livescience.com/24168-glacier-volume-sea-level-rise.htm*

    NASA. 2017. Land Ice. *http://climate.nasa.gov/vital-signs/land-ice/*

63 Oskin, Becky. 2012. World's Glaciers have new size estimate. Live Science. *http://www.livescience.com/24168-glacier-volume-sea-level-rise.html*

64 Skeptical Science. 2015. Are Glaciers Growing or Retreating? *https://skepticalscience.com/himalayan-glaciers-growing.htm*

65 Harvey, Fiona. 2012. The Rare Earth Riches Buried Beneath Greenland's Vast Ice-sheet. Climate Central. *http://www.climatecentral.org/news/the-rare-earth-riches-buried-beneath-greenlands-vast-ice-sheet-14745*

66 Quoted in Klein, Naomi. 2014. This Changes Everything: Simon & Schuster p13.

67 NASA. 2017. Sea-levels. *http://climate.nasa.gov/vital-signs/sea-level/*

68 NASA. 2017. Arctic Sea-ice Minimum. *http://climate.nasa.gov/vital-signs/arctic-sea-ice/*

69 Struzik, Ed. 2016. Shipping Plans Grow as Arctic Sea-ice Fades. Yale360. *http://e360.yale.edu/features/cargo_shipping_in_the_arctic_declining_sea_ice*

70 Hirji, Zahra. 2017. Global Warming Could Thaw Far More Permafrost than Expected, Study Says. Inside Climate News. *https://insideclimatenews.org/news/10042017/permafrost-climate-change-arctic-carbon-release*

71 World Bank. 2012. Climate Change Report Warns of Dramatically Warmer World This Century. *http://www.worldbank.org/en/news/feature/2012/11/18/Climate-change-report-warns-dramatically-warmer-world-this-century*

72 Peasland, Joanna. 2016. Major Cities Threatened by Rapid Sea-level Rise, New Reports Find. Climate Home News. *http://www.climatechangenews.com/2016/02/22/major-cities-increasingly-threatened-by-rapid-sea-level-rise-new-reports-find/*

73 Gillis, Justin. 2017. Climate Change is complex. We've got answers to your questions. New York Times. *https://www.nytimes.com/interactive/2017/climate/what-is-climate-change.html?smid=pl-share*

    Le Page, Michael. 2015. Latest numbers show at least 5 metres sea-level rise rise locked in. New Scientist. *https://www.newscientist.com/article/mg22630253-300-latest-numbers-show-at-least-5-metres-sea-level-rise-locked-in/*

74 Radford, Tim. 2013. Australian Floods of 2010 and 2011 Caused Global Sea-level to Drop. The Guardian. *https://www.theguardian.com/environment/2013/aug/23/australian-floods-global-sea-level*

Endnotes and References

75 Reuters. 2016. Five Pacific Islands lost to Rising Seas as Climate Change Hits. The Guardian. *https://www.theguardian.com/environment/2016/may/10/five-pacific-islands-lost-rising-seas-climate-change*
76 **Radio National** (with Johannes Leutz). 2016. Rising Seas to Push out 500 million. *http://www.abc.net.au/radionational/programs/scienceshow/rising-seas-to-push-out-500-million/4831836.*
77 **Peasland, Joanna.** 2016. Major Cities Threatened by Rapid Sea-level Rise, New Reports Find. Climate Home News. *http://www.climatechangenews.com/2016/02/22/major-cities-increasingly-threatened-by-rapid-sea-level-rise-new-reports-find/*

Chapter 10

78 **Whale Facts.** n.d. What Do Blue Whales Eat? *http://www.whalefacts.org/what-do-blue-whales-eat/*
79 **World Wildlife Foundation.** 2016. Living Planet Index. *http://www.livingplanetindex.org/projects?main_page_project=LivingPlanetReport&home_flag=1*
80 **Animal Ecology Lab.** n.d. Flying Fox Heat Stress Forecaster. *http://www.animalecologylab.org/ff-heat-stress-forecaster.html*
81 **Bhandari, Neena.** 2013. Climate Change compound rising threats to koala. The Guardian. *https://www.theguardian.com/environment/2013/apr/30/climate-change-threats-koalas*
82 **McGee, Tim.** 2009. Moving Up: Climate Change forces species to higher elevations. Treehugger. *https://www.treehugger.com/natural-sciences/moving-up-climate-change-forces-species-to-higher-elevations.html*
83 **Cho, Renee.** 2015. Climate Change poses challenges to plants and animals. Columbia University. *http://blogs.ei.columbia.edu/2015/02/03/climate-change-poses-challenges-to-plants-and-animals/*
84 **IPCC.** 2014. SPM. p13.
85 **Cho, Renee.** 2015. Climate Change poses challenges to plants and animals. Columbia University. *http://blogs.ei.columbia.edu/2015/02/03/climate-change-poses-challenges-to-plants-and-animals/*
86 **NASA.** 2017. Arctic Sea-ice Minimum. *http://climate.nasa.gov/vital-signs/arctic-sea-ice/*
87 **Amstrup, Steven.** n.d. Are Polar bear populations increasing: in fact, booming? *https://polarbearsinternational.org/research/research-qa/are-polar-bear-populations-increasing-in-fact-booming/*
88 **The Centre for Biological Diversity.** n.d. The Extinction Crisis. *http://www.biologicaldiversity.org/programs/biodiversity/elements_of_biodiversity/extinction_crisis/*
89 **Drake, Nadia.** 2015. Will Humans Survive the Sixth great Extinction? National Geographic. *http://news.nationalgeographic.com/2015/06/150623-sixth-extinction-kolbert-animals-conservation-science-world/*
90 **Carrington, Damian.** 2016. The Anthropocene Epoch: Scientists Declare Dawn of Human Influenced Age. The Guardian. *https://www.theguardian.com/environment/2016/aug/29/declare-anthropocene-epoch-experts-urge-geological-congress-human-impact-earth*
91 **University of Queensland.** 2016. Online course: Making Sense of Climate Denial. Week 5, Part 2. Expert Interviews *https://www.edx.org/course/making-sense-climate-science-denial-uqx-denial101x-5*

Chapter 11

92 World Bank. 2013. Helping India Combat Persistently High Rates of Malnutrition. http://www.worldbank.org/en/news/feature/2013/05/13/helping-india-combat-persistently-high-rates-of-malnutrition

93 Kanji, Laura. 2016. Famine or Feast: Climate Change and the Future of Food Production. Harvard International Review. http://hir.harvard.edu/famine-feast-climate-change-future-food-production/

94 IPCC. 2014. SPM. p15. Note that this may not take into account other changes (eg technological) which may increase food production.

95 Food and Agriculture Organisation. 2014. Direct and Indirect Effects of Sea Level Rise. http://www.fao.org/nr/climpag/pub/EIre0047_en.asp

96 Food and Agriculture Organisation. 2014. Report highlights growing role of fish in feeding the world. http://www.fao.org/news/story/en/item/231522/icode/

97 McVeigh, Karen. 2017. 'Alarm Bells we Cannot Ignore': Global Hunger Rising for the First Time this Century. The Guardian. https://www.theguardian.com/global-development/2017/sep/15/alarm-bells-we-cannot-ignore-world-hunger-rising-for-first-time-this-century

Chapter 12

98 IPCC. 2014. SPM. p16.

99 Water Footprint. n.d. What is a Water Footprint? http://waterfootprint.org/en/water-footprint/what-is-water-footprint/

The Guardian datablog. 2013. How Much Water is Needed to Produce Food and How Much Do We Waste? https://www.theguardian.com/news/datablog/2013/jan/10/how-much-water-food-production-waste

100 CNA Corporation. 2007. National Security and the Threat of Climate Change. https://www.cna.org/cna_files/pdf/National%20Security%20and%20the%20Threat%20of%20Climate%20Change.pdf

101 Worldatlas. n.d. Indo-Pakistan wars – 1947, 1965, 1971, and 1999 http://www.worldatlas.com/articles/indo-pakistan-wars-1947-1965-1971-1999.html

102 Nabeel, Fazilda. 2017. How India and Pakistan are competing over the mighty Indus River. The Conversation. https://theconversation.com/how-india-and-pakistan-are-competing-over-the-mighty-indus-river-77737

Kugleman, Michael. 2016. Why the India – Pakistan War over Water is so Dangerous. http://foreignpolicy.com/2016/09/30/why-the-india-pakistan-war-over-water-is-so-dangerous-indus-waters-treaty/

103 Perez, Ines. 2013. Climate Change and Rising Food Prices Heightened Arab Spring. Scientific American. https://www.scientificamerican.com/article/climate-change-and-rising-food-prices-heightened-arab-spring/

Zurayk, Rami. 2011. Use Your Loaf: Why Food Prices Were Crucial in the Arab Spring. The Guardian. https://www.theguardian.com/lifeandstyle/2011/jul/17/bread-food-arab-spring

104 McAlister, Terry. 2010. Climate Change could lead to Arctic Conflict, Warns Senior NATO Commander. The Guardian. https://www.theguardian.com/environment/2010/oct/11/nato-conflict-arctic-resources.

RT News. 2014. Climate Change May Cause Conflict in the Arctic, Threats to Security Worldwide: Former US Generals. https://www.rt.com/usa/159036-climate-change-military-generals/

105 **Bodansky, Daniel.** 2011. Governing Climate Engineering: Scenarios for Analysis. *http://citeseerx.ist.psu.edu/viewdoc/download?doi=10.1.1.260.897&rep=rep1&type=pdf*

Chapter 13

106 **Thatcher, Margaret.** 1988. Margaret Thatcher Foundation. Speeches, Interviews & Other Statements. *https://www.margaretthatcher.org/document/107346*

107 **World Bank.** 2012. Climate Change Report Warns of Dramatically Warmer World This Century. *http://www.worldbank.org/en/news/feature/2012/11/18/*Climate-change-report-warns-dramatically-warmer-world-this-century and *https://www.vox.com/2014/4/22/5551004/two-degrees*

108 **Pope Francis.** 2015. Laudato Si: On Care for Our Common Home. paragraph 161.

109 **Anderson, Kevin.** 2014. We seem to be headed for a 4C World. Climate Scientist Kevin Anderson imagines what it would be like. Citizen Action Monitor. *https://citizenactionmonitor.wordpress.com/2014/12/09/we-seem-to-be-headed-for-a-4c-world-climate-scientist-kevin-anderson-imagines-what-it-would-be-like/*

Chapter 14

110 **Goldenberg, Suzanne.** 2015. Will '1.5 to stay alive' deal be enough to save Seychelles? The Guardian *https://www.theguardian.com/environment/2015/dec/12/climate-change-seychelles-cop21-economy-collapse*

111 At least, at this stage the relationship is roughly linear. In the long-term, it is a logarithmic relationship, meaning that doubling CO_2 levels from 280 to 560 ppm should cause the same temperature increase (estimates range from 1.5-4.5 C) as doubling from 560 to 1020.

See **Skeptical Science.** 2011. Fast-rising CO_2 levels accelerate global warming. *https://skepticalscience.com/exponential-increase-CO$_2$-warming.htm*

Lindsey, Rebecca. 2014. How Much Will the Earth Warm If Carbon Doubles Pre-Industrial Levels. NOAA. *https://www.climate.gov/news-features/climate-qa/how-much-will-earth-warm-if-carbon-dioxide-doubles-pre-industrial-levels*

112 **IPCC. SPM.** 2014. p10.

113 **IPCC SR.** 2014. p63.

114 **IPCC SR.** 2014. p64.

Why is the budget for 1.5°C so much less than the budget for 2°C (400 compared to 1000Gt)?

Basically because we've already warmed the earth by almost a degree, with more warming in the pipeline even if we stopped emitting tomorrow. This makes achieving the 1.5°C target look unlikely.

115 **IPCC.** 2014. SPM. p5. Note that we are using the IPCC report, which, though published in 2014, contains figures from 2010 (this is because it takes the IPCC a long time between collecting its material and publishing its final report). For more recent figures, see:

PBL Netherlands Environmental Assessment Agency, Joint Research Centre. 2016. Trends in Global CO_2 emissions, 2016 report. *http://edgar.jrc.ec.europa.eu/news_docs/jrc-2016-trends-in-global-co2-emissions-2016-report-103425.pdf*.

This gives a figure of 36 Gt CO_2 from fossil fuels and industrial processes (unlike the IPCC, which includes land use). The graph on p.13 shows growth in the period 2010-2014, with carbon emissions having stalled since.

116 **Carrington, Damian.** 2017. Global carbon emissions stood still in 2016, offering climate hope.

The Guardian. *https://www.theguardian.com/environment/2017/sep/28/*

Endnotes and References

global-carbon-emissions-stood-still-in-2016-offering-climate-hope

Note, however, that this is only CO_2 emissions. Methane emissions are still growing.

117 **United Nations Human Development Programme 2008.** Human Development Report. Pages 44-52 examines carbon budgets

118 **Skeptical Science. 2015.** CO_2 Emissions Stay in our Atmosphere for Centuries. *https://www.skepticalscience.com/co2-residence-time.htm*

 Nature Reports. 2008. Carbon is Forever. *http://www.nature.com/climate/2008/0812/full/climate.2008.122.html*

 Hansen, James et al. 2007. Journal of Atmospheric Chemistry & Physics. pp 2287-2312.

119 **Oil Change International. 2016.** The Sky's Limit: Why the Paris Climate Goals Require a Managed Decline of Fossil Fuel production. *http://priceofoil.org/2016/09/22/the-skys-limit-report*

 McKibben, Bill. 2016. Recalculating the Climate Math. New Republic. *https://newrepublic.com/article/136987/recalculating-climate-math*

120 **Carbon Tracker Initiative. 2013.** Unburnable Carbon: Wasted Capital and Stranded Assets, p4. *http://carbontracker.live.kiln.digital/Unburnable-Carbon-2-Web-Version.pdf*

 Note that this report gives 2860 Gt. However, this is inclusive of the 942 Gt in existing coal mines and oil & gas wells.

121 For an explanation of why other GHGs are not included in the IPCC's carbon budgeting, see Oil Change International (2016) The Sky's Limit, p 12. Basically, because CO_2 has a longer and more stable atmospheric lifetime, it is much easier to consider its emissions alone. This also makes it easier to do calculations involving fossil fuel reserves. For our purposes, however, we wish to consider the effects of other greenhouse gases (see Science Geek (6), CO_2 vs CO_2e). To get a figure in CO_2e, I multiplied by 4/3 (as carbon dioxide accounts for about 3/4 of total emissions), yielding 150 tonnes over a person's lifetime. Of course, this is highly unjust in that future generations, from a baby born tomorrow to a person living in 2200, get no share of the carbon budget. We give this figure merely as a very rough guide.

122 **IPCC. 2014.** SPM. p5 GWP is the technical term for how many times more potent than CO_2 a greenhouse gas is. We are using GWP 100 (comparing the gases over a 100 year time frame). Different time frames lead to different numbers. See:

 IPCC. 2007. Physical Science Basis: Direct Global Warming Potential. *http://www.ipcc.ch/publications_and_data/ar4/wg1/en/ch2s2-10-2.html*

 IPCC. 2014. SP p87, for explanation. p121 and 124, for definitions of GWP and CO_2e

123 **PBL Netherlands Environmental Assessment Agency, Joint Research Centre. 2016.** Trends in Global CO_2 emissions, 2016 report. *http://edgar.jrc.ec.europa.eu/news_docs/jrc-2016-trends-in-global-co2-emissions-2016-report-103425.pdf*

124 **OECD. 2015.** Greenhouse gas emissions per capita. *https://stats.oecd.org/Index.aspx?DataSetCode=AIR_GHG*

 Note that these figures are the total GHG emissions produced in that country, divided by its population. Britain's emissions are remarkably low at 7.9. This is partially because it imports a lot: the emissions from producing the stuff it buys from China, for instance, are counted as China's emissions. Note that consumption-based emissions reporting, in general, results in even starker inequalities in emissions per capita between 'developed' and 'developing' world. For an exploration of consumption-based emissions reporting, see:

 Davis, Steven & Caldiera, Ken. 2011. Consumption based accounting of CO_2 emissions. *http://www.pnas.org/content/107/12/5687.full*

Endnotes and References

Chapter 15

125 **Department of Environment and Energy.** 2017. Quarterly Update of Australia's National GHG Inventory. *http://www.environment.gov.au/system/files/resources/6cc33ded-14aa-4ddc-b298-b6ffe42f94a1/files/nggi-quarterly-update-march-2017.pdf*

This gives a sectoral breakdown of Australia's 550 Mt CO_2e emissions. Australia's population at time of writing: 23.8 million. Note that the World Bank figures (below) which we use for India put Australia's emissions significantly higher, at 760 Mt CO_2e, but we opt for the more conservative figures of the Australian government. The difference probably stems from different accounting techniques of land use change emissions. *https://data.worldbank.org/indicator/EN.ATM. GHGT.KT.CE?end=2012andstart=1970andview=chartandyear_high_desc=true.*

126 **Engineering Toolbox.** n.d. Densities and molecular weights of some common gases. *http://www. engineeringtoolbox.com/gas-density-d_158.html*

Density of CO_2 at Normal Temperature & Pressure = 1.84 kg/m3.

23,000 kg ÷(50 x 25 x 3 m3)÷(1.84 kg/m3) = 3.33 Olympic swimming pools.

127 The Australian GDP was AUD$1.7 trillion at the time of writing, yielding an overall emissions intensity of 0.32 kg CO_2e/$. Assuming this emissions intensity, and $20,000/ year spent on buying goods, equates to about 6 tonnes CO_2e.

128 **Ting, Inga.** 2015. Australia is the Meat Eating Capital of the World. Sydney Morning Herald *http://www.smh.com.au/national/health/australia-is-the-meateating-capital-of-the-world-20151027-gkjhp4.html*

129 **Department of Environment and Energy.** 2017. Quarterly Update of Australia's National GHG Inventory. p7. *http://www.environment.gov.au/system/files/resources/6cc33ded-14aa-4ddc-b298-b6ffe42f94a1/files/nggi-quarterly-update-march-2017.pdf*

In Australia, agricultural and waste emissions together account for 86 Mt CO_2e. Farms also consume significant diesel, resulting in 8 Mt CO_2e. Transport, processing and retail of food also takes significant energy, allowing us to estimate emissions at 4 t CO_2e per person per year.

130 The average light passenger vehicle in Australia is driven 13,000 km per year; there are 13 million passenger vehicles in Australia. This corresponds to about 7,500 km per person. With typical mileage of 10.6L/100 km and 2.31 kg CO_2 released per litre of petrol burnt, this equates to almost 2 tonnes.

Australian Bureau of Statistics. 2013. Car Nation. *http://www.abs.gov.au/AUSSTATS/abs@.nsf/Lookup/4102.0Main+Features40July+2013*

Bureau of Infrastructure, Transport and Regional Economics. 2017. Fuel economy of Australian passenger vehicles: a regional perspective. *https://bitre.gov.au/publications/2017/files/is_091.pdf*

University of Exeter. n.d. Calculation of CO_2 emissions. *https://people.exeter.ac.uk/TWDavies/energy_conversion/Calculation%20of%20CO2%20emissions%20from%20fuels.htm*

131 We realise that some long-distance trips are made by car, but for simplicity's sake, we equate 'local travel' with cars and 'long distance travel' with flights.

Berners-Lee, Mike & Clark, Duncan. 2010. What's the Carbon Footprint of a New Car. The Guardian. *http://www.theguardian.com/environment/green-living-blog/2010/sep/23/carbon-footprint-new-car*

Australian Bureau of Statistics. 2013. Car Nation. *http://www.abs.gov.au/AUSSTATS/abs@.nsf/Lookup/4102.0Main+Features40July+2013*

132 **Public Transport Users Association.** 2015. Myth: Public Transport Doesn't Really Save Energy. *http://www.ptua.org.au/myths/energy/*

133 8.7×10^6J (recommended daily nutritional intake) x 365 (days per year) x 31 years = 10^{11}J

8,850m (height of Mount Everest) x 9.8m/s2 (gravitational acceleration) x 5 x 10^3 kg (weight of elephant) x 230 elephants = 10^{11}J

4×10^6 J/km x 2.5×10^4 km = 10^{11} J. See *http://www.ptua.org.au/myths/energy*

134 **Berners-Lee, Mike & Clark, Duncan.** 2010. What's the Carbon Footprint of a New Car. The Guardian. *http://www.theguardian.com/environment/green-living-blog/2010/sep/23/carbon-footprint-new-car*

135 **Department of Infrastructure & Regional Development.** 2017. Domestic Aviation Activity. *https://bitre.gov.au/statistics/aviation/domestic.aspx*

Department of Infrastructure & Regional Development. 2017. International Aviation Activity. *https://bitre.gov.au/statistics/aviation/international.aspx*

Approximately 60 million domestic flights each year, and 40 million flights into or out of Australia (we can assume that 20 million of these are taken by Australians). Assuming 0.2 tonnes CO_2e per domestic flight (1500 km, eg Brisbane to Melbourne) and 1.1 tonne CO_2e per international flight (8,000 km, eg Sydney to Tokyo), this amounts to 34 Mt total – about 1.5 tonnes per person. Note that governments do not include emissions from international aviation in their national count.

136 **Department of Environment and Energy.** 2017. Quarterly Update of Australia's National GHG Inventory. *http://www.environment.gov.au/system/files/resources/6cc33ded-142a-4ddc-b298-b6ffe42f94a1/files/nggi-quarterly-update-march-2017.pdf*

Australian Energy Regulator. 2017. National Electricity Market electricity consumption *https://www.aer.gov.au/wholesale-markets/wholesale-statistics/national-electricity-market-electricity-consumption*

Australian Bureau of Statistics. 2012. Energy Use. *http://www.abs.gov.au/ausstats/abs@.nsf/Lookup/by%20Subject/1301.0~2012~Main%20Features~Energy%20use~201*

Energy Information Administration. 2016. How Much Carbon Dioxide is Produced When Different Fuels are Burnt. *https://www.eia.gov/tools/faqs/faq.cfm?id=73andt=11*

197 TWh of electricity is consumed in Australia, the generation of which releases 188 Mt of CO_2. About a quarter of Australia's electricity consumption is residential (with other major consumers being manufacturing, services, and mining), thus 47 Mt CO_2 (2t/person). 144 PJ worth of natural gas is also consumed by households, for cooking and heating, leading to a further 8 Mt CO_2 (0.3 t per person).

137 **Australian Bureau of Statistics.** 2011. Census QuickStats. *http://censusdata.abs.gov.au/census_services/getproduct/census/2011/quickstat/0*

138 **Berners-Lee, Mike.** 2010. What's the Carbon Footprint of... Building a House? The Guardian. *https://www.theguardian.com/environment/green-living-blog/2010/oct/14/carbon-footprint-house*

139 **Market Forces.** n.d. Bank Comparison Table. *https://www.marketforces.org.au/info/compare-bank-table/*

140 Government spending is about 25% of the economy, but this is significantly less emissions intensive than the economy overall (as it involves providing services) leading to an estimate of around 1.4 tonnes.

Australian Government. 2015. Budget Paper 1 – Statement 6. *http://www.budget.gov.au/2014-15/content/bp1/html/bp1_bst6_chart_data.htm*

The approach of Shrink that Footprint leads to an estimate in this ballpark. *http://shrinkthatfootprint.com/what-is-a-carbon-footprint*

Total scope 1 & 2 mining emissions (see next endnote) are 91 Mt, equating to 3.8 tonnes per person. Total: 5.2 tonnes per person

Endnotes and References

141 Gas: 314 PJ x 0.06 Mt CO_2/PJ = 17 Mt. Diesel: 147 PJ x 0.07 Mt CO_2/PJ = 10 Mt. Some CO_2 and methane is also unintentionally released from the extraction of fossil fuels. This is termed 'fugitive emissions', and accounts for about 47 Mt CO_2e. Total 'scope 1' direct emission: 74 Mt.

   Australian Bureau of Statistics. 2012. Energy Use. *http://www.abs.gov.au/ausstats/abs@.nsf/Lookup/by%20Subject/1301.0~2012~Main%20Features~Energy%20use~201*

   Department of Environment and Energy. 2017. Quarterly Update of Australia's National GHG Inventory. *http://www.environment.gov.au/system/files/resources/6cc33ded-14aa-4ddc-b298-b6ffe42f94a1/files/nggi-quarterly-update-march-2017.pdf*

142 The electricity consumed by mines results in about 17 Mt CO_2. 64 PJ x 0.26 Mt CO_2/PJ = 17 Mt.

   Australian Bureau of Statistics. 2012. Energy Use. *http://www.abs.gov.au/ausstats/abs@.nsf/Lookup/by%20Subject/1301.0~2012~Main%20Features~Energy%20use~201*

143 Australia exported 200 Mt of thermal coal in 2015-16. This yields about 480 Mt CO_2 of scope 3 emissions.

   Department of Industry, Innovation and Science. 2016. Australia's Major Export Commodities: Coal. *https://industry.gov.au/resource/Mining/AustralianMineralCommodities/Documents/Australias-major-export-commodities-coal-fact-sheet.pdf*

   Boles, Steve. n.d. What are the differences between scope 1, 2 & 3 emissions. *http://www.icomplisustainability.com/index.php/ask-the-expert/ghg-management/item/63-what-are-the-differences-between-scope-1-2-and-3-greenhouse-gas-emissions/63-what-are-the-differences-between-scope-1-2-and-3-greenhouse-gas-emissions*

144 Global emissions (49 Gt CO_2e in 2010) / Global population (7.4 billion) = 6.6 t CO_2e/person. **IPCC.** 2014. SPM. p5.

Chapter 16

145 By average, we mean a person representative of the mean carbon emissions. This figure was obtained by dividing 3 Gt, India's total emissions, by its population of 1.3 billion people. Ruksana herself probably has a carbon footprint lower than this.

   World Bank. 2012. Total Greenhouse Gas Emissions. *http://data.worldbank.org/indicator/EN.ATM.GHGT.KT.CE?end=2012andstart=1970andview=chartandyear_high_desc=true.*

146 This is a crude estimate, based on having a 'disposable income' of US$400 per year, and the emissions intensity of the Indian economy of about 1.3 kg CO_2e/US$ (3 Gt CO_2 ÷ US$2.3 trillion (nominal GDP)).

   Indian manufacturing consumes about 410 Twh of electricity, accounting for 0.3 tonnes/person – the bulk of emissions in this category.

   International Energy Agency. 2014. India: Electricity and Heat. *http://www.iea.org/statistics/statisticssearch/report/?country=INDIAandproduct=electricityandheatandyear=2014*

147 Indian agriculture consumes quite a lot of electricity, primarily to pump irrigation water, amounting to 0.12 t CO_2e per person. A government source claims that agriculture (excluding its electricity consumption) accounts for 17% of India's emissions, that is, about 0.5 t CO_2e per person. Hence I've given an estimate of 0.6 t. A substantial proportion of these emissions are from cows: India has the world's largest cattle herd, at 300 million. The estimates of how much methane each cow produces vary widely, from about 0.5 t CO_2e per year, to 2.3 t CO_2e.

   International Energy Agency. 2014. India: Electricity and Heat. *http://www.iea.org/statistics/statisticssearch/report/?country=INDIAandproduct=electricityandheatandyear=2014*

   Beef2Live. 2014. World Cattle Inventory: Ranking Of Countries. *http://beef2live.com/story-world-cattle-inventory-ranking-countries-0-106905*

Silverman, Jacob. 2007. Do Cows Pollute as Much as Cars? How Stuff Works. *http://animals.howstuffworks.com/mammals/methane-cow.htm*

Time For Change. 2008. Are Cows the Cause of Global Warming? *http://www.timeforchange.org/are-cows-cause-of-global-warming-meat-methane-CO2*

Aggarwal, Pramod & Prathak, Himanshu. n.d. Climate Change, Agriculture and Food Security. GHG emissions from Indian Agriculture: Opportunities for Mitigation. *http://www.ncaer.org/uploads/photo-gallery/files/1427095828PK%20Aggarwal.pdf*

148 There are only about 2 cars per 100 people in India. They consume about 20 Mt of diesel and 15 Mt of petrol, releasing a total of about 90 Mt of CO_2e, amounting to 0.07 t CO_2e per person. Given the emissions intensity of car manufacture (3 million cars x 15 tonnes/car / 1.3 billion people = 0.03 t per person), electricity consumption of local trains (0.02 t per person) and other sources, we round up to 0.2 tonnes per person. The real Ruksana doesn't own a car, but we're using her to represent the 'average Indian'.

Ministry of Petroleum & Natural Gas. 2013. All India Study on Sectoral Demand for Petrol & Diesel. *http://www.ppac.org.in/WriteReadData/Reports/201411110329450069740AllIndiaStudyonSectoralDemandofDiesel.pdf*, p17, p34.

149 About 100 million passengers fly each year in India, of which 60 million are domestic and the other 40 million international (flights to and from India). Assuming 0.2 t CO_2e per domestic flight, and 1 t per international flight (assume there are 20 million of these by Indian citizens), yields 32 Mt of CO_2e, amounting to 0.03 t per person. 1050 billion passenger km by train annually, but this is remarkably efficient, resulting in only 10 Mt, or 0.01 t per person. Long-distance bus journeys would add a bit too, so round up to 0.1.

International Air Transport Association. 2014. New IATA Passenger Forecast Reveals the Fast Growing Markets of the Future. *http://www.iata.org/pressroom/pr/Pages/2014-10-16-01.aspx*

World Bank. 2013. Passenger Kilometres by Train. *http://data.worldbank.org/indicator/IS.RRS.PASG.KM*

International Union of Railways. 2012. Railway Handbook: Energy Consumption & CO_2 emissions. *http://www.uic.org/com/IMG/pdf/iea-uic_2012final-lr.pdf*, p77

150 About 225 TWh of electricity are consumed by Indian homes annually. The emissions intensity is about 1 kg CO_2 per kWh. This equates to 0.17 tonnes per person. Add a bit more for gas consumption (18 Mt x 3 t CO_2/t LPG ÷1.3 billion population = 0.04 t per person), and electricity that's been stolen (and hence doesn't show up on the records as 'residential').

International Energy Agency. 2014. India: Electricity and Heat. *http://www.iea.org/statistics/statisticssearch/report/?country=INDIAandproduct=electricityandheatandyear=2014*

Energy Information Administration. 2017. How Much Carbon Dioxide is Produced When Different Fuels are Burnt. *https://www.eia.gov/tools/faqs/faq.cfm?id=73andt=11*

151 Much of the emissions from housing construction are from the manufacture of cement. In India, emissions intensity of cement production is somewhat higher than the global average, at about 0.9 t CO_2e/t cement. Producing about 280 Mt of cement each year thus equates to 0.2 t CO_2e per person. I've rounded up to 0.3 t, given use of other building materials too, such as bricks, and energy involved in construction.

Indian Brand Equity Foundation. 2016. Indian Cement Industry Analysis. *https://www.ibef.org/industry/cement-presentation*

Hendriks, C.A. et al. 2004. Emission Reduction of Greenhouse Gases From Cement Industry. IEA *http://www.wbcsdcement.org/pdf/tf1/prghgt42.pdf*

152 The Indian government spending is about 11% of the country's GDP; this might equate to around 0.2 tonnes / person. Of this, the largest share is probably military spending. If, as some estimates suggest, the US military emits as much as 5% of the world's CO_2 emissions, that could

mean the Indian military (which spends about 1/10th the money of the US military) may be responsible for up to 200 Mt of emissions – amounting to about 0.15 tonnes/person.

Shrink That Footprint. n.d. What is a carbon footprint? *http://shrinkthatfootprint.com/what-is-a-carbon-footprint*

The GlobalEconomy.com. 2015. India: Government spending, proportion of GDP. *http://www.theglobaleconomy.com/India/Government_size/*

Hynes, Patricia. 2011. The Military Assault on Global Climate. Truthout News. *http://www.truth-out.org/news/item/3181:the-military-assault-on-global-climate*

153 Approximately 50 Mt CO_2e of fugitive emissions. 90 Twh of electricity consumption → 90 Mt CO_2e. Total: 140 Mt CO_2e → approximately 0.1 t per person.

Singh, Ajay K & Kumar, Jaywardhan. 2016. Fugitive Methane Emissions from Indian Coal Mining and Handling Activities: Estimates, Mitigation and Opportunities for its Utilization to Generate Clean Energy. Energy Procedia, Volume 90, pp336-348. *http://www.sciencedirect.com/science/article/pii/S1876610216314114*

International Energy Agency. 2014. India: Electricity and Heat. *http://www.iea.org/statistics/statisticssearch/report/?country=INDIAandproduct=electricityandheatandyear=2014*

154 **Raworth, Kate. 2012.** A safe and just space for humanity: can we live within the doughnut? Oxfam Discussion Paper. *https://www.oxfam.org/sites/www.oxfam.org/files/dp-a-safe-and-just-space-for-humanity-130212-en.pdf*

Chapter 17

155 **Whitman, Richard. 2017.** Global Advertising Revenue Reached US$532 billion in 2016, will reach US$590 billion in 2017. Media Post. *https://www.mediapost.com/publications/article/292082/global-advertising-revenue-reached-532-billion-in.html*

156 **Hadhazy, Adam. 2016.** Here's the Truth about the Planned Obsolescence of Technology. British Broadcasting Corporation. *http://www.bbc.com/future/story/20160612-heres-the-truth-about-the-planned-obsolescence-of-tech*

157 **Elmhirst, Sophie. 2016.** Liquid Assets: How the Business of Bottled Water went Mad. The Guardian. *https://www.theguardian.com/business/2016/oct/06/liquid-assets-how--business-bottled-water-went-mad*

158 **Chen, Angus. 2015.** Here's how much Plastic enters the Ocean each Year. Science. *http://www.sciencemag.org/news/2015/02/here-s-how-much-plastic-enters-ocean-each-year*

159 **Department of Environment and Energy. 2013.** Australia's Waste and Resource Recovery Infrastructure. *http://www.environment.gov.au/protection/national-waste-policy/national-waste-reports/national-waste-report-2013/infrastructure*

160 **Atkin, Emily. 2017.** The Media has Essentially Stopped Covering Climate Change. New Republic. *https://newrepublic.com/minutes/141567/media-essentially-stopped-covering-climate-change*

161 **Milman, Oliver. 2013.** One third of Australia's Media Coverage Rejects Climate Science, Study Finds. The Guardian. *https://www.theguardian.com/environment/2013/oct/30/one-third-of-australias-media-coverage-rejects-climate-science-study-finds*

162 **Goldberg, Suzanne & Bengtsson, Helena. 2016.** Biggest US Coal Company Funded Dozens of Groups Questioning Climate Science. The Guardian. *https://www.theguardian.com/environment/2016/jun/13/peabody-energy-coal-mining-climate-change-denial-funding*

Gibson, Connor. 2016. Koch Front Groups are Defending ExxonMobil's Anti-Science Campaigns. Greenpeace. *http://www.greenpeace.org/usa/koch-cash-in-defense-of-exxonmobil-climate-denial-investigations/*

163 Mandel, Charles. 2016. US coal giant owed money to Canadian climate change deniers. National Observer. *https://www.nationalobserver.com/2016/06/16/news/exclusive-us-coal-giant-owed-money-canadian-climate-change-deniers*

Union of Concerned Scientists. n.d. Global Warming Skeptic Organizations. *http://www.ucsusa.org/global_warming/solutions/fight-misinformation/global-warming-skeptic.html#.Wh5DUt9fhOA*

Chapter 18

164 Department of Environment and Energy. n.d. Montreal Protocol on Substances that Deplete the Ozone Layer. *http://environment.gov.au/protection/ozone/montreal-protocol*

165 Nelder, Artur. 2013. Why carbon capture and storage will never pay off. ZD Net. *http://www.zdnet.com/article/why-carbon-capture-and-storage-will-never-pay-off/*

166 Carbon Capture and Storage Association. 2017. Affordability. *http://www.ccsassociation.org/why-ccs/affordability/*

167 David Suzuki Foundation. 2009. The Problems with Carbon Offsets from Tree Planting. *https://web.archive.org/web/20100212232904/http://www.davidsuzuki.org/Climate_Change/What_You_Can_Do/trees3.asp*

168 Narain, Sunita. 2015. How to plant trees for development. *http://www.downtoearth.org.in/blog/how-to-plant-trees-for-development-49760*

169 IPCC. 2014. SPM. p5.

170 Vidal, John. 2016. Oil Drilling Underway Beneath Ecuador's Yasuni National Park. The Guardian. *https://www.theguardian.com/environment/2016/oct/26/oil-drilling-underway-beneath-ecuadors-yasuni-national-park*

171 Scheirmeier, Quirin. 2012. Dumping iron at sea does sink carbon. Nature. *https://www.nature.com/news/dumping-iron-at-sea-does-sink-carbon-1.11028*

172 Center for Science Education. 2012. Mount Tambora and the Year Without a Summer. University Corporation for Atmospheric Research. *https://scied.ucar.edu/shortcontent/mount-tambora-and-year-without-summer*

173 IPCC. 2014. SR. p89.

174 Iles, Carley, et al. 2013. The Effect of Volcanic Eruptions on Global Precipitation. The Journal of Geophysical Research: Atmospheres. *http://onlinelibrary.wiley.com/doi/10.1002/jgrd.50678/pdf*

175 Brower, Kenneth. 2010. The Danger of Cosmic Genius. The Atlantic. *https://www.theatlantic.com/magazine/archive/2010/12/the-danger-of-cosmic-genius/308306/*

176 Avienaash. 2016. Assembly Elections 2016: One in Three MLAs have Criminal Record. The Hindu. *http://www.thehindu.com/data/Assembly-elections-2016-One-in-three-MLAs-have-criminal-record/article14342438.ece*

177 Queensland Government. 2016. Queensland Government Steps Up to Progress Adani Mine Project. *http://statements.qld.gov.au/Statement/2016/10/9/queensland-government-steps-up-to-progress-adani-mine-project*

Chapter 19

178 World Health Organisation. 2017. Reproductive Health. *http://www.wpro.who.int/reproductive_health/data/en/*

NB We are avoiding the debate about the ethics of contraception, which rages in some Christian circles.

Endnotes and References

179 **Nanitashvili, Nana.** 2014. Infant Mortality and Fertility: Population Horizons Factsheet 5. *http://www.ageing.ox.ac.uk/download/143*

180 **Murti, Mamta et al.** 1995. Mortality, Fertility and Gender Bias in India: A District Level Analysis. *http://www.histecon.magd.cam.ac.uk/docs/mortality.pdf*

181 **World Bank.** 2016. Population Growth Rates. *http://data.worldbank.org/indicator/SP.POP.GROW*

   Admittedly, net immigration makes up a significant proportion of Australia's population growth.

182 **Economic Survey of Delhi.** 2012-13. Chapter 12: Transport. *https://docs.google.com/file/d/0B9aAj1yhm51paUxVeXJiZWF5QTA/edit*

   We've extrapolated from 2.3 million cars in 2012 up to 3 million in 2017.

183 **World Economic Forum.** 2016. Which are the World's Most Polluted Cities? *https://www.weforum.org/agenda/2016/05/which-are-the-world-s-most-polluted-cities/*

184 **Lukacs, Martin.** 2017. Neoliberalism has conned us into fighting climate change as individuals. The Guardian. *https://www.theguardian.com/environment/true-north/2017/jul/17/neoliberalism-has-conned-us-into-fighting-climate-change-as-individuals*

Chapter 20

185 See endnote 136.

186 **Australian Bureau of Statistics.** 2012. Energy Use. *http://www.abs.gov.au/ausstats/abs@.nsf/Lookup/by%20Subject/1301.0~2012~Main%20Features~Energy%20use~201*

187 **Your Home.** 2013. Energy. *http://www.yourhome.gov.au/energy*

188 **Bulman, May.** 2017. Brexit vote sees highest spike in religious and racial hate crimes ever recorded. The Independent. *http://www.independent.co.uk/news/uk/home-news/racist-hate-crimes-surge-to-record-high-after-brexit-vote-new-figures-reveal-a7829551.html*

Chapter 21

189 Percentages rounded to sum to 100%. This is for the world overall, although the breakdown in Australia is probably quite similar.

   IPCC. 2014. Synthesis Report. p5, p47.

   US Environmental Protection Agency. n.d. Overview of Greenhouse Gases. *https://www.epa.gov/ghgemissions/overview-greenhouse-gases#nitrous-oxide*

   For a breakdown of methane emissions, see: **Global Methane Initiative.** n.d. Global Methane Emissions and Reduction Opportunities. *http://www.globalmethane.org/documents/analysis_fs_en.pdf*

190 **Food or Fuel.** 2012. US corn harvested for ethanol could feed 412 m people. *http://foodorfuel.weebly.com/*

191 **Beyond Zero Emissions.** 2010. Stationary Energy Report. P32.

192 41 Mt divided by 24 million population = 1.7 t/person. Round up given emissions associated with car maintenance.

   Commonwealth of Australia. 2016. Australia's Emissions Projections 2016. Department of Environment. *http://www.environment.gov.au/system/files/resources/9437fe27-64f4-4d16-b3f1-4e03c2f7b0d7/files/aust-emissions-projections-2016.pdf*

193 **Palmer, Kate et al.** 2018. Total cost of ownership and market share of hybrid and electric vehicles in the UK, US and Japan. Science Direct, Volume 209, pp 108-119. *http://www.sciencedirect.com/science/article/pii/S030626191731526X?via%3Dihub*

194 EasyJet in the UK claim they will have electric flights for short distances operational by 2027. However these short distance trips really should not be made by flights, but rather by train. Furthermore, the low number of passengers per flight would have severe limitations.

> Monaghan, Angela. 2017. EasyJet says it could be flying electric planes within a decade. The Guardian. *https://www.theguardian.com/business/2017/sep/27/easyjet-electric-planes-wright-electric-flights*

195 Beyond Zero Emissions. 2014. High Speed Rail. *http://bze.org.au/high-speed-rail-plan/*

196 BZE. 2014. High Speed Rail Report. p xiv. *http://bze.org.au/high-speed-rail-plan/*

197 World Health Organisation. 2016. Household Air Pollution and Health. *http://www.who.int/mediacentre/factsheets/fs292/en/*.

> This type of burning biomass is classified as producing emissions because, in many cases, gathering firewood contributes to deforestation. Furthermore, these stoves often burn quite inefficiently, and the methane and black carbon resulting from partial combustion are potent GHGs.

Chapter 22

198 Neslen, Arthur. 2015. Wind Power Generates 140% of Denmark's Electricity Demand. The Guardian. *https://www.theguardian.com/environment/2015/jul/10/denmark-wind-windfarm-power-exceed-electricity-demand*

199 EnerData. 2016. Global Energy Statistical Yearbook. *https://yearbook.enerdata.net/electricity-domestic-consumption-data-by-region.html*

> World Bank. 2015. World Development Indicators: Power and Communications. *http://wdi.worldbank.org/table/5.11*

200 Comparison of renewable energy sources. Figures, where possible, are from 2015, and are rounded. Growth rate refers to average annual growth rate between 2010 and 2015. 1000 TW = 1 PW.

> REN21. 2017. Renewables 2017, Global Status Report. *http://www.ren21.net/status-of-renewables/global-status-report/*.

> World Nuclear Association. 2015. Nuclear Share Figures, 2004-14. *http://www.world-nuclear.org/information-library/facts-and-figures/nuclear-generation-by-country.aspx*

> World Nuclear Association. 2017. Nuclear Power in the World Today. http://world-nuclear.org/information-library/current-and-future-generation/nuclear-power-in-the-world-today.aspx

201 Union of Concerned Scientists. n.d. How Hydroelectric Energy Works. *http://www.ucsusa.org/clean_energy/our-energy-choices/renewable-energy/how-hydroelectric-energy.html#.Wh-S999fbOA*

202 National Geographic. n.d. Hydropower. *https://www.nationalgeographic.com/environment/global-warming/hydropower/*

203 The Guardian. 2016. Hydroelectric Dams Emit a Billion Tonnes of Greenhouse Gases, Study Finds. *https://www.theguardian.com/global-development/2016/nov/14/hydroelectric-dams-emit-billion-tonnes-greenhouse-gas-methane-study-climate-change?utm_source=espandutm_medium=Emailandutm_campaign=Poverty+Matters+2016andutm_term=199803andsubid=14934314andCMP=EMCGBLEML1625*

204 Approximately 89PW striking the earth's surface at any time (once reflection and scattering by the atmosphere has been accounted for). Global electricity consumption in 2015: 22 TWh.

> Tsao, Jeff et al. 2006. Solar FAQs. US Department of Energy. *http://www.sandia.gov/~jytsao/Solar%20FAQs.pdf*

205 Sinovoltaics. 2015. What is the Energy Payback time for Solar Systems. *http://sinovoltaics.com/learning-center/solar-panels/energy-payback-time-for-solar-systems/*

Endnotes and References

206 **Beyond Zero Emissions.** 2010. Stationary Energy Plan. pp23-28 *http://media.bze.org.au/ZCA2020_Stationary_Energy_Report_v1.pdf*

207 **ABC.** 2017. Solar Thermal Plant announced for Port Augusta 'biggest of it's kind in the world'. *http://www.abc.net.au/news/2017-08-14/solar-thermal-power-plant-announcement-for-port-augusta/8804628*

208 **Union of Concerned Scientists.** 2014. How Geothermal Power Works. *https://www.ucsusa.org/clean_energy/our-energy-choices/renewable-energy/how-geothermal-energy-works.html#.WjtiBrpuJMs*

209 **World Energy Council.** 2016. World Energy Resources Geothermal. *https://www.worldenergy.org/wp-content/uploads/2017/03/WEResources_Geothermal_2016.pdf*

210 **Geoscience Australia.** n.d. Ocean Energy. *http://www.ga.gov.au/scientific-topics/energy/resources/other-renewable-energy-resources/ocean-energy*

211 **Osborne, Samuel.** 2016. Sweden phases out fossil fuels in attempt to run completely off renewable energy. Independent. *http://www.independent.co.uk/news/world/europe/sweden-phases-out-fossil-fuels-in-attempt-to-run-completely-off-renewable-energy-a7047306.html*

Chapter 23

212 **Environmental Protection Agency.** 1998. Enteric Fermentation – Greenhouse Gases. *https://www3.epa.gov/ttnchie1/ap42/ch14/final/c14s04.pdf*

213 **Hutching, Gerard.** 2016. NZ scientists say seaweed cure for methane emissions comes up short. NZ Farmer. *http://www.stuff.co.nz/business/farming/88009884/nz-scientists-say-seaweed-cure-for-methane-emissions-comes-up-short*

214 **Global Forest Atlas.** 2017. Soy Agriculture in the Amazon Basin. *http://globalforestatlas.yale.edu/amazon/land-use/soy*

215 **Worldwatch Institute.** 2009. Global Palm Oil Demand Fuelling Deforestation. *http://www.worldwatch.org/node/6059*

216 **US Environmental Protection Agency.** n.d. Overview of Greenhouse Gases. *https://www.epa.gov/ghgemissions/overview-greenhouse-gases#nitrous-oxide*

217 **IPCC.** 2006. Guidelines for National Greenhouse Gas Inventories. Volume 2, Chapter 4: Fugitive Emissions. *http://www.ipcc-nggip.iges.or.jp/public/2006gl/pdf/2_Volume2/V2_4_Ch4_Fugitive_Emissions.pdf*

218 **Cement Industry Federation.** 2017. Cement Emissions. *http://cement.org.au/SustainabilityNew/ClimateChange/CementEmissions.aspx.*

219 **Physics and Maths Tutor.** n.d. Extraction of Metals. *http://pmt.physicsandmathstutor.com/download/Chemistry/A-level/Notes/AQA-Old/Unit-2/Set-A/2.07%20Extraction%20of%20Metals.pdf*

220 **Johnston, Chris et al.** 2016. Climate Change: Global Deal Reached to Limit Use of Hydrofluorocarbons. The Guardian. *https://www.theguardian.com/environment/2016/oct/15/climate-change-environmentalists-hail-deal-to-limit-use-of-hydrofluorocarbons*

Chapter 24

221 **United Nations Framework Convention on Climate Change.** 2014. Kyoto Protocol. *http://unfccc.int/kyoto_protocol/items/3145.php*

222 **US Environmental Protection Agency.** 2017. Global Greenhouse Gas Emissions data. *https://www.epa.gov/ghgemissions/global-greenhouse-gas-emissions-data*

223 **The White House, President Barack Obama.** 2014. U.S.-China Joint Announcement on Climate Change. *https://obamawhitehouse.archives.gov/the-press-office/2014/11/11/us-china-joint-announcement-climate-change*

Endnotes and References

China's target was very unambitious: indeed, emissions may have peaked already. See:

Harvey, Chelsea. 2016. China vowed to peak emissions by 2030. It could be way ahead of schedule. Washington Post. *https://www.washingtonpost.com/news/energy-environment/wp/2016/03/07/china-vowed-to-peak-carbon-emissions-by-2030-these-researchers-think-it-could-already-be-there/?utm_term=.78b9164a037d*

224 **Narain, Sunita.** 2014. US-China Climate Deal: Maker or Breaker? Centre for Science and Environment. *http://www.cseindia.org/content/us-china-climate-deal-maker-or-breaker*

225 **Rogelj, Joeri.** 2016. Why Paris Climate Pledges Need to Overdeliver to Keep Warming to 2C. Carbon Brief. *https://www.carbonbrief.org/guest-post-why-paris-climate-pledges-need-to-overdeliver-to-keep-warming-to-2c*

Chapter 25

226 **Cunningham, Nick.** 2016. The Decline of the Coal Industry is "Long Term" and "Irreversible". Oil Price. *https://oilprice.com/Energy/Coal/The-Decline-Of-The-Coal-Industry-Is-Long-Term-And-Irreversible.html*

Business Today. 2017. Coal India plans to shut 37 mines this financial year. *http://www.businesstoday.in/current/corporate/coal-india-plans-to-shut-37-mines-this-fiscal-year/story/254022.html*

227 **World Bank.** 2015. State and Trends of Carbon Pricing. *http://documents.worldbank.org/curated/en/636161467995665933/pdf/99533-REVISED-PUB-P153405-Box393205B.pdf*

228 **Hill, Jess.** 2015. The great energy spend that is costing us billions. ABC. *http://www.abc.net.au/news/2015-11-10/hill-the-great-energy-con-that-is-costing-us-billions/6924272*

Robertson, Joshua. 2017. 'Way off the planet': regional businesses use renewables to slash costs. The Guardian. *https://www.theguardian.com/environment/2017/oct/28/way-off-the-planet-regional-businesses-use-renewables-to-slash-costs*

229 **Carbon Tax Center.** n.d. Softening the Impact. *https://www.carbontax.org/softening-the-impact/*

230 **Delaney, Thomas.** 2015. Is Economic Growth Sustainable? *https://mixedpickle4u.wordpress.com/page/2/?s=economic+growth*

231 **Eisenstein, Charles.** 2015. Sacred Economics. Banyan Tree Publishing.

232 **Wilkinson and Pickett.** 2009. The Spirit Level. Allen Lane.

Chapter 26

233 **Keany, Francis.** 2015. Peter Dutton Overheard Joking about Rising Sea-levels in Pacific Island Nations. ABC News. *http://www.abc.net.au/news/2015-09-11/dutton-overheard-joking-about-sea-levels-in-pacific-islands/6768324*

234 **Schwartz, John.** 2016. Investment Funds Worth Trillions are Dropping Fossil Fuel Stocks. New York Times. *https://www.nytimes.com/2016/12/12/science/investment-funds-worth-trillions-are-dropping-fossil-fuel-stocks.html?_r=0*

Carrington, Damian. 2016. Fossil fuel divestment funds double to $5tn in a year. The Guardian. *https://www.theguardian.com/environment/2016/dec/12/fossil-fuel-divestment-funds-double-5tn-in-a-year*

235 **Carrington, Damian.** 2015. Norway Confirms $900bn Sovereign Wealth Fund's Major Divestment. The Guardian. *https://www.theguardian.com/environment/2015/jun/05/norways-pension-fund-to-divest-8bn-from-coal-a-new-analysis-shows*

Endnotes and References

236 Norway's national superannuation scheme is worth US$1 trillion, of which $8 billion will be divested from coal. This fund has been built up primarily from petroleum revenue. In a similar irony, the Rockefellers were major players in the establishment of the fossil fuel industry in the US.

350.org. n.d. Campaign Update: Divestment. *https://350.org/350-campaign-update-divestment/*

237 **Morales, Alex.** 2014. Fossil Fuel Investors Risk Being Stranded by Tougher Climate Rules. Sydney Morning Herald. *http://www.smh.com.au/environment/climate-change/fossil-fuel-investors-risk-being-stranded-by-tougher-climate-rules-20141202-11yvlh.html*

238 **Elliot, Tim.** 2016. Decision on Coal Mine 'Defies Reason'. Sydney Morning Herald. *http://www.smh.com.au/federal-politics/political-news/decision-on-coal-mine-defies-reason-20160403-gnxbc6.html*

239 **ABC.** 2016. Adani coal mine gains 'critical' status as Queensland Government moves to kick start project. *http://www.abc.net.au/news/2016-10-10/adani-coal-mine-gains-critical-status-queensland-kick-start-move/7917506*

240 **ABC.** 2015. Adani Carmichael Project: Commonwealth Bank Walks Away from Financial Advisor Role for $16 Billion Coal Mine Project in Central Queensland. *http://www.abc.net.au/news/2015-08-05/cba-terminates-adviser-role-for-adani-carmichael-coal-mine/6675722*

241 **Robertson, Joshua.** 2017. Big four banks distance themselves from Adani coalmine as Westpac rules out loan. The Guardian. *https://www.theguardian.com/environment/2017/apr/28/big-four-banks-all-refuse-to-fund-adani-coalmine-after-westpac-rules-out-loan*

242 **Neslen, Arthur.** 2015. Dutch Government ordered to cut carbon emissions in landmark ruling. The Guardian. *https://www.theguardian.com/environment/2015/jun/24/dutch-government-ordered-cut-carbon-emissions-landmark-ruling*

243 **Wangan and Jagalingou Family Council.** 2017. *http://wanganjagalingou.com.au/*

Chapter 27

244 **Nevins, Joseph.** 2017. Mitigating Climate Disaster will Require both Systemic and Lifestyle Changes. Truthout News. *http://www.truth-out.org/news/item/40237-mitigating-climate-disaster-will-require-both-systemic-and-lifestyle-changes*

245 **Beaurepaires.** n.d. *https://www.beaurepaires.com.au/advice/about-us/tyre-stewardship-australia*

246 **Shrink That Footprint.** n.d. Shrink your service footprint. *http://shrinkthatfootprint.com/shrink-your-service-footprint*

Chapter 28

247 Note, however, that the documentary does use shoddy emissions accounting techniques to claim that 51% of all GHG emissions are caused by animal agriculture. In reality, the figure is closer to 15%.

Boucher, Doug. 2016. Movie Review: There's a Vast Cowspiracy about Climate Change. Union of Concerned Scientists. *https://blog.ucsusa.org/doug-boucher/cowspiracy-movie-review*

248 **Gimmenez, Eric.** 2012. We already grow enough food for 10 billion people – and still can't end hunger. Huffington Post. *https://www.huffingtonpost.com/eric-holt-gimenez/world-hunger_b_1463429.html*

249 **Roser, Max & Ritchie, Hannah.** 2017. Yields and Land Use in Agriculture. Our World in Data. *https://ourworldindata.org/yields-and-land-use-in-agriculture/#breakdown-of-global-land-area-today*

250 **Ting, Inga.** 2015. Australia is the Meat Eating Capital of the World. Sydney Morning Herald. *http://www.smh.com.au/national/health/australia-is- the-meateating-capital-of-the-world-20151027-gkjhp4.html*

251 **Wilson, Lindsay.** 2013. The Carbon Footprint of 5 Diets Compared. Shrink That Footprint. *http://shrinkthatfootprint.com/food-carbon-footprint-diet*

252 **Familydoctor.org.** 2017. Vegetarian diet: How to get the nutrients you need. *http://familydoctor.org/vegetarian-diet-how-to-get-the-nutrients-you-need/*

253 **O'Connor, Annahad.** 2015. Report Links Some Types of Cancer With Processed or Red Meat. New York Times. *http://www.nytimes.com/2015/10/27/health/report-links-some-types-of-cancer-with-processed-or-red-meat.html*

254 **Chrisafis, Angelique.** 2016. French Law Forbids Food Waste by Supermarkets. The Guardian. *https://www.theguardian.com/world/2016/feb/04/french-law-forbids-food-waste-by-supermarkets*

255 **Food Wise.** 2017. Fast Facts on Food Waste. *http://www.foodwise.com.au/foodwaste/food-waste-fast-facts/*

256 **McKinnon, Alan.** n.d. CO_2 Emissions from Freight Transport: an Analysis of UK data. *http://www.greenlogistics.org/SiteResources/d82cc048-4b92-4c2a-a014-af1eea7d75d0_CO2%20Emissions%20from%20Freight%20Transport%20-%20An%20Analysis%20of%20UK%20Data.pdf*

Chapter 29

257 **Colville-Anderson, Mikael.** The 20 most bike-friendly cities on the planet. Wired. *https://www.wired.com/2015/06/copenhagenize-worlds-most-bike-friendly-cities/*

258 **Hutchens, Gareth.** 2014. Air Pollution takes toll on Australian Lives, Economy: OECD Report. Sydney Morning Herald. *http://www.smh.com.au/federal-politics/political-news/air-pollution-takes-toll-on-australian-lives-economy-oecd-report-20140522-38rre.html*

White, Alexander. 2014. What Kills 3000 Australians a year? The Guardian. *http://www.theguardian.com/environment/southern-crossroads/2014/may/28/air-pollution-australia-greg-hunt*

259 **Sharma, Rahul et al.** 2011. Conventional, Hybrid and Electric Vehicles for Australian Driving Conditions. Part 2: Lifecycle CO_2 emissions. *http://citeseerx.ist.psu.edu/viewdoc/download?doi=10.1.1.718.7976&rep=rep1&type=pdf*

260 Australia's electricity has an average emissions intensity of around 950 g CO_2e/ kWh (see endnote 136), and an electric vehicle typically uses 0.25 kWh/km. Interestingly, this is about 4 times more efficient energy-wise than a conventional car (which uses 4 MJ, or 1.1 kWh, per km). The inefficiency of burning fossil fuels to generate the electricity means that the emissions are ultimately quite similar. Australian petrol vehicles have an average mileage of 10.6 litres per 100 km, and burning a litre of petrol releases 2.31 kg CO_2, yielding 244 g CO_2 per km.

Shrink that Footprint. n.d. The 'Electric Cars aren't Green' Myth Debunked. *http://shrinkthatfootprint.com/electric-cars-green*

261 **GreenPower.** 2017. About Us. *http://www.greenpower.gov.au/About-Us/*

262 Of course, if they didn't have an electric car, they could feed more electricity into the grid – thus, in a sense, offsetting their carbon emissions – see Chapter 33.

Chapter 30

263 **NSW Trainlink.** n.d. *http://www.nswtrainlink.info/* .

Firefly Express. n.d. *https://www.fireflyexpress.com.au/FFNew/Index.asp*

Endnotes and References

264 **Green Ration Book.** 2010. The Cost of Everyday Living. *http://www.greenrationbook.org.uk/resources/footprints-air-travel/*

265 **Public Transport Users Association.** 2015. Myth: Public Transport Doesn't Really Save Energy. *http://www.ptua.org.au/myths/energy/*

266 Estimated using the following carbon footprint calculator, including radiative forcing: *http://calculator.carbonfootprint.com/calculator.aspx?tab=3*

267 Estimated using the following carbon footprint calculator, including radiative forcing: *http://www.carbonfootprint.com/calculator.aspx*

268 **Carbon Independent.** 2015. Aviation Sources. *http://www.carbonindependent.org/sources_aviation.html*

269 Longer flight legs have the disadvantage of needing to carry more fuel, however.

270 **Clark, Duncan.** 2011. A complete guide to Carbon Offsetting. The Guardian. *https://www.theguardian.com/environment/2011/sep/16/carbon-offset-projects-carbon-emissions*

Chapter 31

271 Note in this regard that solar potential (that is, the intensity and duration of sunlight) varies significantly around the world. Australia households can generate their electricity needs from rooftop solar PV relatively easily, while households in north Europe and Canada may struggle a bit. In this regard, it's embarrassing for us Australians that we have an 8 times lower solar PV installed capacity than Germany, despite our vastly greater solar resource.

British Business Energy. 2016. World Solar PV Potential Maps. *https://britishbusinessenergy.co.uk/world-solar-map/*

272 **Solar Quotes.** 2017. 5 kW systems. https://www.solarquotes.com.au/systems/5kW/ . The solar panels themselves cost around $1/Watt, but installation costs a significant amount.

273 **Bill Republic.** n.d. Average Household Electricity Usage. *https://www.billrepublic.com/average-electricity-usage/* .

Finn Peacock. 2017. Will a Solar System save you money in the long run? Solar Quotes. *https://www.solarquotes.com.au/solarpanelpayback.html*

We say 5 to 10 years, because of the cost of remaining connected to the grid, and some of the electricity produced will be sold back to the grid rather than used to offset your electricity consumption. The price given for feeding electricity back into the grid is lower (typically 6-8c) than the cost of electricity from the grid (typically 18-30c). This means that, if you have solar, it is financially beneficial to use more electricity in the middle of the day, when your panels are producing. Your payback time will depend on what proportion of the electricity you use during the day.

Chapter 32

274 **The Guardian.** 2010. What's the Carbon Footprint of a House? *https://www.theguardian.com/environment/green-living-blog/2010/oct/14/carbon-footprint-house*

Chapter 33

275 **Australian Bureau of Statistics.** 2013-14. Household Income and Wealth. *http://www.abs.gov.au/ausstats/abs@.nsf/mf/6523.0*

After having paid tax, and spent money on housing, electricity, food and transport, a typical Australian might have a disposable income of about $20,000/yr. As the average carbon intensity of the Australian economy is about 0.3 kg CO_2e/$ (550 Mt CO_2e emissions divided by GDP of

Endnotes and References

$1.55tn), this corresponds to about 6 tonnes. Of course, the way this money is spent also has a significant impact, as some sectors are far more carbon intensive than others.

276 6000 km/yr in a car with 3 people in it, with good fuel efficiency (200 g CO_2e/km) = 0.4 tonnes. Purchase new car only once in 25 years = 0.6 tonnes.

277 Purchase a new bicycle, with embodied emissions of 300kg, once every 20 years → 15 kg/year. Spare parts → 5 kg/year. 30 kg CO_2e/year worth of additional food requirements This figure is based on cycling 10 km/day, with a carbon footprint from additional food requirements of under 20 g CO_2e/km but with a 40 kg/year deduction for the likelihood that this energy would otherwise have been burned playing sport or in a gym.

   Berners-Lee, Mike. 2010. What's the Carbon Footprint of Cycling? The Guardian. *http://www.theguardian.com/environment/2010/jun/08/carbon-footprint-cycling*

278 5000 km/yr @ 40g CO_2e/passenger km.

279 It would only be reasonable to claim this as a reduction in your carbon footprint if you don't sell the Renewable Energy Certificates from installing your solar panels. This would typically mean that the solar system would be around 30% more expensive.

280 Note that about this area would be necessary to house enough solar panels, assuming that ¼ of roof space can be used, and that a 250 W solar panel is 1.6 m2. Joe or others with tiny houses might get around this by investing in solar on public buildings.

Chapter 37

281 **Kingsley, Patrick & Timur, Safak. 2015.** How Alan Kurdi's death changed the world. The Guardian. *https://www.theguardian.com/world/2015/dec/31/alan-kurdi-death-canada-refugee-policy-syria-boy-beach-turkey-photo*

282 **Kakkar, Rahul, 2014.** History of Chipko Movement. Important India. *https://www.importantindia.com/11686/history-of-chipko-movement/*